PAT
McCARRAN:
POLITICAL BOSS OF NEVADA

Jerome E. Edwards

University of Nevada Press
Reno, Nevada
1982

Nevada Studies in History and Political Science No. 17

Studies Editor
WILBUR S. SHEPPERSON

Editorial Committee

DON W. DRIGGS   JOSEPH A. FRY
JEROME E. EDWARDS   ANDREW C. TUTTLE

Library of Congress Cataloging in Publication Data
Edwards, Jerome E., 1937-
    Pat McCarran, political boss of Nevada.

    (Nevada studies in history and political science ;
no. 17)
    Bibliography: p.
    Includes index.
    1. McCarran, Pat, 1876-1954.   2. Nevada—Politics
and government.   3. Politicians—Nevada—Biography
4. Legislators—United States—Biography.   5. United
States. Congress. Senate—Biography.   I. Title.
II. Series.
E748.M142E38   1982   979.3'03'0924   82-8576
ISBN 0-87417-071-0   AACR2

University of Nevada Press, Reno, Nevada 89557 USA
© Jerome E. Edwards 1982. All rights reserved
Printed in the United States of America

*Dedicated to my mother
and in memory of my father*

CONTENTS

Contents

Introduction

THIS STUDY emphasizes Senator Patrick McCarran's role in Nevada state politics. It does not attempt to be a personal biography, or even a comprehensive political biography. Rather it analyzes the ways McCarran gained, consolidated, and used his great power within Nevada. It is a case study of how a single individual—a U.S. senator—dominated an entire state. Thus, it treats his career in the United States Senate, where McCarran gained national fame, only insofar as that career affected Nevada politics. It does not discuss his legal cases, although McCarran was an unusually competent defense lawyer and the cases are a most attractive part of his record. Such biographical details will be treated only as background.

During Senator McCarran's lifetime, Nevada—although considerably larger than the United Kingdom in area—was the least populous of American states. In fact when McCarran first became a senator, the entire state had fewer than 100,000 people—not too many more than a typical Chicago ward at the time. Because of this small size, any Nevada politician worth his salt knew a considerable proportion of his constituents. Politics was gossipy, personal, immediate, in a way unknown in larger states. Nevada's intimate scale made it much easier for an individual, a group, or a corporation to establish political or economic primacy.

Also, the political system in twentieth-century Nevada was not fully developed. There was no significant difference between the two political parties, and party loyalties were fluid. Party discipline was almost nonexistent. Nevada's Republican and Democratic parties have both tended to be conservative and both have emphasized state over national issues. In part, this reflects the common perception that the state is terribly vulnerable to the federal government. McCarran made skillful use of these traits in accruing and using his power.

In other ways, too, the analogy with a Chicago ward—or with Tammany Hall—holds. Although party organization in Nevada was much looser, McCarran's use of patronage, his bestowing of personal favors for political ends, and his insistence on undeviating personal loyalty all have counterparts among the Irish political bosses in the major cities of the northeast. Although they ran urban, municipal governments, and McCarran's bailiwick was a sparsely populated state, many of the political methods were similar, as will be seen.

I am indebted to many people for assistance with this work.   Two must be particularly acknowledged. Unfailingly helpful and generous was Sister Margaret Patricia McCarran, the senator's eldest daugher. As the child of McCarran's who was most intellectually attuned to him, Sister Margaret is a profoundly loyal defender of her father. She placed no restrictions on the use of her father's papers, and made them all available while they were still under her control. She was always ready with insights and information. Second is Mary Ellen Glass, head of the Oral History Project at the University of Nevada in Reno. Mrs. Glass has always been most encouraging about this project. Under her leadership, the Oral History Project has become a splendid repository of information on the senator. She has also been instrumental in securing for the library of the University of Nevada-Reno, manuscript resources such as the outstanding Pete Petersen collection, which was especially important for this study. I also wish to thank my colleagues, Wilbur Shepperson, Russell Elliott, William Rowley, and Michael Brodhead, for their professional and personal help, and Elizabeth Raymond for her insightful editorial assistance. It has been deeply appreciated. I am grateful to the University of Nevada-Reno for time and research moneys which helped to further and complete this project. Finally, my wife, Elsie, should be thanked for her continuing encouragement of this work, and her unfailing patience with the time it took.

J. E. E.

Reno, October 1981

CHAPTER 1

BEGINNINGS

PATRICK A. MCCARRAN, who would become Nevada's first native-born senator, was born on August 8, 1876, in Reno. He was the son of Irish immigrants.

His father, Patrick, born in County Londonderry in 1834, had come to the New World around 1848—the "starving time." He came west with the U.S. Army, and in November, 1861, joined the California Volunteers. He was sent to Fort Churchill, in the new Nevada Territory, but deserted in 1862, before being mustered in. He then bought the land on the Truckee River which later became the nucleus for the McCarran ranch. The elder Patrick was later remembered for his "wild temper and his fiery red hair and beard." He was once charged with "assault with intent to kill" when he shot a sheepherder who had trespassed on the family ranch with his flock. McCarran, Sr. was a man of some substance, and the 1875 state census listed his assets at $1,150, mostly in real estate.

The senator's mother, Margaret, was born in County Cork in 1852. She had come to the United States in 1872, and worked as a domestic servant. After coming to Reno, she met Patrick, and they were married in October, 1875. Her granddaughter remembers her as a strong, sturdy woman, with a beautiful singing voice, able to recite poems and tell stories about "fairy godmothers and old castles."[1]

When Patrick was two, the family moved to a ranch on the Truckee River, approximately fifteen miles east of Reno. There they raised sheep. Beautifully situated, and located on the Central Pacific Railroad, the ranch is still held in the family.

Patrick was an only child and grew up alone (except for his parents) on the ranch. Because of the ranch's isolation, Patrick's schooling began late; through his college years, he was always approximately four years older than other members of his classes. At age ten, he was sent to the nearest public school, the one-room schoolhouse at Glendale. By then he was big enough to ride the ten miles to and from school, although his attendance was often intermittent. It was still necessary for young Patrick to milk a dozen cows each morning,and bring them home in the evening to milk them again.[2]

Regular church attendance was impossible, although his mother undoubtedly saw to his religious instruction. The one day that required church attendance was Easter Sunday, when Patrick and his mother (significantly not his father) would go to mass in Reno.[3] This annual event imprinted itself indelibly in McCarran's memory. Fifty years later, he reminisced about the annual trek to his eldest daughter, then a nun. The letter illustrates his sensitivity and charm:

> Well Pal, Easter will soon be here again. It always brings back fond memories. I can recall with what joy a freckled faced country boy looked forward to the afternoon of Easter Saturday when he would be dressed in his best (none too good) and by his mother's side on an old spring wagon drawn by two sturdy horses—they together would go from the old ranch and drive to Reno to arrive there about 6 P.M. that evening ... then about seven to the dear little old church way up by the University where we would together kneel and examine the conscience and read the prayers before Confession, then to the dear little Confessional where the freckled faced boy told all the terrible sins which a freckled faced boy with only a dog for a playmate might be guilty of committing.

McCarran remembered how he played with other boys on Saturday afternoon and evening. Easter Morning soon came:

> By his mothers side to church before the sun was quite arisen. (He was told and believed that the sun danced on Easter morning). To the dear old church, where easter lillies were banked and flowers of all kinds prevailed, where the easter sun that had danced itself into existence shone through the old stained glass windows. Where the old priest whose face was to the freckled faced boy, the face of God; turned to hold high, the body and being of the Living God and while he did the whisper of his mother wafted to the ear of the boy "have mercy on us." Then to the rail and the lightening glory akin to the new born sun filled the boy, and joy was everywhere.[4]

When Patrick turned fifteen, his father offered to send him to public school in Reno, where he was placed in the seventh grade. The young man must have presented an awkward sight, as he made his appearance before the school principal clad in a new pair of overalls and a chinchilla coat. "My garb evidently was a matter of much comment," McCarran later recalled, "but I knew no different and was content."[5]

Initially Patrick did not do well as a student, taken in as he was by the distractions of Reno. Probably his being so much older than his classmates also caused problems. His record was poor until he came under the spell of a teacher he later described as a "great woman" and an "outstanding teacher," Libbie C. Booth. Mrs. Booth was one of the two people (his mother was the other) who made him look beyond sheepraising for a career. The teacher saw the young man's promise, encouraged him, occasionally lectured him, and gave him an interest in and a will to apply himself to his studies. Through her influence, he became interested in public speaking and declamation, in public events, in athletics, "and in the building of school spirit."[6]

When McCarran was a Nevada Supreme Court justice, he wrote to Libbie Booth about how much her influence had meant to him. It was praise which any teacher would be proud to receive:

> The lessons you taught, and the rules you laid down, have been with me constantly, and I look back to you as the beginning of my public career, and whatever temple I may build in that respect, the foundation was laid by you; and however I may round out my career, it is with extreme gratitude that I always look back to the one who awakened me to the realization that it was possible for me to achieve something in life.[7]

Pat McCarran attended Reno High School and was valedictorian of a class of sixteen in 1897. His graduating address was on the conventional theme, "In the Footsteps of the Sands of Time." With special pride he noted in his later years how he had excelled in school athletics at Reno High; he broke school records of 10.2 seconds in running the 100-yard dash, and 5.2 seconds for the 50-yard dash. Only one of his high-school teachers, Mary S. Doten, was singled out for later mention; in his words, she was "teacher, poetess, writer, molder of the character of youth."[8]

In 1897, he began work at the University of Nevada, in Reno. McCarran's college work was indifferent; his grades were satisfactory in his first year but then began to slide. Political science was by far his best course. His deeper interests were athletics (he briefly played on the football team) and debating, and he was adjudged the best debator at the college in 1900. He also wrote for the school newspaper, the *Student Record.* He never entered into the social scene, and, as he wrote later, was "never sufficiently popular to become a member of any fraternity." He also believed fraternities represented cliques, "peculiar segregation," and denied "the democracy of life." Socially, young McCarran was rather a lone wolf.[9]

His grades dropped and McCarran left the university in the spring of his senior year. His father, then almost 70, had been injured in a fall from a wagon, and Patrick took over active operation of the ranch. When the time came for the class of 1901 to graduate, he took his mother to see twenty-six other members of the class receive their diplomas: she sat in the auditorium with him and cried.[10]

After his college training, young McCarran took up sheep raising on a full-time basis. In October, 1901, a Reno newspaper referred to him as "the youngest sheep man in Nevada and one of the most successful." He must have been strongly tempted to make the sheep business his career, and his father certainly argued for this. But other pressures worked to force McCarran away from a life as an agriculturalist. Both his mother and his former teacher, Libbie C. Booth, believed he had the talent and intelligence to pursue a career in law. Then, too, his well demonstrated, and ego-boosting, talent for oratory bent him toward a legal or political career.[11]

The key decision appears to have been made in 1902, when the Democrat-Silverite party in Nevada was in a tight race for control of the state legislature. The race was important because the legislature would elect a United States senator to succeed thirty-year veteran John P. Jones. The party candidate was Francis G. Newlands, a prominent silver advocate and Nevada's lone congressman from 1890 to 1902. The Newlands Reclamation Act of 1902, which opened the west to federally financed irrigation projects, was named for him. Newlands was a wealthy Yale graduate whose father-in-law was banker William Sharon, one of the developers of the Comstock Lode.

As McCarran later told the story, William E. Sharon (William Sharon's nephew) drove out to the McCarran ranch and asked Patrick to run in the legislative race: "I wasn't a likely looking candidate for office. I was out working in the corrals and had about two weeks' growth of beard and was dressed in the usual sheepherder's outfit. And I had a lot of sheep to take care of. But I decided to make a try for it, bearded or not."[12]

Certainly this meeting was one of the crucial turning points in McCarran's life. He was nominated at the Silver-Democratic convention in Reno for one of the seven assembly seats representing Washoe County. He ran on a platform that urged passage of an eight-hour-working-day law, to apply to the mines, mills, and smelters of the state. Such an eight-hour law was to be extended to "other classes of labor so far as it can be made to apply." The platform also recognized the right of laboring men to organize into unions, and demanded the curbing of the trusts. Many were impressed with McCarran's remarks when he accepted his nomination, at least if the enthusiastic testimony of the Democratic *Nevada State Journal* can be believed: "There is but little doubt of his in the future being elected to a higher position than a place in the State legislature."[13]

The intensity of McCarran's purpose may be gauged by his mortgaging the ranch for $2,000 to raise necessary campaign funds. His campaign heavily emphasized his support of the eight-hour law, and perhaps gained some impetus when William Jennings Bryan, his personal oratorical and political hero, came to Reno to speak on the ticket's behalf. When the votes were counted, McCarran ran sixth out of a group of fourteen candidates competing for the seven seats. So at the age of 26, his new political career was in the making.[14]

It did not take McCarran long to be mentioned in the newspapers. He wanted to make his mark from the session's beginning. One way of insuring this was his arrangement with the *Reno Evening Gazette* to become its assembly reporter in Carson City. The *Gazette* gained a correspondent, and McCarran made sure that his copy was filled with news of himself. In fact his name was mentioned in every story he filed; in the *Gazette's* columns, he and his close associate H. R. Cooke appeared to dominate the legislative proceedings. This may not have been a distortion of reality, however. Even a cursory reading of the dry but official assembly *Journal* lends credence to the impression that McCarran was very much in the thick of things. In his *Gazette* reporting, McCarran made sure that his personal arguments in favor or against a bill were elaborated fully, with all the proper supporting adjectives. Other assembly members, except for his friend Cooke, received only the barest mention.

The burden of being an assemblyman in a state with a population of 40,000 was not particularly heavy. The only session was over in two months. McCarran gained important recognition for his oratorical talents, his energy, and his quick mastery of parliamentary tactics. The *Reno Evening Gazette* praised him for being one of the assembly's "most careful and painstaking members." The legislative session was important in firing McCarran's ambition for still higher office, and it stamped him as a young man very much in the political mainstream of the Progressive Era.[15]

In the meantime, McCarran had fallen in love with a young woman from Elko County, Martha Harriet Weeks. He had met Harriet while he was attending the University of Nevada and she was a student at the affiliated Normal School. They corresponded after Patrick left college; and, after her graduation and a year of teaching in a one-room school in Clover Valley, east of Elko, they married on August 10, 1903. They were married by the Protestant Episcopal bishop, which was all right with Patrick, since it was before the 1906 Roman Catholic edict on intermarriage. However, at Harriet's suggestion, they remarried in the Catholic church on August 14, 1903. Otherwise she feared that Patrick's mother would not accept her as his wife. Harriet subsequently adopted the Catholic faith herself, and two of her daughters were to become sisters of the church.[16]

The couple honeymooned in San Francisco, then rented a house in Reno. They also spent several months living at the ranch. They were to have five children. the first, Margaret Martha, was born on July 22, 1904, "the biggest and handsomest young lady, for the years to be found in a week's journey" according to the enthusiastic birth notice in a Reno newspaper.[17] Temperamentally and intellectually, Margaret came to be closer to her father than any of the other children. In time she joined the Order of the Holy Names, received a Ph.D. in History in 1950, and wrote several historical works, including a warm appreciation of her father.[18]

Another girl, Mary Ladwina, was born on August 31, 1906. Mary followed her sister into the Order of the Holy Names. She developed considerable talent as a musician and an artist, and had a calmer, more pious disposition than her elder sister.[19] A third girl, Norine Isabelle, was born January 30, 1911. When she was a teenager Norine contracted encephalitis, which permanently crippled her. A fourth girl, Sylvia Patricia, was born April 19, 1919, and finally—

the long-awaited son—Samuel Patrick on September 28, 1921, when McCarran was 45. Sam eventually entered the practice of medicine.

McCarran developed an obvious taste for politics. Refusing another bid for the assembly, he ran for state senate against Harry Martin, the brother of one of his university instructors, Anne Martin. But 1904 turned out to be a strongly Republican year in Nevada, and McCarran was defeated by a margin of 1,298 to 1,114 votes. This may have increased his determination to remove himself and his family from the Reno area.[20]

The sheep business had become discouraging, and there were obvious problems of balancing sheep, the law which he had begun reading, and politics. Soon after passing his bar examinations in 1905, McCarran decided to move to Tonopah. Although he kept his Reno real estate, and the family ranch remained in the hands of his parents, McCarran made the move with Harriet and daughter Margaret in the fall of 1905.

Tonopah was then a lonely, windswept, barren town situated high in the mountains and desert of central Nevada. On May 19, 1900, a prospector named Jim Butler had come across some promising ore outcroppings at the site, which turned out to be amazingly rich in silver and gold. The resulting boom town of Tonopah was to produce a hundred million dollars of ore—mostly silver—in two decades, and an immediate end to the twenty-year depression that had afflicted Nevada. Tonopah was not alone. On December 4, 1902, a gold discovery was made thirty miles south, and by 1904, the thriving new town of Goldfield was being developed. Whereas Tonopah produced silver, Goldfield, as its name indicates, produced mostly gold, with a yield of eighty million dollars over the following twenty years. Both towns became bustling centers, the two largest cities in the state.

Other people important to the state's future were moving to Tonopah and Goldfield at approximately the same time. Among them were: Key Pittman (later U.S. senator for 28 years), his brother Vail (governor for 5 years), George Wingfield (the state's dominating political and economic influence for a quarter-century), Tasker Oddie (later governor and then U.S. senator for 12 years), George Bartlett (congressman), and Ray Baker and George Thatcher (prominent Democratic leaders). These people represented two generations of leadership, an infusion of political and financial power which would dominate Nevada from 1910 to 1950.

The reasons for McCarran's move were twofold. First, his political instincts made him realize that the political center of Nevada had gravitated to the mining-boom towns. Tonopah was new; there was no established element jealously guarding its political and financial prerogatives. Everyone was in on the ground floor, everyone was a carpetbagger. McCarran had been defeated politically in Reno; Tonopah thus presented political and legal opportunity. The second reason for moving was that McCarran wanted to make money. He desired to be rich, and was strongly attracted by hoped-for bonanzas, and by the speculative atmosphere permeating a young, exuberant mining town on the way up. The sheep business had proved discouraging, and Tonopah was a fertile new field.

McCarran emphasized criminal law in his Tonopah practice. It is interesting that he avoided the lucrative field of mining law, where Key Pittman was to find his wealth. After a series of cases that brought him a modest, local reputation, McCarran was nominated by the Democrats for district attorney of Nye County. The Republicans did not nominate an opponent, so McCarran won the election by default in November, 1906.

McCarran's tenure as Nye County district attorney was not uniformly successful. He considered the post a political way station, and he found it increasingly difficult to work closely with fellow Democratic leaders. However, a certain discomfort with the duties and philosophy of the office itself is also evident. Temperamentally McCarran was a much better defense attorney than prosecuting attorney. As a defense attorney, McCarran always extended himself all the way for his clients. However, as a prosecuting attorney he displayed a certain hesitancy to prosecute to the fullest possible extent. His heart was with the sinner.

CHAPTER 2

DEFEATED AMBITION

IN TONOPAH, a deep political rift developed between McCarran and leading state Democrats. He appears to have irritated the incumbent Democratic governor, John Sparks, by refusing in 1907 an appointment as judge of the newly created Fourth Judicial District, embracing Nye County. Since McCarran had only two years of legal experience, this proffered appointment illustrates the rapid mobility possible at that time and place. In a letter written thirty years later, the then senator expressed his mixed feelings about his refusal:

> I have always regretted that I declined that appointment. . . . The Governor wanted to express his gratitude to me. He was very much put out when I declined and I have since continued to regret it. . . . That was the first and only appointment that was ever offered to me. I have always had to fight for everything I have received.[1]

More important were his problems with George Wingfield, who would be a dominating political influence impeding McCarran's career for the next quarter-century.

Wingfield was born in Arkansas on August 16, 1876. He was eight days younger than McCarran. He came to Nevada in 1896, and worked for four years as a cowboy on ranches near Winnemucca. In Winnemucca he made the acquaintance of George S. Nixon, the local banker, who gave him a loan when Wingfield decided to go to Tonopah in 1901. Because of this generosity, Wingfield is alleged to have declared that Nixon would be his partner in everything he acquired in southern Nevada. He kept his word and Nixon reaped millions of dollars from the bargain.

When Wingfield moved to Tonopah, he interested himself successfully in gambling, mining, and banking. When the Republican Nixon
was elected U.S. senator from Nevada in 1905, Wingfield took over
active control of the business. When Nixon died in 1912, Wingfield
gained sole financial control. In 1904, Wingfield and Nixon organized the Tonopah Banking Corporation; in 1906, the Reno National
Bank; and by 1907, they had gained control of the John S. Cook &
Company bank in Goldfield. By 1905, Wingfield and Nixon had
moved into Goldfield, and Wingfield made his home there. In 1906,
he and Nixon, with financial backing from Bernard Baruch, organized the Goldfield Consolidated Mines Company, the dominant
company in Goldfield, capitalized at $50,000,000.[2]

Wingfield's political enmity for McCarran probably had a personal foundation. In 1906, McCarran represented May Wingfield in
a suit for divorce against George. The divorce case was a seamy one,
and George Wingfield won it, receiving instead of a divorce, an
annulment. May Wingfield stated in her complaint "that she knew
that because of her husband's high political position, she had reason
to believe that he would buy the judgment." She asserted George was
guilty of extreme cruelty, "forcing her to having marital relations
with him when he had syphilis." George Wingfield and McCarran
were to spar in the courtroom again. If McCarran conducted this
case in his usual forceful fashion, it may well have been the basis for
future opposition on Wingfield's part. McCarran, of course, was far
too stubborn to change his defense of May to suit George.[3]

But McCarran and Wingfield had deep-seated political differences
as well. These stemmed in part from differing attitudes toward the
famous Goldfield strike of 1907-08. The Wingfield financial empire
had its first major labor troubles in 1907, when the Western Federation of Miners, affiliated with the I.W.W., called a strike on November 27. Relations between the workers and the mine owners,
dominated by Wingfield, had deteriorated after the owners insisted
upon the imposition of "change" rooms, where the miners were
forced to switch from street clothes to work clothes and vice versa,
watched by company guards. This was to prevent the practice of
"high grading," whereby millions of dollars of gold had been stolen
by miners who hid particularly rich ore in their clothes. But the
immediate cause of the strike was that the union members refused
to accept their pay in scrip, supposedly necessitated by the 1907
financial panic.[4]

Because of pressure from mine owners, Governor John Sparks formally requested the presence of federal troops. Sparks almost gave the game away by stating that "a committee of mine owners, mine operators, and mill operators from the Goldfield district" had decided county authorities could not handle the situation. He asserted that an insurrection was imminent unless President Roosevelt immediately sent in troops. Sparks' request was supported by Senator George Nixon (Wingfield's business partner) and Representative George Bartlett (a friend of Wingfield's). The Esmeralda County authorities were not consulted. Theodore Roosevelt acceded to the request.[5]

When federal troops arrived on December 6, the mine owners, led by Wingfield, used the opportunity to break the union. On December 9, wages were reduced a dollar a day, and the companies began hiring nonunion workers. The mines reopened in early January, 1908, under federal protection.[6]

Roosevelt soon had second thoughts and sent a commission to investigate the situation. The commission telegraphed back to Roosevelt that the governor had misled the President:

> We do find no warrant for statement that there has been or is a complete collapse of civil authority here. . . . Our investigation so far completely has failed to sustain the general and sweeping allegations in the governor calling for troops, and the impression as to conditions here given in that call is misleading and without warrant. We do find no evidence that any condition then existed not easily controlled by the local authorities. . . .
>
> So far as can be learned no county officer was consulted by governor previous to calling for troops. All still resent his action and consider it was unnecessary. . . . In other words, the State authorities propose to do nothing, but wholly rely on the Federal authorities. [7]

After further correspondence, President Roosevelt gave notice that he would withdraw the troops. "The State of Nevada," he wrote Governor Sparks, "must itself make a resolute effort in good faith to perform the policy duties incident to the existence of a State." The owners, dominated by Wingfield, then demanded the creation of a state police force which would substitute for the federal troops and keep the mines open. Governor Sparks, who was gravely ill (he was to die on May 22, 1908), acquiesced, as did most of the Republican and Democratic party organizations. The bill to create a state police force was ramrodded through the state senate unanimously and the state assembly by a vote of 31-7 over the vociferous objections of union labor.[8]

The political importance of this legislation cannot be overemphasized. The state police bill became the chief issue in Nevada in the 1908 elections, and perhaps more important, it conditioned the way people such as George Wingfield looked at candidates. Although George Wingfield was a Republican, and not interested in higher office himself (he was to refuse appointment to the U.S. Senate on Nixon's death in 1912), he kept an active interest in the candidates nominated by both parties (see pp. 27–31).

McCarran opposed Wingfield by publicly criticizing the call for federal troops, and also the creation of a state police force. By so doing he set himself against most of the state Democratic organization; luminaries such as Representative George Bartlett and future senator Key Pittman supported the federal intervention and creation of a state militia. In Rhyolite, District Attorney McCarran emphatically expressed his views:

> I am very much opposed to armed intervention at Goldfield, but if such a thing is necessary at all, I would rather see the regular troops of Uncle Sam kept in Goldfield. The plan of Governor Sparks to equip a body of Texas Rangers and vest these horsemen with power to use their shooting irons at will in the settlement of labor controversies would be more than a state disgrace. Instead of stopping trouble the adoption of the ranger system would start trouble that would be never-ending in Nevada, and it would set us back several notches in the scale of civilization.[9]

Because of this stand, McCarran began gaining a reputation as a dangerous radical. Not coincidentally, McCarran's political career, which had prospered through 1906, ground to a dead halt in 1908. McCarran decided not to run for reelection as Nye County district attorney. For one thing, he had by now discovered that the role of prosecuting attorney did not particularly suit him. Also he thought that his career should always move upward and did not wish to be stalled in any job. Four years earlier he had refused to run for reelection to the state assembly and had tried for the state senate instead. When he was unsuccessful he had changed his address. Furthermore, a decision to run for reelection as district attorney would have meant committing himself to living in Tonopah, where the boom appeared to be subsiding.

Instead McCarran decided to run for the United States House of Representatives. The seat was already held by Democratic incumbent George Bartlett, who was quite close to major Nevada leaders such as Key Pittman and George Wingfield, and Bartlett was not willing to resign his seat voluntarily. But McCarran was never one to mind dividing the party if it meant the furtherance of his own political ambitions.

His candidacy went nowhere. In April, 1908, he announced that he would seek the Democratic nomination for the House of Representatives. Party leaders such as Key Pittman, however, believed that McCarran was too radical, undoubtedly because of his stand on the state police bill, and that he would divide the party.[10] Pittman also believed that McCarran was not an entirely loyal Democrat, arguing that McCarran was a weak candidate "by reason of the fact that nearly all who know him doubt his sincerity, and believe that he would sacrifice everything for his own political ambitions."[11] Pittman added insult to his description by declaring in one letter that McCarran's "reputation as a double-crosser is too well established throughout the state."[12]

The fight between Bartlett and McCarran was fought in the precincts, and by the time the state convention met in September, 1908, the steam had gone out of the McCarran candidacy. Bartlett was the only name presented to the convention and he was nominated 136-46, with 13 delegates not voting. The state police bill was the hottest issue at the convention, and Bartlett's renomination rested in part on his unequivocal support of the measure.[13]

Upon the completion of his term as Nye County district attorney, McCarran moved his family, which now included two girls, back to Reno. He purchased a home there with the intention of making that city his permanent residence. By 1909, the Tonopah and Goldfield booms had leveled off, his speculations in mining stock had failed to make him rich, and the center of Nevada's political community and population was shifting rapidly to Reno. Indicative of this shift was the fact that George Wingfield moved from Goldfield to Reno in the same year. By 1909, Reno was once again the largest community in Nevada; with 10,000 people it had far outstripped both Tonopah and Goldfield.

From 1909 to 1912 McCarran practiced law, as he had during his term as Nye County district attorney. After serving six years on the Nevada Supreme Court, he returned to his practice in 1919 and continued with it through 1932. ✗

He was one of Nevada's outstanding criminal attorneys. McCarran defended all types: accused murderers, ladies of the night, bank robbers, an abortionist (twice, which was rather surprising for a prominent Roman Catholic layman). Perhaps his greatest fame came from the murder cases. Reno's morning newspaper, the *Nevada State Journal,* pointed out in 1911 that attorney McCarran had the reputation "sometimes claimed by surgeons of never sending a man to the cemetery."[14] It is significant that no defendant of McCarran's ever was executed by the state. In a jam, McCarran was the man to call for help. Like Clarence Darrow, he was an eloquent and fearless advocate and extended himself to the utmost for his clients. ✗

His style in the courtroom could be evocative and emotional. A longtime politician observed, "He would start in a low voice, then die down. He would almost cry and the audience felt the same way. He held people spellbound." Another observer noted that "McCarran was a very good orator. He got to be a good trial lawyer. McCarran could make you weep. He could completely sway his audience."[15]

Even when McCarran lacked a strong case, he could overwhelm a courtroom with his emotional effusions. Occasionally this was sufficient to win. One witness, a Reno newspaperman of many years' experience, remembered a courtroom drama of the late 1920s:

> Pat was at his very best. He was involved with a half-caste Chinese gal from down the line who'd stuck a knife in her boyfriend, and Pat came in there as the attorney for the defense. And I guess he was just out of practice and wanted to get into his dramatics again. [Laughing] He did! He went on to claim, oh, this poor little beaten down lotus flower of the Orient, who'd been raised in a convent, and so on and so forth, and now, who knows, but if she comes out from under this blush, she may return to the friendly shadow of a convent, and so on. Oh, talk about your tear jerkers! He was the very best. Well it worked. The jury acquitted her. And that night, so they tell me, she did not go back to the shelter of that convent. They held the damndest party there was in town [laughing] there in one of the old time 'houses.'[16]

But constant repetition of this point can be misleading. One must not confuse the McCarran who spoke in grand, bloviating phrases with the real McCarran. His emotional oratory was only one facet of McCarran, and he used it when it expressly suited his purpose and the taste of his audience.

In both private correspondence, and courtroom behavior, McCarran could demonstrate thinking of the most rigorously logical order when there were complex issues at stake. He could, when he wished, explain complicated ideas in a simple, but never simpleminded, way. And in the courtroom he was always exceedingly well prepared, whether he chose to work on the juror's intellect or emotions or both. He had a considerable repertoire of rhetorical tools at his command.

McCarran was also an eminent divorce lawyer. His most famous case was the sensationally publicized divorce of actress Mary Pickford from her first husband, Owen Moore, in 1920—with all its implications for Nevada law.[17] But most divorce cases were not so glamorous. Instead they demonstrated the seamier side of human relationships. McCarran usually represented the aggrieved woman. The McCarran files for this period reveal grounds for terminating marriage such as "maimed and nearly killed her," "cruelty, blows, throws, curses," "frequent adultery, cruelty, innoculated her with gonnerhea [sic] by forced intercourse," "insanely jealous, angry, violent," "blows, beatings," *ad nauseum.* Such cases must have given McCarran an understanding of the darker side of human character. Since divorce was relatively rare during this period, the causes forcing a partner to seek it as a remedy to a loveless marriage were violent indeed.[18]

McCarran's legal experience gave him a deep understanding of human frailties. Although the sin was doubtless wrong, it was a natural part of the human beast. It needed interpretation and compassion, and, at any rate, who among men was in a position to cast the first stone? In a disbarment case which McCarran heard when he was on the Nevada Supreme Court, the jurist put it this way:

> Condemnation is the first blush that comes to the cheek of shocked propriety. But propriety should be an exacting, a charitable mistress. Condemnation neither explains nor rectifies; and, while it may scourge, it teaches no lesson. We may enforce the laws of man; we may interpret his constitutions and his codes, but we can offer no solution for the varying and conflicting laws, that, emanating from an unseen power, seem to govern the idiosyncrasies we find in mankind.[19]

As the 1912 elections approached, McCarran demonstrated anew his ever restless ambition. At first he made tentative plans to seek the congressional seat, and he wrote Key Pittman in the fall of 1911, asking for his support. Although Pittman's reply was noncommittal, McCarran received enough discouragement elsewhere that he decided not to make the race. Instead, he announced for a justiceship of the state supreme court, an elective office in Nevada. In his campaign he refused to specify his political opinions, but promised to work diligently in his office and "apply the law without regard to person, power or influence." He also publicly supported the principle of judicial recall.[20]

McCarran did not enjoy general support from the legal profession. A poll of lawyers in the *Nevada State Journal* showed 7 supporting McCarran and 51 his Democratic opponent in the primary. However, he handily won the nomination of his own party, defeating A. A. Heer by 3,577 votes to 2,650.[21]

In the general election, he won by the greatest margin of any Democrat in Nevada, placing far ahead of either presidential candidate Woodrow Wilson or senatorial candidate Key Pittman. Garnering 9,721 votes, or 51 percent of the total vote, he decisively defeated former congressman George Bartlett (Independent), who had considerable support from the Democratic leadership but only 4,466 votes; J. M. Lockhart (Republican), who had 2,701; and W.R. Thomas (Progressive), who had 2,183. It was obvious that although neither the legal profession, the newspapers, nor the Democratic party leadership entirely supported McCarran,[22] he enjoyed great popular appeal. This was no doubt due to his passionate defense of the underdog in his legal practice, and partly to his persuasive oratory over the previous years, which had brought his name to the attention of voters. He never was to lead his ticket in plurality again.

There is no place on earth that constitutes so fine a political burying ground, as the bench. That's where men are really buried, politically. I was buried there once myself, but I was like the Irishman who was much given to drink. It was his custom to get stupidly drunk quite frequently, and during the summertime would take up his nightly abode in the gutter. There was to be a funeral in the town in which this Irishman lived and the grave had been opened and prepared to receive the corpse. A group of boys were out marauding one evening and found their Irish friend in the gutter. As a prank they picked him up, carried him to the cemetery, lowered him down into the grave and put the cover on the box. The next morning our Irish friend awakened, pushed the cover off the box, climbed out of the grave, and said, "Dead, buried

and resurrected, and the first son of a gun out." So I got off the bench
and was the first to get out.[23]

With these words, written many years later, Patrick McCarran expressed his disdain for the period during which he was a member of the Nevada Supreme Court, 1913-18. He never publicly emphasized this period, and when he died the newspapers also tended to ignore his service on the court. But McCarran had a judicial record he could have been proud of. Even today decisions he wrote remain eloquent and important. His judgeship was a continuation of his distinguished legal career.

Two basic themes stand out in McCarran's decisions on the court. One of these is an emphatic defense of the rights of defendants. Once he admonished prosecutors, "The duty of district attorneys to be fair to defendants on trial is scarcely less obligatory than the duty which rests upon the courts, whose officers they are. Both are bound, while holding a defendant accountable for his acts, to protect him in his substantial rights."[24] He also argued vehemently for a defendant's right to adequate counsel: "Of all the rights secured to one accused of crime, it is, I think, quite safe to say that there is none more important or vital than that of being represented by counsel."[25]

Another major theme of McCarran's decisions is that the legislative branch should be given the widest possible latitude in passing progressive statutes to advance the economic and social status of the people. As a corollary, the courts should be chary of tampering with the legislative process, even when it produces defective statutes. Basically, the courts should leave the legislative branch of government alone, and give it considerable discretion. McCarran was not a judicial activist. Probably that is why he so strongly preferred membership in the legislative branch of government over the judiciary; in his conception of government, the legislative branch was the more active, and gave more scope for his talents.[26]

And that is where he wished to be. For the time being, however, his position on the court stymied his ambition for higher legislative office. McCarran soon discovered that gaining election to the supreme court had been a grievous mistake from a political standpoint. The position was a dead end instead of a way station to something better. For one thing, the Nevada Constitution quite explicitly forbids judges to run for other nonjudicial offices during the term for which they have been elected or appointed; the election of such a judge to another office "shall be void."[27]

This restriction meant that becoming a Nevada Supreme Court justice was an impediment to political advancement during tenure on the court, and this was doubtless the intention of the constitution makers. McCarran must have been aware of this constitutional prohibition when he ran for the court in 1912; but he discovered early that the court did not satisfy his abundant energies and ambition, which focused increasingly on the United States Senate. He does not appear to have been discouraged. He ran for the Senate anyway without resigning his seat on the court, in complete contradiction to the spirit and letter of the state constitution.

Perhaps he sought a court test on the article's constitutionality, since the U.S. Senate is, after all, a federal office. However, such a court test would have placed his party and his own candidacy in a most awkward position if he had won nomination. Needless to say, McCarran's action afforded plenty of ammunition to an ever-growing list of political enemies. He was the only Nevada Supreme Court justice in this century who openly used his office to further his political ambition, and the consequences were disastrous.

Another major difficulty confronting McCarran in his quest for the U.S. Senate was the fact that Nevada was already represented in the Senate by two eminent men of his own party. Francis G. Newlands, the son-in-law of wealthy comstock financier William Sharon, was an experienced Nevada politician. Born in 1848, he had been a member of the United States House of Representatives from 1893 to 1903, and had represented Nevada in the Senate since 1903.[28] McCarran, in fact, had seconded his nomination to the Senate in the 1903 legislative session. Key Pittman, born in 1873, had come to the state during the Tonopah boom and first took his seat in the United States Senate in 1913.[29] Neither man would be easy to dislodge, and any attempt was certain to divide the party.

Restless as a judge, McCarran began acting in a political fashion from the very beginning. In 1913, when President Wilson nominated A. B. Gray as the United States Marshal for Nevada, on the advice of Newlands and Pittman, McCarran conducted a lonely fight against the appointment. He wrote an acquaintance in Denver requesting information about Gray's earlier Colorado years: "Am anxious to get history of Mr. Gray. I am doing this in the interest of Decency." He wrote a number of letters protesting the appointment.[30] Although McCarran was not successful in this endeavor, he believed he had gained considerable support throughout the state. He certainly earned no plaudits from the two incumbent Democratic senators.

Newlands came up for reelection in 1914. He would probably have been the easier of the two senators to dislodge because of his age and lengthy absences from the state of Nevada. In fact he was to win his battle against the Republican candidate in the fall by only forty votes. McCarran's letters, to correspondents scattered over Nevada, did not disguise his ambitions for Newlands's seat: "My position demands that I remain silent, but that does not prevent me from answering the inquiries of friends and I receive those quite often."[31] He fooled no one. A prominent Carson City journalist complained to Key Pittman, "He is hardly seated on the bench before he shies his castor into a new ring."[32]

One of McCarran's most intimate friends, Joe M. McNamara of Elko, realized McCarran's ambition as early as January, 1913. Warning the justice against any premature revelation of plans, McNamara stated that "a faint rumor has reached here that you may be a candidate for the office of United States Senator at the next general election."[33] McCarran's reply is not available, but by the beginning of the following year his plans were an open secret. Writing to Reno attorney James D. Finch in January, 1914, McCarran asked, "By the way, Jim, there are just three men of prominence in the State of Nevada, who have not written to me personal letters requesting me to run for U.S. Senate. You are one of them. What's the matter?" Although McCarran did not realize it, a copy of this letter was delivered to Key Pittman, and probably to Senator Newlands.[34] The extent of McCarran's indiscretion is indicated by the fact that Finch had been Newlands's secretary from 1905 to 1907.[35]

McCarran certainly made no bones about his ambitions in his private correspondence, and openly sought the advice of friends as to whether or not he was strong enough to defeat Newlands. He maintained that Newlands was "weaker . . . than he ever was in the history of his public career" and that his own candidacy was an answer to a "spontaneous expression" on the part of the good citizens of Nevada.[36] To further his prospects, he made himself freely available on the oratorical circuit, and the newspapers whispered that a challenge to Newlands was in the offing.[37]

McCarran eventually decided, on the insistent advice of his friends, that he was not strong enough to challenge Newlands. Joe McNamara offered the opinion that Senator Newlands was too formidable an opponent because of his money and machine. Finch pointedly declared that a McCarran fight would prove an embarrassment to his friends.[38] Instead of a go-ahead, what McCarran reaped was a harvest of ill will within the Democratic party. He himself

blamed Emmet Boyle, successful Democratic candidate for governor in 1914, for turning the party against him,[39] but Boyle was not
alone in his enmity. U.S. Marshal A. B. Gray wrote Pittman, de-
nouncing Patrick McCarran for his "brain backed with egotism . . .
I am going to let him think that I have gone to sleep now and when
the awakening comes I will have old Rip Van Winkle skinned a
thousand ways."[40]

Pittman had been forewarned, and McCarran, ever the optimist,
now trained his ambitions upon 1916, when the junior senator would
be coming up for reelection. McCarran's thinking moved in this
direction even before the campaign of 1914 was completed:

> At the present time I am watching men and events very closely with
> a view of determining whether it is advisable for me to enter the fight
> at the next election. At the present time I am inclined to become a
> candidate.[41]

An amusing incident may have furthered McCarran's ambitions
for Pittman's seat. The junior senator, who had an alcohol problem,
was in Reno just before the final voting in 1914. According to the
Nevada State Journal, he had been drinking heavily:

> United States Senator Key Pittman, Nevada's junior Senator, was felled
> and sent prone in the gutter on Virginia Street yesterday after he had
> made an unprovoked attack on Lytton Stoddard, striking him without
> a word. Stoddard retaliated once with the result stated.
> The scene which occurred in full view of scores of persons on the street
> at 11 o'clock in the morning, was the culmination of a series of affrays
> precipitated by Pittman. The aggregate results follow:
> . Struck Zeb Ray, democratic politician
> Struck United States Marshal A. B. Gray
> Struck Senator William F. Sharon
> Struck Supreme Justice P. A. McCarran
> Struck Deputy Sheriff Lee Updike
> Struck H. Fraley, republican leader
> Struck Lytton Stoddard
> Struck Virginia Street

The story related how Pittman, when he saw McCarran, removed
the cigar from his mouth, and "with the same hand struck McCarran
who squared off but forebore to strike back, grappling with Pittman."[42]

Although McCarran did not realize it, Key Pittman, because of his youth and ability, was a more formidable adversary than New-lands. Also, in 1915, the Nevada legislature passed a law changing the method of nominating candidates from popular vote back to the convention system. This hurt McCarran's chances, since it reduced the effectiveness of his oratory, and put party control more securely in the hands of experienced professionals. Not surprisingly, Francis G. Newlands warmly supported his colleague, Pittman, as did most of the party organization.[43] Woodrow Wilson also wrote a letter of endorsement for the junior senator, which was published, and the federal employees in the state worked for his reelection. It was possibly no coincidence that Pittman was placed on the Foreign Relations Committee in April, 1916, over seven other applicants. Ironically, considering McCarran's later hearty support from labor, the unions went down the line for Pittman.[44]

McCarran officially announced his candidacy for Pittman's Senate seat in July, 1915. Always sanguine, he claimed to be aware of the odds against him. Early in the campaign he wrote, "Lined up against me I find Newlands, Dickerson, Bartlett, and Thatcher, as well as Pittman. This is the old machine, and I had them against me in 1912."[45] To combat the machine, McCarran relied mainly on his considerable personal charm and his many contacts. William Wood-burn wrote Pittman that the saloon element was solidly lined up for McCarran.[46] Even so, McCarran's campaign was difficult and dis-couraging, in contrast to that of Pittman, who did not even bother to return to the state to campaign. McCarran was particularly an-gered at Wilson's public support of his opponent, so he drafted a hot-tempered telegram to the president, telling him he could "bid goodbye to the three Presidential Electors in this State, and they can bid goodbye to a Democratic Senator from this state at the next election." The telegram was never sent, but it was privately leaked and circulated among McCarran's enemies.[47] He campaigned until he was exhausted. In a letter of unusual self-revelation, McCarran confessed that he had become chronically tired: "However, such is the fate of one guilty of being overly ambitious. I remember that in my early days I was told that 'He aims too low who aims beneath the stars,' but I have later found out that to keep up such an aim requires a mountain of vanity."[48]

The issues of the campaign did not run deep. Ambition, not issues, was the reason McCarran had challenged Pittman. In announcing his candidacy, McCarran implied that his opponent was more inter-ested in the welfare of other states than in his own. His argument was, in short, a repetition of the tired, provincial assertion, heard often in Nevada, that he would do for the state more than the incumbent. In his own words, McCarran argued that fighting for Nevada's progress would be his "first consideration."[49]

McCarran made Pittman's refusal to support the national suffrage amendment for women a prime issue. Since women had the right to vote in Nevada, this provided a potential aid to his candidacy. Mrs. Denver Dickerson wrote Pittman, "McCarran seems to be gaining among the Women's Civil League."[50] McCarran attempted to get additional mileage out of a Pittman amendment to a land bill. This amendment provided for the sale of seven million acres of federal land in Nevada, by parcels, to the highest bidders. In a public letter to Pittman, McCarran asked whether his amendment did not "open the door to land monopoly in this state by affording opportunity for the wealthy to secure the land to the exclusion of the settler and home builder of moderate means." Elsewhere he stated that the Pittman amendment would perpetuate the system where "25 persons in the state controlled 64 per cent of the private property."[51] Surprisingly enough, foreign policy was not a prime issue, even after Pittman's inclusion on the Foreign Relations Committee, and both candidates gave at least lip service to Wilson's policies. In his private correspondence, McCarran was staunchly anti-British in his views, but this did not produce any public denunciation of Wilson's foreign policy. Perhaps he did not dare to do so. Furthermore, it was by no means clear in 1916 that Wilson's foreign policy would lead the United States into war. Thus the thrust of McCarran's campaign focused on state issues, and which candidate would do the most for Nevada.

Even before the convention met in August, 1916, the contest was obviously hopeless for the challenger. Although McCarran's popularity was admitted, the general feeling was that he had "overstepped the mark" in going for Pittman's seat. Pittman wrote Woodburn one month before the convention that McCarran was a beaten man and that Pittman's supporters should attempt to conciliate him.[52] McCarran independently reached the same conclusion and in a public, rather grandiloquent letter to Pittman, dropped out of the race before the delegates assembled.[53] He offered his full support to the junior senator in the November election, personally nominated Pittman at the convention, and campaigned indefatigably for the ticket in the fall. The niceties were observed, but nobody was fooled.

In retrospect, McCarran's decision to run against Pittman was probably the single worst error of political judgment he ever made. He earned the undying enmity of a strong portion of the party and the reputation among party leaders of being selfishly interested only in his own political advancement, to the detriment of party unity. A. B. Gray harshly characterized him as an "egotistical ass."[54] Pittman, whose opinion was obviously important to McCarran's future, was devastating:

> McCarran has nothing to recommend him for this position except his nerve, energy and social qualities. He is violating the policy, if not the constitution of our state. He is degrading the dignity of the bench. He is threatening the success of our party, and he is selfish and ungrateful. He is utilizing the great office that has been conferred upon him from every stump in Nevada at the time that he ran. His term of office has not expired. He has no right to run. . . .
> I do believe that Judge McCarran's selfishness has endangered the success of the whole party in the State. I do believe that he has forfeited the support of the party for anything that he may ever aspire to.[55]

Why, it must be asked, did McCarran wage this doomed fight? His daughter believes that her father was possibly egged on by what he thought was an anti-Catholic attitude prevalent in the state.[56] This may well have been one reason for McCarran's decision, which may also have sprung from Pittman's drunken physical attack on the justice in 1914. However, McCarran seems to have been primarily governed by a driving, blinding ambition which warped his political judgment. He was consumed by the desire to become senator. Since he realized that Pittman's reelection would probably give him the seniority to continue for a long tenure, McCarran undoubtedly saw the moment as a crucial one. Pittman's triumph closed the doors leading to the only office McCarran really wanted. Also, McCarran turned forty in 1916, and he may well have been apprehensive over the passage of time, believing as he did that the moment had arrived to make a bid for the Senate.

After the humiliation of defeat, McCarran began pulling strings to obtain a lifetime judicial post, preferably outside his beloved state of Nevada. He telegraphed Senators Pittman and Newlands concerning the possibility of being appointed to the U.S. District Court of Nevada and was immediately turned down.[57] Undaunted, he believed he had discovered something more concrete when, in December, 1917, he heard of a vacancy on the Court of Appeals for the District of Columbia. McCarran wasted no time in requesting an endorsement from the two Nevada senators, and this time they were happy to comply, doubtless thinking it would be a splendid way to get rid of McCarran for good. His ostensible, although disingenuous, reason for seeking the position was that it would "afford the opportunity which I seek to continue my work, and . . . give my little girls the education that the city of Washington supplies." He asked a variety of people, including the chief justice of the California Supreme Court, whom he did not know and had never met, to write letters in his behalf.[58] The upshot of this opéra bouffe was that President Wilson wrote Newlands and Pittman that there was a major misunderstanding somewhere, as no vacancy existed on the District of Columbia Court of Appeals.[59] The fact that McCarran sought to permanently leave the state of Nevada, which he loved, was a measure of his desperation and embarassment.

But an unexpected opportunity developed when Senator Francis Newlands died suddenly on Christmas Eve, 1917. It took McCarran no time at all to organize a campaign to pressure Governor Emmet Boyle (whom he not so privately despised) to appoint him to the vacant senatorial seat.[60] The governor, naturally enough, ignored McCarran's entreaties and appointed instead the more compatible Charles Henderson of Elko. Unknown to McCarran, certain elements among the party leadership were also grooming District Judge Edward Ducker of Winnemucca to run for McCarran's seat on the Nevada Supreme Court. According to that ever faithful enemy, A. B. Gray:

> McCarran wired all over the state and was endorsed accordingly, and is a mighty sore man, said he would be a candidate in the primaries but don't think he has the nerve to try it. That constitutional hodoo has about got his goat. I am of the opinion that Ducker will beat Pat if he makes the race for the judgeship and that Henderson will beat him if he tries for the senate, so let our beloved friend practice law, it is a noble profession.[61]

McCarran did weigh the possibility of challenging Henderson in 1918 for the remainder of the two-year term. While he was still mulling over his decision, writing letters all over the state, bitter at Governor Boyle, and respectful of the money behind Henderson,

Ducker was persuaded to run. "We want a judge that will not monkey with politics and try to be a United States senator every other year," stated one politician.[62] McCarran decided in late February, 1918, not to challenge Henderson; but realizing Ducker's growing strength, and not liking the office of justice much anyway, he delayed his decision concerning his reelection candidacy. He drifted until June, 1918, when he finally announced he would run again. It was too late. He was defeated by a margin of 12,101 to 11,566. In only one other twentieth-century election has an incumbent Nevada supreme court justice been defeated. Many party leaders rejoiced at the loss. William Woodburn wrote Pittman:

> P.S. By the way, do you remember one P. A. McCarran? Well, the task of retiring him to private life was completed the other day when Judge Ducker beat him mercifully in the election. McCarran complained that the Pittman wing of the party was against him. For once he made a good decision.[63]

A. B. Gray was not so confident that McCarran was politically dead, and he foresaw another McCarran race for the Senate in 1920.[64]

McCarran further alienated the Nevada Democratic party leaders when he attempted to defeat Governor Boyle in the 1918 primary by openly supporting the candidacy of his chief rival, party chairman Sam Pickett. He wrote J. H. Causten of Lovelock that it made no difference to him whether the new governor was to be a Democrat, a Socialist, an anarchist, or even an I.W.W.—"anybody but Boyle."[65] Joe McNamara received the news that McCarran would vote Republican if by some unforeseen chance Boyle should defeat Pickett: "So far as I am concerned and so far as friends of mine are concerned, it is anybody but Boyle, regardless of political lines."[66] McCarran's promise to bolt the party if Boyle won the nomination indicated how limited his party regularity had become by this time. This inclination to refuse to give blanket support for the entire ticket was to grow with the years. Unfortunately for McCarran, Boyle easily won renomination and went ahead to defeat Republican candidate Tasker Oddie in the general election. Defeated in his own bid for reelection, McCarran was cast into the political wilderness.

The story of McCarran's political career from 1907 to 1918 is that of a man who steadily antagonized the Democratic leadership by refusing to conform to any set principles of party loyalty. By compulsive electioneering while serving on the bench, in defiance of the state constitution, McCarran not only ruined his chances for an early Senate nomination, but also for keeping his seat on the high court. His machinations were not only never-ending, they were ultimately self-destructive. Despite his brains, his huge talent, his warm charm, and his nerve, McCarran had reached a political dead end by 1918.

After his defeat he left Carson City with relief. He remembered his time on the court as "six years of exile."[67] "I am very much pleased at the outcome," he stated. "Another six years on the bench would mean six years retirement from active life, whereas, I hope when I am free to enter into life with a new determination and a new activity."[68] It would take fourteen more years of determination and activity, however, before his ultimate ambition would be satisfied, because the power structure was still in the hands of George Wingfield and his associates.

CHAPTER 3

McCARRAN AND WINGFIELD

BY THE mid-1920s, George Wingfield had risen to the apogee of his power in Nevada. His influence remained at a high level until 1932, when his banks were forced to close their doors. By 1932, Wingfield owned 13 of Nevada's 32 banks and had a branch in every considerable town in the state with the important exception of Las Vegas. Although the banks were separate corporations, since Nevada had a law against branch banking, this device fooled no one and the newspapers generally wrote of the "Wingfield chain." In 1932 the Wingfield banks controlled 57.2 percent of all bank deposits and 59.9 percent of the total assets and liabilities of all banks in the state,[1] dominance of the banking system unparalled in any other state.

After 1909, when Wingfield moved to Reno, the financier also obtained important real-estate holdings, including the two largest Reno hotels, the Riverside and the Golden. In the 1920s, it was rumored he controlled the bootlegging and gambling interests in the wide-open city, in conjunction with Jim McKay and Bill Graham. McKay and Graham, incidentally, were sentenced to the federal penitentiary on mail-fraud charges in 1938.[2]

Financial power gave Wingfield political power. The extent of Wingfield's political power, although debated, was considerable, and certainly inimical to McCarran's aspirations. Surprisingly, Wingfield himself was not ambitious for higher office, remaining content in the role of kingmaker. In 1912, for example, when his partner, Republican Senator George Nixon, died, Governor Tasker Oddie accommodatingly offered Wingfield Nixon's seat in the upper house. After considerable reflection, Wingfield refused the office, on the ground

27

that he could retain more power by remaining in Nevada. "Were I to accept the office," he declared in a remarkable statement, "what ever might be the character of my senatorial service, the state would inevitably lose something which I can give only by remaining for a time in private life."[3]

The only office he ever ran for was member of the Board of Regents for the University of Nevada, in 1928. He claimed he was not interested in politics, writing in 1910, for example, to Representative George A. Bartlett, "Of course I am not in politics and am a free lance and split my ticket any way I see fit."[4] But his impact on the political sphere was considerable, even in 1910, and it grew steadily. Wingfield was personally a Republican, but he had close contacts with members of both parties and this helped diffuse party differences. Then too, Nevada problems seemed larger than national problems, the state was unusually vulnerable to federal policies, and it seemed necessary that Nevada representation in congress, whether Democratic or Republican, should reflect state interests.

Wingfield's power was increased by the fact that, from 1910 to approximately 1950, the political and financial power of Nevada was to an amazing extent concentrated in Reno. Most political and financial leaders lived within one-half mile of each other on Reno's near-south and southwest side. McCarran and Wingfield in fact lived only one-half block apart. The Nevada leadership worked in close proximity, they attended many of the same social and business functions, ate lunch together, and belonged to many of the same clubs. They are even buried together in Mountain View Cemetery in Reno. Because of his dominating financial power, Wingfield was generally acknowledged to be the most powerful of this group.

This web, as indicated, crossed party lines. Among Republicans, Tasker Oddie (governor 1911-14, senator, 1921-33), Lester Summerfield, Fred Balzar (governor 1927-34), and Morley Griswold (lieutenant governor, 1927-34, governor, 1934) were close to Wingfield. Among Democrats, Key Pittman (senator, 1913-40), William Woodburn, George Thatcher, Sam Pickett, Ray Baker, George A. Bartlett, and James Scrugham (governor, 1923-26) had ties with Wingfield.[5] Pittman always denied any alliance with Wingfield, and it is probable his association was not direct, but rather through his close political friends Woodburn and Thatcher. Thus Pittman's political allies were also Wingfield's political allies. George Thatcher was attorney for the Wingfield banks, and Wingfield's chief adviser, in short, the power behind the kingmaker.

One anti-Wingfield newspaperman, John Sanford, later editor of the *Reno Evening Gazette,* put it this way:

> Every little thing that went on around the here, everybody said, "Well, now, how's that gonna get along with the boys up there in 'the cave'?" By that, they meant the upstairs of that old Reno National Bank Building there. And in one political campaign, those who opposed the Wingfield machine used to bring up the war cry of "4111 in Nevada politics." That was a telephone number. And 4111 gave you the Reno National Bank, George Wingfield, George Thatcher, and Bill Woodburn. George Thatcher at that time—let's see, I believe he was Democratic national committeeman, Bill Woodburn was state chairman, and George Wingfield was national committeeman for the Republicans. So you can see what 4111 meant. And every one of the state conventions that was held around here, Republican or Democrat, the influence of that machine was in there.[6]

A 1920 letter from Thomas Miller to Tasker Oddie demonstrates how the former Republican governor, and that party's candidate for U.S. senator, was expected to toady to the Wingfield line:

> I want to give you some straight advice, and I talked it over with George [Wingfield] as to what I would write you. You have made mistakes in your past political performances, the same as all of us, and I think that one of your greatest faults is not taking advice as to the policies to be followed from those of your friends who know how to give advice in matters political. If nominated, I would place myself absolutely in the hands of your State Committee or in Wingfield, and confer with them and follow along the lines suggested by them in your campaign.[7]

Unfortunately, no extensive, scholarly biography of Wingfield has been attempted, and probably none will be forthcoming. The Wingfield papers are under seal at the Nevada Historical Society, and will not be opened to researchers until 1997. It is possible they would have little to reveal to a researcher anyway. The present evidence is that Wingfield was a rough character who dealt harshly with opponents. Apparently he was not above using his considerable financial clout to force adherents to adopt proper doctrines, and to punish antagonists. John Sanford, always a bitter enemy, believed that Wingfield used his banking strength to force James Scrugham and his *Nevada State Journal* to follow a generally subservient line:

And it had its influence even over the newspaper business around the state through its loans that it had made, and that was one of the things that haunted the *Nevada State Journal* for years and years when Scrugham bought the paper. He gave a $60,000 note to the—well, the Wingfield banks, and more particularly, Thatcher and Woodburn. And when Fred McKechnie bought the paper from Scrugham, he thought that was just a plain legitimate note, one that could be handled and paid off. He found out afterwards that wasn't so. That was a club over the paper and its publisher.[8]

Wingfield did not hesitate to intervene in the political situation to suit his own personal needs. In the early 1920s, George Springmeyer was the U.S. Attorney for Nevada. His great fault, at least according to Wingfield and his powerful friends, was that he took the Volstead Act much too seriously, and insisted on its zealous enforcement. Conditions became so intolerable that Wingfield and Senator Oddie appealed personally to the proper authorities in Washington for Springmeyer's removal, and the authorities compliantly obtained his resignation.[9]

Wingfield, not Senator Oddie, asked Harry Atkinson, a Tonopah Republican to be the new U.S. attorney. Atkinson agreed, was confirmed, and promptly obtained offices "at the Reno National Bank building . . . right next to the president's [Wingfield's] office." Atkinson satisfied Wingfield sufficiently that he served two full terms, from 1926 until 1934, when McCarran was to have a major hand in naming his successor, Edward P. Carville. Under Carville, some of Wingfield's associates were put into prison. Many years later Atkinson told an interviewer the realities of the situation:

Enforcing prohibition was one of my chief jobs as U.S. Attorney. Prominent people owned bootlegging places. Wingfield might have owned the Reno Social Club. He might have been the undercover, but there was Bill Graham and Jim McKay on the outside. Later, Bill was sent to Leavenworth on account of some deal in which he was found guilty, and I think also that McKay was, too, found guilty. They owned lots of places during prohibition. . . .

It was hard to enforce prohibition, awfully hard. Of course, I told the fellows that we wouldn't stack against anybody. We wouldn't do any underhanded work to catch them or to break in or anything like that.

Some of the fellows coming in from the outside were these prohibition agents that you couldn't control, hardly. They were a little bit too fast about doing things. They tried to catch me, too. Oh, you bet your life! And they also tried to get Wingfield because I think his cook or someone like that gave some records to them, or was alleged to have done it. They used a search warrant to search his house. They tried to get the goods on him, but they didn't. Prohibition was a bad "noble experiment."[10]

The Wingfield machine (the term "machine" perhaps indicates too structured a situation to describe these informal connections) did have its critics, most notably the conservative Republican *Reno Evening Gazette,* edited by Graham Sanford. At this time the *Gazette* was Nevada's largest and most important newspaper. The neighboring *Sacramento Bee,* which had a considerable circulation and editorial influence in western Nevada, also opposed Wingfield. In 1935 the *Bee* won a Pulitzer Prize for meritorious public service, for a series of articles by Arthur B. Waugh that it ran in early 1934, which exposed some of Wingfield's mode of operation. Among politicians, however, by far the most eminent Nevadan to cross swords with Wingfield was Patrick A. McCarran, who refused to take orders from anyone. Although McCarran was generally publicly discrete (except during the Cole-Malley trial, when he attempted to expose Wingfield's excesses in the face of yawning public apathy), his attitude was well known. Wingfield's retribution was to keep McCarran out of the United States Senate for many years.

Partly because of Wingfield, and partly because of his own differences with the Democratic leadership in Nevada, McCarran's political ambitions were stymied for well over a decade after his 1918 defeat, although his legal career prospered and his public fame continued. On foreign policy issues, his views were opposed to the dominant sentiment of the Democratic party. Thus he refused to vote for Democratic presidential candidate James Cox in 1920, because of Cox's espousal of U.S. membership in the League of Nations, a fact McCarran readily admitted and that furnished considerable ammunition to his political enemies within the state. In 1924 and 1928, he supported Al Smith for President.

His ultimate goal remained the U.S. Senate. Sometime in the early 1920s a friend, Joe McDonald, asked McCarran whether he would make another try for that office, and McCarran replied, as McDonald was to remember almost a half century later, "Does anybody lose that ambition?" McDonald answered, "I don't think so." McCarran finally responded, "I'm going to be a candidate again. I don't know just when; whenever the time is right."[11]

In 1926, he declared once again for the Senate, but the attempt was ill advised. As in 1916, the Democratic establishment united against his candidacy, this time backing Ray Baker for the office. Baker had all the political and social connections McCarran lacked. Born in Eureka in 1879, he had been the personal escort to Elinor Glyn on her famous visit to Rawhide in 1907. Baker was warden of the Nevada State Prison from 1911 to 1912; assistant secretary to his close friend, Senator Key Pittman, from 1913 to 1914; secretary to the American ambassador to Russia, George T. Marye, from 1914 to 1916; and director of the Mint, from 1917 to 1922. Baker was married to Margaret Emerson Vanderbilt, the widow of Alfred Vanderbilt, who had gone down with the *Lusitania.* In 1926, Baker was a lobbyist in Washington for the Dollar Steamship Line, and he was chairman of the Wingfield United Nevada Bank in Reno.[12]

McCarran's campaign strategy was to emphasize those issues which differentiated him from other Democrats. Ultimately, and not surprisingly, this backfired. One popular issue that McCarran did argue for, in common with most Nevadans, was modification of the Volstead Act so that private parties could drink in the privacy of their homes. He tempered this by advocating the continued abolition of saloons and public drinking places.[13] More at variance with standard Democratic principles, he forthrightly announced his opposition to United States membership in the League of Nations and the World Court. One campaign brochure for McCarran quoted him, "The interest and prosperity of America does not depend on alliances with alien powers. This nation should avoid participating involvement in any court, compact or league which may endanger our being drawn into foreign wars."[14] When heckled for this stand, McCarran declared in a Reno speech just before the primary that, "whenever the question arises when a young man may be called abroad to die on foreign soil it is an issue," and asserted that if elected, he would oppose any measure which would throw the United States into the "maelstrom of international disputes."[15]

Baker, on the other hand, could point out truthfully that he was in the mainstream of the Democratic party, "in complete accord with the views and plans of Senator Pittman." One of Baker's newspaper ads announced that "he is a democrat, and is the only democrat standing squarely on the democratic platform."[16]

Baker's victory was expected, as the entire Democratic organization from Governor Scrugham on down worked in his behalf. One
prominent correspondent wrote Key Pittman that he was hopeful
McCarran could be "so decisively defeated in the primary that he
cannot possibly do much harm hereafter." William Woodburn wrote
Pittman that he and Thatcher were supporting Baker. "Of course our
desire to pay our respects to McCarran may have something to do
with it."[17] But the size of the victory was surprising. Baker amassed
4,732 votes, McCarran received only 2,755, and two other candidates
split 2,003 between them.[18] McCarran carried only one county, and
in the words of a friend, the election was "an awful blow." Although
McCarran campaigned for Baker in the final election, he probably
was not overly disturbed when Republican Tasker Oddie soundly
defeated him. It must have looked increasingly unlikely, even to
McCarran, that he would ever be elected to the United States Senate.
He was now fifty, and the state Democratic organization appeared
determined, and able, to prevent any further progress.

The Cole-Malley case in 1927 provided McCarran with his most
public confrontation with George Wingfield, and demonstrated quite
clearly the nature of the power structure in the state of Nevada. By
all odds it was the most important legal case in which McCarran was
ever to be involved as an attorney and the one with the greatest
political implications.

George Cole had been state controller of Nevada from his initial
election in 1914 until his defeat in 1926, when he narrowly lost a bid
for a fourth term. His close friend, Ed Malley, was first elected state
treasurer in 1914. More popular than Cole, he was reelected three
consecutive times and still held the position in 1927.

On the evening of April 27, 1927, these two men paid a surprise
visit to George Wingfield at his Reno home. They had a shocking
story to divulge. They announced that $516,322.16 of state money
was missing from the Wingfield-owned Carson Valley Bank in Carson City. They added that they and cashier H. C. Clapp of the bank
were responsible for the defalcation.[19] Over a period of years, the
money had been sunk by the three men in the Signal Hill Oil Company, and the company had come up with nothing but dry holes.

Wingfield had inadvertently caused the scandal to blow up at that
particular time, by discharging H. C. Clapp because of his heavy
drinking. With the firing of the cashier, who was anxious to get even,

the defalcation could no longer remain hidden. The fact that Cole and Malley went to Wingfield with their story, rather than to a responsible government official such as the governor or attorney general, indicates the true nature of the power structure. Certainly they desperately hoped and believed that Wingfield would cover up for them.

For some time there had been uneasy rumors among state officials in Carson City that something was amiss. It is possible that James Scrugham, governor from 1923 through 1926, had some idea of the sloppiness with which state finances were handled, although he did little to investigate such rumors. The son of the then editor of the *Reno Evening Gazette,* which was strongly anti-Wingfield, said that the new state administration of Governor Fred Balzar "knew there was something wrong; they didn't know what. It began to be rumored around during the '27 session of the legislature. Our man over there said they suspected something was wrong."[20]

Cole and Malley explained to Wingfield how the defalcations had occurred. The procedure was a complicated one of issuing false cashier's checks. The transactions had begun in 1919 and had steadily continued over the ensuing years.

Although Wingfield denied it at the trial, Cole and Malley were to testify on the witness stand that at this meeting they had been promised immunity. They declared under oath that George Thatcher, attorney for the Wingfield banks, who had been called in immediately, told them that very day (April 27) that everything "was fixed up." They asserted that Wingfield had made similar assurances and quoted him as saying that he had never "squealed" on friends and would not begin now.[21]

Despite Wingfield's denial on the stand, either he or Thatcher probably did at least imply that Cole and Malley would receive immunity; Wingfield doubtless was afraid of a run on his banks if the story leaked. Furthermore, Nevada was run by a clubby type of government, the political leaders had for the most part known each other for many years, first in Tonopah and Goldfield, and then in Reno. By common consent mistakes were covered up. Sins were not to be publicly confessed, and no one, least of all the public, was usually much enlightened about the inner workings of Nevada politics. Wingfield does appear to have implied some grant of immunity until he received the hard-nosed advice of San Francisco attorney J. F. Schuman, who represented the Crocker banking interests.[22]

For nine days, Wingfield and his attorneys sat on the story. There were several other tangled questions, aside from the one of immunity, which necessarily had to be resolved. For one thing, was the $516,322.16 loss to be borne by Wingfield's Carson Valley Bank, or by the state? So far, all state checks had been honored, so the shortage would appear to have been with the bank, a situation which certainly would have been distasteful to Wingfield. But if the loss were to be borne by the state, Wingfield still had problems. He owned the Nevada Surety and Bonding Company, which had bonded Malley and Cole in their official capacities as state treasurer and state controller, for $100,000 apiece. There was also the problem of how to avert a major run on the Carson Valley Bank, which was after all capitalized at only $50,000. Even worse, there might be runs on the other Wingfield banks.[23]

On the advice, or more probably the orders, of attorney Schuman, Wingfield decided to prosecute, which was probably his only possible course of action anyway. For one thing, the conviction of Cole and Malley could possibly put financial responsibility for the defalcation on the state rather than the bank. Also, on Schuman's advice, Wingfield immediately placed a large sum of money in the Carson Valley Bank to insure confidence. Seeing their chances for immunity disappearing, in early May, 1927, Cole and Malley sought the services of Patrick McCarran, the most prominent anti-Wingfield attorney in the state. Although the two men were broke, McCarran became attorney for the Nevada Signal Hill Oil Company for two years, at a retainer of $10,000 a year. The third conspirator, H. C. Clapp, decided to continue his independent course by publicly confessing to the embezzlement.[24]

On May 6, 1927, after keeping the secret for nine days, Wingfield invited leading Nevada government officials to dinner at his home, where he released the bad news. Among those present were Governor Balzar, Attorney General M. A. Diskin, and Bank Examiner True Vencil. It must have been a cheerless dinner. It certainly reflected the realities of Nevada politics that the state officials were summoned to see the banker instead of the other way around. By mutual agreement, although Wingfield had certainly already worked this out with his lawyers, it was decided that Cole, Malley, and Clapp were to be prosecuted. The state on its part agreed not to interfere with the functioning of the Carson Valley Bank, although under the circumstances it had the lawful authority to do so.[25] The following day, the story broke in considerable detail in the *Reno Evening Gazette*. Wingfield gave assurances to the public that they need feel no loss of confidence in his banks, as he had personally deposited $600,000 in the Carson Valley Bank:

> Pending such investigations I have personally deposited in the Carson Valley bank the full amount of money involved to be there held to meet and liquidate whatever liability may be legally imposed upon the bank.
>
> I am taking this course in order to guarantee to the people of the state of Nevada and to the depositors of the Carson Valley bank that whatever shortage in the funds of the state legally chargeable against the bank will be paid without a cent to anyone, other than myself.[26]

The most powerful newspaper in the state, the *Reno Evening Gazette*, strongly Republican but anti-Wingfield, editorially asked some pointed questions. Hitting very hard at the central issue it declared:

> The wonder of it all is that so huge a shortage should have so long escaped detection. Seemingly there has been an inexcusable amount of looseness in the financial administration of the state when more than one-half million dollars of the people's money could be lifted from the treasury and replaced by paper which may prove worthless.

The *Gazette* asked why the bond of the state treasurer was only $100,000, when the bond for comparable county fiscal officers was several times larger. It further pointed out, correctly, that if the state had lived up to its own statutes, the fraud could not have occurred.[27]

Reno's morning newspaper, the *Nevada State Journal*, was owned by James Scrugham, who was in the embarrassing position of having been governor from 1923 through 1926. Since Scrugham obviously had been negligent in his fiscal housekeeping, the *Journal* more or less hoped the matter would simply go away. On May 8, it declared, "The State Will Survive." This editorial offered no criticisms of state or bank officials, nor were any forthcoming.

Cole, Malley, and Clapp were arrested, whereupon bank cashier Clapp confessed everything and turned state's evidence. Malley was in due course removed from office, bail was set at $200,000, which could not be raised, and in August, 1928, the trial began in Carson City.

Clapp's confession made it difficult for Cole and Malley to protest their innocence. For the record, McCarran publicly stated that his clients were innocent, but during the trial he placed little emphasis upon this dubious point. Instead his defense of Cole and Malley mainly depended upon three shrewdly chosen arguments. McCarran's contentions were quite courageous, since they hit critically at the way Nevada was governed. His strategy was to absolve his clients by spreading the blame throughout the state administration and ultimately to George Wingfield himself. Needless to say, this strategy did not endear him to his political opponents.

First, McCarran argued incontrovertibly that the state of Nevada had not lived up to the requirements of its own statutes. If it had done so, the defalcation could not have mounted to such proportions. A 1913 statute which stated that no bank could be the depository of public funds in excess of seventy-five percent of its paid-up capital was still in effect in 1927; yet the Carson Valley Bank was capitalized at only $50,000, and it held $750,000 in state funds.[28]

McCarran also attempted to expose the cozy relationship between the state administration and George Wingfield by bringing out in the trial the fact that the state had demanded no security on its deposits. This same 1913 statute provided that "banks receiving such deposits should secure the state by depositing with the Treasurer, subject to acceptance by the board of examiners, bonds of the United States, or those of the state of Nevada or its political subdivisions to an amount fifteen percent in excess of the deposits received." Yet when McCarran cross-examined George Russell, Malley's successor as treasurer, Russell was forced to admit the state had no security whatever for the cashier's checks held from Wingfield banks.[29]

McCarran's second strategy was to attempt during the course of the trial to destroy the credibility of George Wingfield, certainly a dangerous task for a man who must still have retained some political ambitions. It may be that McCarran's ambition had temporarily waned after his crushing defeat in 1926. More likely his bulldog determination to do everything possible for his clients forced him upon this course of action. And beneath it all was unquestionably a deep-seated hatred of Wingfield, a desire to embarrass the financier and gain revenge for previous defeats.

For whatever reasons, when Wingfield took the stand, McCarran did his best to put him in an unflattering and uncomfortable position. Wingfield did not enjoy this unaccustomed role. According to the unfriendly *Reno Evening Gazette,* Wingfield appeared nervous under

McCarran's insistent examination and "spoke in such a low voice
that he was requested by the attorneys of both sides to speak louder."
In his questioning, McCarran attempted to bring out Wingfield's
rough-and-tumble background, his involvement in gambling activities, and his meddling in politics. He asked Wingfield why James
McKay, a notorious dealer in illegal gambling and liquor operations,
was in his home when Malley and Cole paid their celebrated visit.
He repeatedly queried Wingfield about why there was a nine-day
delay in notifying state officials about the embezzlements.[30]

In his summary argument, McCarran contended that, like some
evil Midas, everything Wingfield touched somehow turned corrupt.
According to the *Gazette,* McCarran

> pictured Nevada under the grip of a multimillionaire and saw Malley
> and Cole as two men caught in the machinery of gold controlled by
> George Wingfield.
>
> "Ed Malley can go to prison," he said. "George Cole can go to prison
> and come out just as they went in—but can individuals go into bondage
> and come out; can this sovereign state go into the bondage of gold and
> come out?"
>
> "Where do I get my authority for this statement?" he demanded. "I
> get it from one statement made by a multi millionaire—it's the permeat-
> ing thing in this case, 'They know what I want.' "
>
> That statement, made by Wingfield on the witness stand in response
> to a question asked him concerning the directions given his attorneys,
> George Thatcher and William Woodburn, was the motif of McCarran's
> appeal to the jury.
>
> "They know what I want," McCarran shouted time and again.
>
> "There is but one question involved in this case," McCarran said.
> "Shall Ed Malley and George Cole go to the penitentiary or shall the
> Carson Valley Bank pay $516,000.[31]

This last sentence led into McCarran's third argument. He began
with the question of who was going to make good the $516,322.16:
the bank (Wingfield) or the state? Since bank cashier Clapp had
already pleaded guilty, if Cole and Malley were found innocent, the
state would then be off the hook. McCarran even went so far as to
argue, probably accurately, that Wingfield had sought the prosecution of Cole and Malley so the state of Nevada would have to make
up part of the defalcation and he, Wingfield, would not have the sole
responsibility for the amount.[32]

If one accepted the disputed cashier's checks as legitimate,
McCarran argued, then the state had no shortage. And if no shortage

existed, the state had no valid case against Cole and Malley.[33] In a sense, by prosecuting Cole and Malley, the state was laying itself open to being responsible for making up the $516,000. Even before the trial's beginning, McCarran made plain the nature of this argument:

> No fraudulent transactions or transactions of a fraudulent nature are admitted or could be admitted by either Mr. Cole and Mr. Malley, because no fraud or defalcation appears in their offices nor with reference to public moneys.
>
> If the Carson Valley Bank after enjoying the use of these moneys in the bank circulation for years, now refuses to honor these checks of its cashier, the matter is not chargeable to Cole or Malley as controller or treasurer.[34]

State law—although admittedly it had never been consistently followed—seemed to indicate the bank's responsibility. A 1911 act to regulate banking stated:

> Any director, officer or other person who shall participate in any violations of the laws of this state relative to banks, shall be liable for all damages which the said bank, its stockholders, depositors or creditors shall in consequence of such violation sustain.[35]

The state's accounts were balanced at the time charges were brought. In his summary, McCarran declared that the choice was clear: "Whether George Cole and Ed Malley would have to go to state prison or whether the President of the Carson Valley bank, George Wingfield, would have to pay the amount of the alleged defalcation." McCarran thundered, "There is one thing to decide—which is greater, the gold of life or the gold of George Wingfield."[36]

The plea was ignored. Cole and Malley were found guilty by the jury and sentenced to 5 to 15 years in prison.

From a later perspective, it is obvious that the trial left many loose ends and unanswered questions, although McCarran appears to have done his best to raise them. In order to defend his clients properly he had to attempt an exposure of Nevada's power structure, and too many individuals wanted to prevent the opening of that particular can of worms. The prosecution deliberately chose to narrow the scope of proceedings rather than widen it. For one thing, other people were implicated in the defalcations, yet nothing was done to indict them, or even solicit their testimony. A significant example is

that the Carson Valley Bank had previously covered up for Bank
Examiner Gilbert Ross. McCarran could later write that the Cole-
Malley mess was all Ross's fault: "He was the bank examiner who
initiated the whole thing." Malley's defalcations began in 1919 when
Clapp began covering up for Ross.[37] The *Reno Evening Gazette*
published the court testimony:

> Dwelling at length in this phase of the case Clapp testified when
> questioned by McCarran, that Ross would buy stock through a broker
> and that the stock with draft attached would be sent to the Carson
> Valley Bank and when Ross failed to take up the drafts that Malley
> took them up.
> "When did you go in with Ross?" asked McCarran.
> "I didn't go in with him," Clapp replied.
> "Did the bank honor the Ross drafts?" he was asked.
> "Yes, it paid them."
> "Did he have an account at the bank?" was the next question.
> "Yes, but there was rarely anything in it," Clapp said.
> "Did the bank directors know of these drafts?"
> "Yes, I told Doyle and he said to have Ross take them up."
> "Was bank money paid out for those drafts?"
> "Yes."
> "Was there a shortage in cash of the bank from these drafts?"
> "Yes, they were carried as cash."
> Clapp then said in response to a question that some of Ross' checks
> were not returned to him and that $960 in checks of Ross were not
> made good.
> Asked if drafts for other customers of the bank were paid by the bank
> Clapp replied that they were not and that they were returned when not
> paid.
> "Why was Ross treated any different than any other customers,"
> McCarran then asked.
> "Well, he was the bank examiner," replied Clapp, "and he said he
> would take them up."

The bank, it developed, lost a total of $6,915 on Ross.[38]
    Ross was not even asked to testify. He just happened to be on
vacation at the time. James Scrugham, who was governor when the
defalcations had reached their height, was also neglected. Scrugham's *Nevada State Journal,* continuing its blind support of Wingfield's machine, refused to carry most of McCarran's
cross-examination. Not surprisingly, its editorial page failed to draw
any implications from the mess.

The court testimony certainly brought out the chummy, club-like atmosphere permeating the state leadership of Nevada. Most of these men had known each other from Tonopah-Goldfield days, and none were going to inquire too deeply into each other's secret dealings, or unpaid bills. There appeared to be, in the words of John Sanford, a "Go to Hell atmosphere." Everyone thought Malley was a good guy and Cole a good guy. With that sense of brotherhood, nobody had paid much attention to what had been going on.[39]

The scandal, although reported with huge headlines, was only a seven-day wonder. The residents of Nevada, as it turned out, were to be the chief losers: but they remained apathetic. Many of the people implicated continued to have prosperous careers. Although Clapp died in prison, Malley and Cole were paroled after serving three and one-half years of their terms. Cole became a dealer in a club at Lake Tahoe. Malley was given a position with the Federal Emergency Relief Administration (FERA) and did well in later real-estate dealings at Tahoe. Gilbert Ross was to hold several important positions with the FERA and the Works Progress Administration (always with the bitter opposition of McCarran), and was a trusted adviser to Governor Vail Pittman in the late 1940s. James Scrugham, instead of being discredited, was elected to the United States House of Representatives in 1932. After serving five terms, he gained election to the U.S. Senate in 1942. Governor Fred Balzar was reelected in 1930. George Wingfield was elected to the University Board of Regents in 1928 without opposition. The scandal was soon forgotten.[40]

But the people of Nevada had to pay. The state continued its policy of depositing most of its funds in the Wingfield banks. When those banks closed their doors in 1932 (see p. 49), although they held "only" 57 percent of the general deposits, they held a disproportionate percentage of the state funds. Wingfield eventually was forced into bankruptcy. It is obvious that the state administration took no greater care with its money after 1927 than it had before 1927, and Wingfield's rather offhand supervision of his own banks continued unchanged.

Another McCarran prophecy turned out to be accurate when the state was forced to sustain the greater part of the immediate financial losses resulting from the defalcations. When the state legislature was called into emergency session in early 1928, it held Wingfield financially responsible for little more than his $100,000 surety bond. A compromise settlement of $154,896.65 (30 percent of the loss) was paid by Wingfield, and the state was held responsible for $361,425.51 in direct costs and $52,000 in indirect costs. This had to be financed by a special state tax. Only the *Reno Evening Gazette* and the *Sacramento Bee* questioned the arrangement. The *Gazette* declared the compromise settlement too low, and thought Wingfield should have made up 50 percent of the loss. The *Bee* asserted that the settlement was an "outrageous imposition and swindle" and only illustrated that Wingfield was "Nevada's financial and political power."[41] McCarran, it is superfluous to note, continued to be frozen out of a leading political role in the state.

It was not until 1932 that McCarran's long-term ambition for the U.S. Senate was finally satisfied. By hard work, excellent organization and planning, considerable luck, and a complete misreading of the situation by his opponents, McCarran was able to beat the hostile Democratic establishment and win election to the office from which he had been systematically excluded for the previous two decades.

There were several reasons for his victory at this time. For one thing, the Wingfield organization underestimated public resentment of the Great Depression and saw no reason why the supposedly popular Republican incumbent senator, Tasker Oddie, should be defeated. It was satisfied with the existing arrangement, with one Democratic and one Republican senator, both close to Wingfield or Wingfield's men, representing the state. Thus there was no real need to groom a bipartisan candidate to head off the McCarran drive. In late 1931, W. A. Kelly, vice chairman of the Nevada Democratic State Central Committee, pointed out to Key Pittman that McCarran was obviously ambitious to run the following year and there was no one around to stop him. He added that "Henderson's absence and Thatcher's refusal to run leave us absolutely without an available candidate unless you have a suggestion to make."[42]

The most obvious candidate, George Thatcher, was a close friend of Senator Oddie and had ambitions only to become state chairman. His law partner, William Woodburn, also refused to make the race. Former governor James Scrugham had ambitions for the Senate, but did not want to run against Oddie. He and Oddie were also friends, and Scrugham even rented his Reno home from the senator.[43] Instead Scrugham decided to run for Nevada's lone seat in the House of Representatives. Ed Clark, the most prominent contender from southern Nevada, was not close to Wingfield and soon announced his lack of interest in a Senate race.[44] This failure of the machine to field a candidate testifies to the prevalent feeling that the well-established Oddie would easily win a third term and Nevada would continue its tradition of bipartisan representation in the U.S. Senate. McCarran, if he won the Democratic nomination, would merely be the party's sacrificial offering, and then he would be finished for good. There was little sensitivity, except on McCarran's part, to the national forces that would modify this scenario.

By early 1932, it was apparent that McCarran had considerable rank-and-file support among Democrats. A straw vote conducted by the *Nevada State Journal* showed McCarran leading every contender, including Oddie. The *Elko Free Press* had him leading every Democrat. The *Las Vegas Review-Journal* poll put him third in the Democratic sweepstakes among southern Nevada voters.[45]

Taking advantage of this seeming popularity, and lacking any obvious opponent, McCarran announced for the U.S. Senate unusually early, on March 17, 1932, a step designed to stop any other major candidate from mounting a campaign. In his public statement, unlike his earlier Senate races, the Reno lawyer was careful to avoid controversial stands that might alienate various party elements. He affirmed his support for the repeal of the Eighteenth Amendment, a position overwhelmingly popular in Nevada. Otherwise he was uncharacteristically vague:

> My platform is so well-known to the people of Nevada and my principles regarding national and international affairs have been so long before the public that it is not necessary to announce them at this time. But at the proper time I will again make a complete and emphatic statement of my platform.
>
> I have always advocated, and do now advocate, home rule and states' rights. . . . I dislike the term "wet" but I believe in individual human liberty."[46]

In 1932, the Democrats were scheduled to hold two state conventions, one in Las Vegas in May and one in Carson City the following month. McCarran carefully prepared the strategy by which he hoped to gain an official endorsement from these two bodies. On the way to the Las Vegas convention, McCarran stopped to gas up his car in the little town of Beatty, and by chance saw Pete Petersen, a prominent Reno labor leader, also on his way to the convention. Striking up a conversation, he told Petersen that he would attempt to get a resolution from the convention recommending that he have no primary opposition "for the reason that the then Senator Oddie was considered to be from three to five thousand votes stronger than the Republican party." As Petersen recounted the story later, he was a bit doubtful that this could be accomplished, and so was McCarran.[47]

The surprising thing is that he did succeed. The Las Vegas State Democratic Convention unanimously endorsed McCarran, an action accompanied by "prolonged cheering."[48] An identical result was obtained from the Carson City conclave on June 28, 1932. According to a delegate who attended this gathering, McCarran forces were well organized, and their timing superb.[49] By thus winning approval from the state party, McCarran had successfully warded off all organizational opposition. Writing after the November election to his eldest daughter, McCarran explained the extent of his preparations:

> Fortune favored me from the very beginning. The Democratic Convention that met at Las Vegas on the 21st of May unanimously endorsed me for the United States Senate. Following that, the Democratic Convention that assembled at Carson City on the 20th *[sic]* of June unanimously endorsed me for the United States Senate. These endorsements were worked out with painstaking, diligent thought. They did not come spontaneously. Every endorsement came as a result of an organization laid carefully months before, and plans that were carried out. These endorsements discouraged any other party from attempting to file in the primary. Hence, I was saved the expense and annoyance and heartache of a primary campaign.[50]

There were no doubt other unstated reasons for the lack of opposition, although this necessarily leads into the realm of speculation. Since the Nevada press unanimously agreed that the Thatcher-Woodburn (read Wingfield) combine controlled both state conventions, and since these forces previously had always been strongly antagonistic to McCarran, one suspects that some type of political accommodation had been worked out. For example, McCarran publicly supported the candidacy of George Thatcher for national committeeman. "I want the world to know that I am for George Thatcher," McCarran shouted at one meeting. "I place my entire political future and hopes of success on the shoulders of George Thatcher."[51] These were strange words indeed from McCarran for an old enemy! The Reno attorney also acquiesced in the election as party chairman of William McKnight, the favorite of the Thatcher-Woodburn crowd, over the incumbent William S. Boyle. McCarran also consistently averred his loyalty to the Roosevelt-Garner ticket, which was popular in the state. The Nevada delegation had supported Roosevelt's candidacy in the 1932 Chicago convention. It is possible that some arrangement for distribution of federal appointments if the Democrats were victorious was also discussed.

Not only did McCarran make an apparent accommodation with the Democratic leadership, he also wisely continued to downplay issues that might have differentiated him from his party. He now never failed to affirm his strong support of both the national and state Democratic platforms.[52] On foreign policy, where he had so violently disagreed with majority party sentiment in previous years, he favored, much less acerbically than in the past, "an honest friendship with all nations but entangling alliances with none."[53] Ironically, considering his later views, he favored recognition of the Soviet Union "and all other countries that offer a potential market for American products."[54] On national issues he hewed closely to the Democratic state platform, campaigning for lower tariffs (he denounced the Smoot-Hawley tariff), a six-hour working day for labor, restrictive immigration laws, and, most vociferously, for immediate repeal of the Eighteenth Amendment, and "the re-establishment of silver as a medium of exchange with a parity fixed on scientific principles."[55] As the campaign developed, he began to denounce the Hoover administration's roughing up of the bonus marchers and supported the principle of a veterans' bonus. But, overall, his chief issue was the remonetization of silver, a most conventional idea within the state of Nevada.

McCarran waged an energetic campaign. As he wrote his daughter after the election:

> A long summer of continuous effort represents your direction, as extended to me in a letter in the early spring, "If you go in this time, go in to win."
>
> Never for a moment, did I lose sight of that motto. I made five laps of this state. I visited every water hole, town, hamlet, valley and place within the State. There was scarcely a man, woman, or child in that State that I did not see personally. Every time I would turn away from a place I thought I had wasted time in, I would think of the motto, "If you go in, go in to win."

... From the 21st of May until eight o'clock on the evening of November 8th, I kept up a continuous "go." I traveled nearly twenty thousand miles during the campaign. Everything seemed to click for once in my career.[56]

His oratorical powers were skillfully used to project his image to the voters. As the campaign developed, McCarran, with his strong support for Roosevelt and his diatribes against Hoover and heavy unemployment, inspired increasing enthusiasm among voters. This increased his self-confidence to a point unattained in previous efforts. One Republican supporter of Oddie found himself mesmerized by McCarran's platform personality. Listening to McCarran in the mining town of Pioche, he described to Oddie his reactions, which could hardly have boosted Oddie's self-confidence:

The speech by Pat McCarran cannot be dismissed so lightly. It is my honest opinion that this man is an able and fully qualified successor to W. J. Bryan; he is a finished orator, and is very adroit in following the attitude of the audience. I sat there spell-bound, not because of any solid reasoning or logic placed before me, but because the man is a master of oratory.[57]

Officially the previous interparty acrimony was forgotten. At one Democratic meeting, William Woodburn told his audience at some length that, although he and McCarran had differed politically many times in the past, they were "now fighting for the same cause." The skeptical, and Republican, *Reno Evening Gazette* thought he was laying it on "a bit too thick."[58] Key Pittman, James Scrugham, and McCarran went off together in an automobile caravan to tour the state.[59] Yet some acrimony obviously remained under the surface, as the narrowness of McCarran's victory in that Democratic landslide year attests. McCarran was required to contribute a large sum ($5,-000) to the state Democratic Central Committee, which he was forced to borrow.[60]

For a candidate who was to be a sacrificial offering, McCarran was doing a good deal better than expected. Even so, Oddie remained a 5-to-4 favorite of gamblers.[61] Oddie was doubtless helped by his labor support;[62] as early as August he realistically foresaw that anti-Hoover feeling in Nevada could defeat him: "The overwhelming anti-Hoover and anti-Administration sentiment in the State ... will carry me down in a landslide if I don't get plain, simple and under-standable facts before the people of the State who do the voting."[63]

Oddie might still have pulled off a victory except for two unfore-seen developments. On October 31, the Wingfield banks closed their doors, permanently as it turned out. Although the consequences to Oddie's campaign were not fully appreciated at the time, the closure could not have failed to hurt the Republican effort. Oddie had been closely associated with Wingfield, and McCarran's independence of the banker was well known and documented.

The other unforeseen development was the huge Democratic vote in Clark County, particularly in Boulder City, which was populated by workers who had recently arrived in the state for the construction of Hoover Dam. The number of votes cast in Clark County was three times greater in 1932 than it had been in 1928, and the increase was almost entirely Democratic.

Even so, Oddie ran a strong race. Roosevelt won Nevada by a landslide margin of 16,082 (receiving 28,756 votes to Hoover's mea-ger 12,674). James Scrugham won election to the House of Represen-tatives by a comfortable margin of 8,846 (24,979 votes to Sam Arentz's 16,133). McCarran, however, eked out a bare 1,692 major-ity, defeating Oddie by 21,398 votes to 19,706. That was 52.1 percent of the votes.[64] McCarran carried normally Republican Washoe County, still the state's most populous, by a slight margin (6,217 to 6,147); and here, since the Republicans had a 2,700 registration margin, the closure of the Wingfield banks may have made some difference. In the "cow counties,"[65] Oddie had a slim victory. McCarran really won, however, because of the strong Democratic vote in Clark County, which had gone Republican in 1928 but went for McCarran by 4,529 to 2,568 votes. Las Vegas voted for McCar-ran by a margin of 2,325 to 1,402, and Boulder City, home of the workers who were erecting Hoover Dam, went for the Reno lawyer by an overwhelming 1,460 to 544 votes.[66] It is significant that Clark County had no Wingfield bank, so the failure of the banks was not a major issue there. The crucial element in McCarran's margin of victory was the inflow of the Democratic-oriented workers into southern Nevada.

On learning of his victory McCarran expressed his appreciation:

> May I . . . express my sincere gratitude to the people of my native state for the honor conferred upon me. I shall in the future dedicate my

life to the welfare of my nation and to the welfare and development of
Nevada, to the end that contentment may come to the masses of the
people and that the forgotten man shall be kept constantly in mind.[67]

To his daughter, McCarran wrote, correctly, that his victory had
been without strings:

> One particular pleasure comes to me on this occasion, and that is that
> I go into the Senate of the United States independently. I owe my
> success to no faction and to no power. I owe my success to the masses
> of the people of this state and especially to the laboring element; to the
> toilers and to the men in the mediocre walks of life. They were my
> backers. They put me over in this. The powers that be, so to speak,
> those who placed themselves in high regard, were not, without a single
> exception, for me.[68]

So, at the age of fifty-six, Pat McCarran had finally attained the office
he had so long coveted. Now it was up to him to make something
of it.

Norman Biltz, who was later a useful political ally of McCarran's,
was in Washington, D.C., to witness the inauguration of President
Roosevelt in 1933. By accident he met Senator McCarran on an
elevator. Biltz went up to McCarran and said, "Senator McCarran,
let me congratulate you. You did a fantastic race." The Senator
replied, "I fooled you and the rest of your gang on the corner, didn't
I?" Biltz could only answer, "You certainly did, Senator."[69] It was
a fitting epigraph for the race.

McCarran's victory marked the gradual end of an era in Nevada's
history. The Wingfield bank debacle hastened the end of one man's
political and economic domination of the state, which had lasted for
a quarter century. The banks had been in trouble for some time,
although the public had been given no inkling of the difficulty until
it was too late. Loose accounting practices, lack of state regulation,
a probable lack of regulation by Wingfield himself, and poorly secured loans to the livestock men and sheepmen of Nevada had all
contributed to the failure.

State regulation had obviously been relaxed. Nothing had been
learned from the 1927 Cole-Malley trial. In 1933, a special legislative
committee condemned the state bank examiner and the banking
board for their affability with the Wingfield interests. It declared:

The relation the banking interests of this state had with the state official
family and in particular with the state board of finance and the bank
examiner contributed to the adoption of a more liberal policy than
would have been possible if the intent of the banking code had been
enforced in all respects.[70]

The banks did not close for lack of outside aid. They had already
received considerable help from private and public sources. In 1932,
the Reconstruction Finance Corporation (RFC) had loaned the
chain $4,000,000, and the Crocker First National Bank of San Fran-
cisco and the Federal Reserve Bank of San Francisco together lent
$863,000. According to a later legislative report, "Officials of the
Crocker National Bank were virtually in charge of all Wingfield
banks for a period of 90 days during the summer of 1932."[71]

By October, 1932, the Wingfield banks were again in serious trouble. Wingfield applied for another $2,000,000 loan from the RFC and
asked the governor for help in obtaining it. Republican Governor
Balzar flew to Washington on October 20 to meet with RFC officials
and President Hoover. Although Balzar received courteous treatment, RFC officials denied the request, because the banks by now
lacked sufficient collateral. According to the head of the RFC, writing many years later, "Under the law requiring us to have full and
adequate security we could render no further help; and we had to
watch the banks go to the wall." This refusal became publicly known
on November 19, 1932.[72]

On October 31, 1932 (eight days before the election), Governor
Balzar telephoned Lieutenant Governor Morley Griswold from
Washington. Balzar asked him to proclaim a bank holiday, beginning the next morning, Tuesday, November 1, and lasting until
November 12. Griswold soon discovered he lacked the authority to
proclaim a bank holiday as such, so instead he proclaimed a general
business holiday, except for "all Courts, the University of Nevada
and all public schools . . . during which said days and for such period
the payment of all debts and obligations of every nature and description except the payment of taxes and obligations prescribed by statute shall be suspended."[73] This was the first statewide bank holiday
of the Great Depression.

This was only a voluntary program, however, since the state
lacked the power to make it mandatory. Thus the First National
Bank of Reno, the state's largest individual bank, remained open.
But all the Wingfield banks closed, and as the bank holiday contin-

ued it was evident that the problem focused exclusively on them. They never did reopen, and eventually George Wingfield was forced to declare bankruptcy. It was not until 1934, however, that the state government in Carson City came under control of people antagonistic to Wingfield's political and financial interests.

McCarran did not become publicly involved in the furor occasioned by the closing of the Wingfield banks and the terms upon which they might be reopened, as he was busy preparing for his senatorial duties. He had consistently avoided putting his own money into a Wingfield bank, so he was not harmed financially, but he was undoubtedly an interested bystander.

As he wrote his daughter, the situation in Nevada was most serious:

> I have no way of describing to you the conditions that prevail here. On the 31st day of October, the Wingfield chain of banks closed their doors and in this respect, I may say all of Nevada excepting Clark County, and it even extended some of its effort into that County. The closing of the Wingfield banks destroyed the financial and industrial life of the State of Nevada. In addition to this, the Wingfield banks, by reason of political affiliation, and by reason of political power had in their custody some one million, two hundred thousand dollars of public funds. This crippled every form of life. School moneys were involved. The funds of the University were tied up. The funds of the schools of every district were tied up and the funds belonging in the State Treasury were tied up—so that State employees were unable to receive their monthly salaries. The business life of the State was the recipient of a solar plexus. Immediately following this, the San Francisco wholesalers issued an order that no credit would be extended for shipment of goods at wholesale to the merchants of Nevada. Cash must be on hand before shipments are made, hence the credit extended by retailers in Northern Nevada to the consumers was immediately curtailed—in fact destroyed entirely. This gives you some color in the picture that represents the State at the present time.

In a final paragraph, McCarran finally ventilated some of the private feelings about Wingfield that had rankled so long. Even in February, 1933, he could not publicly express these thoughts:

> The reason for this is that too much power was vested in one individual, and whenever too much power is vested in one human being, that power usually turns in the form of a flame to destroy the political, financial and moral power of the State—as for the last fifteen years has

been vested in George Wingfield. He was an avaricious controller, demanding the pound of flesh in every line in which he bent his efforts. The God of nature seems to destroy such a condition, and it has come here. It is the greatest blessing that has come to this commonwealth in twenty years. You may wonder why I should say that. It is a blessing of purification, so to speak. The power that controlled the throttle of this state is at an end, and though the people may go back into the throes of impoverishment, they nevertheless will reap the benefit in many ways.[74]

An era of Nevada's history was ending, and McCarran's service to his state, and his great power within the Democratic party was still mostly in the future. One consistent impediment to his advancement was now removed. McCarran was not regretful.

CHAPTER 4

FIRST-TERM MANEUVERINGS

ANY SENATOR from Nevada has to reckon with the fact that the state has a particularly vulnerable relationship with the national government. Because of its small population, and the roller coaster ups and downs of its growth, Nevada over the years has been unusually dependent upon federal largesse and good will. There are at least four aspects of this dependency and vulnerability:

1) From the 1860s until approximately 1955 the most important industry in Nevada generally was mining. An important segment of this mining was precious metals; silver and gold mining were Nevada's initial industries. Over time the previous metals assumed a symbolic importance in the minds of Nevadans. Nevadans have always been defensive about the pricing of gold and silver, believing correctly that pricing decisions were always made elsewhere: in Washington, D.C., or, for that matter, in London or Zurich. Although copper was in fact the most important metal mined in Nevada after 1910, gold and silver (and their pricing) retained their symbolic importance for many Nevadans. It was firmly believed that state, and even national well-being, was tied to their price structure.

2) In 1931, gambling was legalized in Nevada. This was merely a recognition of a situation which had prevailed for many years. But, quite unforeseen by the 1931 legislators, gambling became the state's largest industry by 1955, and Nevada was increasingly dependent upon it. And Nevada gambling cannot flourish without federal acquiescence. Even though legalization may be purely a state matter, gambling could be terminated rather quickly by imposition of a federal tax on gambling transactions.

3) Since the state is so sparsely populated (even in the 1980s its population is mostly concentrated in only two urban areas), most of it is owned by the federal government. In 1970—the figures do not change significantly from year to year—61,049,000 acres of Nevada land were under federal control. This was 86.9 percent of Nevada's total land area (by far the greatest percentage of any state outside of Alaska) and greater than the total land area of Great Britain, for example.

4) The state of Nevada has always been highly dependent upon federal projects for its economic health. The Newlands Irrigation Project of 1905 was responsible for the settlement and growth of the Fallon area. The approval of the Boulder Canyon Project in 1928 and the consequent building of federally controlled Hoover Dam was the catalyst that set off Clark County's sensational growth, which resulted by 1970 in its predominance in state affairs. The Hawthorne Naval Depot, approved in 1928, brought growth to that area. During McCarran's tenure as a United States Senator, Stead Air Base was built near Reno, Nellis Air Base near Las Vegas, and the atomic testing ground in south central Nevada.

Since Nevada is so unusually vulnerable to federal pressures and policies, its citizens believe they have a special need for protection in the national capital. They seek that protection in particular in the U.S. Senate, where their interests are represented equally with those of larger states.

If population is the only criterion, Nevada has always been over-represented in Washington, D.C. This arrangement has been severely criticized, especially by writers from big states. Historian Gilman Ostrander contends in his provocative assessment of Nevada history that Nevada, "the great rotten borough," demonstrated a major failure of the constitution makers in allowing a small, under-populated state such as Nevada to have an equal voice in the United States Senate with far larger, more important states. Moreover, many have argued that Nevada senators have not used that power wisely and have represented only their own parochial interests, to the detriment of the nation at large. Echoing Ostrander, historian Fred Israel asserts in his biography of Key Pittman that the senator consistently served the provincial interests of Nevada rather than the needs of the national government, despite his important position in the Senate and chairmanship of the Senate Foreign Relations Committee.[1]

Much of this is easily documented. Nevada was admitted to the Union during the Civil War, not because of its great population, but partly because the Republican party needed an additional state to ratify the Thirteenth Amendment. No state has ever been admitted with fewer people. From 1864 until 1959, Nevada always ranked last in population among the states. After the collapse of the Comstock mining boom, Nevada's population even declined; by 1900 the state had only 42,335 people. Although the population had grown to 91,058 by 1930, this was no larger than a typical political ward of Chicago or New York City, and a mere 1/1,348 of the total population of the United States. Yet the state had 1/48 of the total representation in the United States Senate and, for that matter, 1/435 of the House of Representatives. It also had 1/177 of the total electoral vote in a presidential election.

There are methods by which small, vulnerable states can heighten the effectiveness of their representation in the Senate, already increased by constitutional protection. Power in the upper chamber is derived basically from seniority, whether the senator represents New York, California, or Nevada constituents. The Senate is built on the committee system, and the chairmanship of the various committees has invariably been a matter of seniority within the majority party.

Therefore, the voters of Nevada have tended to reelect their senators, sensing accurately that this creates power. In the nineteenth century, John P. Jones represented Nevada for 30 years, and William Stewart for 28. In the twentieth century, Key Pittman was senator for 28 years, Patrick McCarran for 22, and more recently, Alan Bible for 20. Howard Cannon has, by 1982, accrued 24 years of seniority.

Elections in Nevada usually are not based primarily on national issues (although election results naturally have a tendency to reflect national trends), but usually on the more primitive question of which individual candidate can and will do more for the state. Even though the senator might have a deep interest in national or foreign affairs, as indeed both Pittman and McCarran had, this interest is often well disguised at reelection time.

McCarran's interest in Nevada affairs was genuine. Although his senatorial concerns extended beyond the confines of his state, the Nevada point of view was well represented during his tenure. He believed, to paraphrase Charles Wilson, "What's good for Nevada is good for the United States."[2] He was also assiduously attentive to his constituents' needs. If Nevada residents had trouble with the federal bureaucracy, or even personal problems, they could always write the senator with the expectation that something would be done. This became the basis of his power.[3]

McCarran's responsiveness stemmed in part from his shrewd evaluation that reelection depended on how well he met the needs of his constituents. More fundamentally, however, McCarran truly did have a deeply felt love for his native state and for its people. Like many politicians who go to Washington, D.C. (and who remain there until they drop dead), McCarran always lamented his absences from his home state. In McCarran's case he appears really to have meant it. He wrote Joe McDonald in 1933, "I would like to see the mountains again and smell the alkali dust, and believe me, the first Jack Rabbit I lay my eyes upon is going to look like a heavenly angel."[4] A highlight of any year was time he could return to Nevada, rest in the desert country, and go hunting. In 1946 he wrote his daughter, "Oh Margie this dear dear old desert has something just dripping from the diadem of God. Here is renewed life and pent up energy blended with hope and promise"[5]

The state that elected McCarran to the Senate was, in 1932, by far the nation's smallest in population. Still, Nevada had changed greatly from the period when McCarran had first entered politics 30 years before. In 1930, it had 91,058 people, less than one person per square mile. Almost exactly 30 percent of these lived in Washoe County, which had 27,158 people. Two northeastern counties in the state placed second and third in population: White Pine, with its copper industry, had 11,771 people; and Elko County, more ranching oriented, had 9,960. Clark County ranked only fourth in population, with 8,532 people; although immediately after the 1930 census workers surged into the Boulder City area, so that by 1932, voting statistics indicated that Clark was the second most populous county.

The state's largest city by far was Reno with 18,529 people, followed in order by Las Vegas (5,165), Reno's sister community of Sparks (4,508), Elko (3,217), and Ely (3,045). The old silver and gold mining towns of Tonopah and Goldfield had dwindled by 1930 to 2,116 and 692 souls respectively.

Nevada had 81,058 whites (about the national percentage), 4,871 Indians, 3,091 Mexicans (not counted by the census in the white totals), 608 Japanese, 516 Negroes, and 483 Chinese. Although the percentage of Indians and Mexicans in the population was high, McCarran was never particularly interested in these groups. Only one person in one hundred eighty was black, and McCarran was never responsive to the problems of this group, either. A large proportion of Nevada's population was foreign born—15,095 (16.6 percent). This figure was significantly higher than the national average of 12.7 percent.

Of 42,885 workers in Nevada in 1930, approximately one fifth (8,938) were in agriculture. From the standpoint of employment, this was the state's largest industry. Despite this primacy, however, Nevada ranked only 47th in the union in the value of agricultural production, and only five percent of the state's land area was in farms. Mining was the second greatest industry, with 6,059 workers, most in copper mining. Despite this small number of mining workers, McCarran focused more on mining problems than on other issues. He concentrated in particular on the pricing of gold and silver, neither of which was especially important to the Nevada economy by this date, but which had huge symbolic significance. It is easy to exaggerate the importance of Nevada mining to the nation in the twentieth century. In 1929, Nevada ranked only 26th among the states in mining. By 1932, it had sunk to 34th. In 1930, Nevada ranked 5th in copper production, 6th in silver, 7th in lead, 8th in gold, and 11th in zinc. The third largest industry in the state in 1930 was railroading, with 4,429 workers.[6]

In religion the state had more Roman Catholics than any other denomination, although most of the population had no church affiliation whatsoever. Catholics made up approximately one tenth of the state's people, indicating that McCarran's Catholicism may have been a political asset to him. There was, by the time of the 1926 religious census, a fast-growing group of Latter Day Saints (Mormons), who were half as numerous as the Catholics and concentrated in the southern and eastern portions of the state. The chief Protestant organizations were far behind.

McCarran had given considerable thought to how he would conduct himself if elected to the Senate. Although the Seventy-Third Congress was not to meet before March, 1933, the lame-duck Senate was in session before that time. McCarran decided to travel back to Washington, D.C. immediately, to put in a bid for some desired committee assignments.

He particularly wished to be on two committees. One, the Judiciary, was a natural for a former state supreme court justice. However McCarran's interest was more than merely being qualified by inclination and background; rather, he was shrewdly aware that much vital legislation was under the control of of the committee, and that it passed on all appointments of federal judges, attorneys, and marshals. This would put him in a strategic position to influence patronage in Nevada.

His choice of the Appropriations Committee was perhaps more surprising for one of his background, but McCarran was anxious to seek out power, and a seat on the that committee indisputably had great potential power. The committee not only exerted national influence, but many federal appropriations had important ramifications for Nevada. Thus a seat on the committee would enhance McCarran's ability to work for his state, and, consequently, his political power within the state.

McCarran was now fifty-six years of age, and although he appeared robust, he must have been aware he was no longer a young man. He was temperamentally incapable of simply biding his time, keeping quiet as freshman senators were supposed to; he wished to make a record as early as possible.

It is not entirely clear just how McCarran obtained a position on these two coveted committees. He fought for them, and somehow talked the Senate leadership into the choice assignments. When he went to Washington, D.C., during the lame-duck session of the old congress, one of the people he talked to was floor leader Joe Robinson of Arkansas. He also saw George Norris of Nebraska, who, although not a Democrat, was highly regarded and was in a position to open doors for him. In fact, McCarran later credited Norris for obtaining his appointment to the Judiciary Committee. Nevada's Key Pittman, *pro tempore* leader of the Senate and a popular figure among his colleagues, also may have been helpful. At the very least he must have adopted a position of benevolent neutrality, since he possessed the power and prestige to thwart McCarran's ambitions. Pittman's apparent generosity, by the way, was in great contrast to McCarran's own later actions when he deliberately tried to keep junior colleagues from Nevada off choice committees (see p. 134). With his ability and his great personal magnetism, McCarran was probably his own best salesman for obtaining the two committee assignments at this time.

Pat McCarran had always been a political renegade before 1933. He had never joined the Wingfield machine, even when it would have suited his ambitions to have done so. Before his successful election drive in 1932, he had never made much attempt to mollify the Democratic leadership in Nevada. Instead he had adopted a lone wolf, independent stance.

Therefore, although he felt no animosity at this time toward Franklin D. Roosevelt, his traditional independence made it impossible for him to support blindly all of the administration program. He was ambitious to make a name for himself in his remaining years. He did not believe he could do this by being someone everyone took for granted. Having succeeded in his endeavor to gain membership on key committees, he now sought to mark out independent positions for himself, positions somewhat different from those of either for the Senate Democratic leadership or of the President. He wished to become expert in and make his views known on national issues, as well as on those primarily affecting Nevada. He was not inclined either philosophically or pragmatically to completely oppose either the Senate leadership or the President; rather he sought to be just unpredictable enough that he would draw attention to himself and never be taken for granted. During Roosevelt's first term, however, he basically worked within the framework of the New Deal.

On the national level, McCarran made a name for himself as an opponent of Roosevelt's early economy bills. He became a champion of the lowly, oft-kicked federal worker, of veterans, and of labor, particularly labor as represented by the American Federation of Labor. He was generally a bigger spender than was the sometimes inconsistent President. He was more prolabor than the President. He fought hard for higher silver prices, adopting a more adamant position on this than Senator Pittman. He became a recognized and respected authority on aviation regulation.

McCarran's press notices during Roosevelt's first term, both in and out of Nevada, were extremely favorable. George Creel, writing in *Collier's,* called him "a large and prickly cocklebur in the cushion of the presidential chair" and was most admiring. "On the whole, however, he always fought for the masses rather than the classes," was one of his conclusions. Still, Creel posed a dilemma which in time was prophetic: "A senator for only two years, and a sagebrush senator at that, yet already a national figure, getting his daily headlines along with Huey Long, Father Coughlin and Good Old Doctor Townsend. Does a tiger turn vegetarian after having tasted blood?"

Time Magazine also found the junior senator from Nevada much more to its liking than it would later:

He does not rate as a conservative, nor as a radical, nor as an opponent of the President. Already one of the best liked members of the Senate, he is considered intellectually honest, frank, logical, and has a way of coming to the point without a smokescreen of oratory. Therefore he is potentially a bigger upsetter of administrator plans than almost any other member of the Senate.[7]

Huey Long named him as one of his favorite men to be President. *Life* called him an "unpredictable mustang." Arthur Krock termed him an "almost unpredictable Senator" except on veterans and labor, a "lone wolf." No one could predict his vote. This increased his national prestige and his importance in the Senate. It also aroused a certain uneasiness about his motives, which became less admiring later on.[8]

To survive in national office, McCarran believed he had to build up an effective state organization. The skillful use of patronage was one of the methods by which he hoped to build this strong political base within Nevada. He believed that if his political friends were shut out of key patronage positions, his enemies would continue to run the state, and eventually effect his political ruin. Clearly it was preferable to ruin his enemies instead. The appointments that a senator would be most directly involved with were those of federal marshal, postmaster, internal revenue collector, and federal attorney. Then there was the major issue of who should be in charge of federal relief projects such as the WPA in Nevada. Before the passage of the Hatch Act, which later controlled the political activities of federal appointees, such patronage was a matter of sheer political survival for McCarran, or at least so he believed.

But McCarran was just a junior senator, and he realized that Key Pittman, with his seniority and influence would insist on the major voice in the selection of appointees. He also believed (not entirely inaccurately) that Pittman acted in consort with his enemies. McCarran realized how close such old antagonists as George Thatcher and William Woodburn were to the senior senator. McCarran therefore determined that if he were to survive, he was going to have to scrap every bit of the way. Perhaps if he were difficult enough, he could gain some of the appointments.

McCarran was not without a certain bargaining leverage. His successful fight to join the Appropriations and Judiciary Committees gave him enormous power over certain patronage positions. Perhaps even more important, he also early discovered that Senator Pittman had a certain softness in his character, a natural tendency to work for the healing of party divisions and old wounds. More than once McCarran found that Pittman would even turn his back on old friends and run away from a fight, if McCarran proved stubborn enough.

Pittman and McCarran did agree on the necessity of booting all Republicans out of federal office just as soon as possible and replacing them with good Democrats. But many of the men in the Roosevelt administration were either old Republicans or considered themselves nonpartisan. McCarran grumbled his frustrations to a friend:

> To begin with, let me give you the atmosphere from the national standpoint. We have Mr. Ickes, Secretary of the Interior, a Republican. We have Mr. Wallace, Secretary of Agriculture, a Republican. We have Mr. Woodin, Secretary of the Treasury, a Republican. We have Mr. Tugwell, Assistant Secretary of Agriculture, a Republican. We have Mrs. Perkins, politically willy-nilly, but not at all pliable to Democratic recommendations. The lady has a code of her own; she even refuses to accept the attentions of the Postmaster General when his card is presented. The nearest that the Junior Senator from Nevada has been able to approach the Lady is by telephone and that was much more grace than has been accorded other Senators. Her voice and attitude over the phone was lovely, but accomplishments from this end, nil.[9]

Then too, McCarran was harried by demands on his time by importunate visitors seeking immediate government employment. As the senator wrote in another letter to McDonald:

> I plan on making a hurried trip home, but the strain and stress of the patronage business being in full swing here now may cause me to put off my trip. Joe, you have no idea of what is going on here. New departments are being created every day. New officers are coming into the swing. Everywhere we hear the word "contact." Those looking for positions are looking first for "contact." There are contact officers connected with every department and it is with this contact officer that the job seeker must make his peace. . . . It was estimated to me by a press representative in the office today that there were over 2,500 lobbyists and special attorneys for big trusts and combinations in Washington now.
>
> In going into one of these departments one must wade through office seekers. The reception rooms are crowded and there are not enough

chairs—they are sitting on the floors, while the heat is unbearable. In the corridors of the Senate Office Building, throngs are assembled everywhere. In every Senator's reception room, delegation after delegation is waiting for an interview with the Senator.

People who visited Nevada years ago, some who went there for divorce and have temporary residence, came rushing to the Nevada representatives, and claim they are citizens of Nevada. Day after day we are confronted with those who were in the State for six weeks or three months. It is struggle enough to find places for our own people.[10]

Perhaps the most crucial patronage position under the control of the two Nevada senators was that of United States Attorney for the state, to replace Harry Atkinson, whose term was to end in 1934. This job was particularly important because, after closure of the Wingfield Banks in 1932, and because of scandals associated with the old power structure, possible indictments of key figures in the Wingfield machine would be handled through the U.S. attorney's office. Consequently it was obviously in the interest of the Thatcher-Woodburn combine to nominate a politician who would be sympathetic to Wingfield's problems, just as Wingfield himself had been instrumental in Atkinson's appointment and had thus shut off any embarrassing enforcement of the Volstead Act.

Senator Pittman, with the concurrence of Thatcher and Woodburn (and doubtless Wingfield), submitted the name of William McKnight, chairman of the state Democratic party. McKnight had been a longtime political friend of the three. Feeling his way carefully, McCarran first indicated he would go along with the nomination.[11] But criticism began mounting in Nevada, suggesting that McKnight was too intimate with the Wingfield organization and that he had not helped McCarran sufficiently in the 1932 election.[12] These reports doubtless had their impact on the junior senator, who was extremely sensitive to rumors that party officials had not fully supported his path to advancement in previous years. Perhaps even more important to McCarran's eventual decision to oppose McKnight is that he somewhere heard that McKnight's secretary (not McKnight) had spread ugly rumors about the senator's private life.[13]

By May 1, 1934, McCarran had concluded that McKnight's nomination as U.S. attorney had to be blocked even if he were forced to declare McKnight "personally obnoxious" on the floor of the Senate.[14] McCarran's position on the Judiciary Committee, which had to consider the nomination, gave him great power over the nomination. McKnight, hearing that McCarran was determined to defeat him, went to McCarran's home to make peace; but McCarran refused to come to terms or confide his reasons for opposing the nomination. In a letter to Senator Pittman, McKnight recounted the details of the disastrous visit:

> My wife and I called on Senator McCarran at his home last night. He received us very graciously and said he was so glad we called to see him. I told him Harry's term expired today and that I was anxiously awaiting word in connection with my application. He said, "Let us not discuss it." My wife said that we must discuss it as we wanted to know. He said he had held no conference with you concerning the appointment. "But just don't call on me." When asked if he had heard I had said or done anything which would justify him in breaking his promise to me at and since the Inauguration he said, "No, not a thing just don't let's discuss it Bill." When asked if he had any reason for not supporting me he said, "no reason at all. Nothing at all against you."[15]

After McCarran threatened to declare McKnight "personally obnoxious," Pittman backed down and, apparently panic-stricken, came up with another name, A. L. Scott of Pioche. Scott was a weak choice, because he too was tied closely to the old machine and lacked McKnight's experience and prestige.[16] When Scott's nomination met with a general outcry, Pittman again hastily withdrew the name. In the meantime, McCarran suggested Judge Edward P. Carville of Elko, an independent-minded Democrat who had no ties to the machine and was universally well regarded. In McCarran's words, "I knew that certain conditions would arise [in re the Wingfield banks] which would require a man of unusual integrity and courage to go through with that situation."[17] Pittman was forced to go along, thoroughly outmaneuvered by McCarran. The *Reno Evening Gazette* stated that McCarran had "evidently decided to cast his lot with the Democratic contingent that is trying to break up the bi-partisan machine that has controlled the party for many years."[18] It was an indication that McCarran had decided to blaze a completely independent path to political advancement, and sensed that the fortunes of the old machine were on the wane.

But McCarran's opposition to McKnight did cause considerable division and bitterness within the party, since McKnight was the state party chairman. At the State Democratic convention in September, 1934, Jack Robbins of Elko, the newly elected state chairman, flayed certain unspecified leaders for "the shameful way in which William McKnight had been treated." Later, when McCarran was asked to address the convention, he refused on the grounds that he had been insulted. At the meeting's close, "McCarran and several of the controlling faction members engaged in heated argument, culminating in one democratic leader inviting McCarran outside, the invitation . . . being declined." McCarran, according to newspaper testimony, allegedly told the group "what he thought of them."[19]

Carville went on to make an estimable record, including indictment and successful trial of two of Wingfield's closest associates, Jim McKay and Bill Graham, on mail-fraud charges. They were sent to prison. Wingfield himself went through the ignominity of personal bankruptcy in 1935; and although he later made a financial comeback, his great, bipartisan political power was ended by the election of 1934. He was defeated in a bid for reelection as regent of the University of Nevada in 1938. He died in 1959.

Another personnel issue which also resulted in a weakening of the now creaky machine concerned a vacancy on the Ninth Circuit Court of Appeals. Frank H. Norcross, U. S. District Judge for Nevada, was nominated by the Justice Department to fill it, on the recommendation of Senator Pittman. Pittman brought up Norcross's name despite his Republican affiliation. This was undoubtedly because nominal party affiliation did not mean much to the bipartisan machine, and, more important, because elevation of Norcross would leave a vacancy in the District judgeship, where Pittman could place one of his Democratic allies.

Norcross had a distinguished background. Born in 1870, he was a graduate of the University of Nevada and Georgetown Law School. He had been a member of the Nevada Supreme Court from 1905 to 1916, where he had sat when McCarran passed his bar examination before the court, and later when the two men were colleagues. After leaving the court, Norcross was a law partner of Thatcher and Woodburn from 1919 to 1924, and was appointed U.S. District Judge for Nevada in 1928. Even as a judge, he had retained his close ties with the bipartisan machine.

Since the elevation of Norcross opened the position of U.S. District Judge for Nevada, Pittman succeeded in persuading the Justice Department to nominate his close political friend, and Wingfield's longtime attorney, William Woodburn, to the post. As in the McKnight nomination, McCarran initially indicated he would cooperate, and actually put this in writing in a letter to Woodburn.[20]

However, disturbing opposition to the two appointments soon developed. In Nevada there was protest that the two positions should not be given to such close associates of Wingfield. Since at this time it was increasingly apparent that Wingfield would probably face personal bankruptcy—and his banks in fact did go into receivership in November, 1933—those two courts might ultimately have to pass judgment on such an event.

Even more serious for the nominees, opposition to the appointment of Norcross to the Circuit Court of Appeals developed in California. This was spearheaded by several newspapers, most notably the *Sacramento Bee,* which ran a Pulitzer-Prize-winning exposé of the workings of the Wingfield machine in the early months of 1934. Consequently the two powerful California senators, Hiram Johnson (whom McCarran greatly admired) and William McAdoo, announced their opposition to the appointment.[21]

The charges against Norcross arose out of an investigation by the Senate Committee on Bankruptcies and Receiverships held in 1933. Its chief investigator, William Neblett, had uncovered evidence that there had been serious mistakes of judgment in the bankruptcy proceedings of the Owl Drug Company in the District Court of Nevada, presided over by one Judge Frank Norcross.

The Owl Drug Company was one of the largest retail drug companies in the world. Although headquartered in San Francisco, it was incorporated under the more lenient laws of Nevada. However, it had no retail outlets in Nevada. Because of continuing financial losses and a high overhead paid on rental fees, it declared bankruptcy in October, 1932. Judge Norcross appointed Nevada Savings & Trust, a Wingfield bank, as receiver. This receivership continued even after the bank closed its doors on November 1, 1932. A friend of Wingfield's, George K. Edler, was appointed trustee, and the bank attorneys, Thatcher and Woodburn, were rumored to have made $80,000 off the bankruptcy. In the end, the Owl Drug Company relieved itself of its most pressing liabilities, but, peculiarly enough, remained under the control of the very men who had operated it before the bankruptcy.[22]

The Senate Committee on Bankruptcies and Receiverships asserted that the bankruptcy proceedings were unconscionable and declared sternly:

> As we review in perspective the tortuous course of that proceeding, we are led to pause and to wonder how long a system of laws, so

administered, can endure or continue to have or to merit the confidence of the people. . . . Judge Norcross allowed himself as a court, not unknowingly, to be the instrument through which the unlawful arrangement was consummated.[23]

These disturbing revelations forced McCarran to rescind his earlier support. Indeed, aside from his earlier promises, there was no reason why he should support the appointments of Norcross and Woodburn, and with rising sentiment against the Wingfield machine in Nevada, some excellent political reasons why he should not. McCarran was appointed to head a Judiciary Subcommittee to evaluate the nomination of Frank Norcross to the circuit court. That Norcross's confirmation would not be an easy task was indicated by the choice, among others, of Senators Hugo Black of Alabama and George Norris of Nebraska as members of the subcommittee. Their often belligerent, and always skilled, questioning during the hearings indicated their skepticism over Norcross's version of the bankruptcy.

The rejection of the Norcross nomination became a certainty when William Neblett, who had uncovered much of the material on the Owl Drug bankruptcy for the Senate Bankruptcy and Receivership Committee, volunteered his services to the subcommittee. Significantly, McCarran accepted the offer. Neblett conducted hearings in Reno and San Francisco, and reported that Norcross had, in fact, acted in collusion with company officials.[24] In a strongly worded report to the subcommittee, Neblett declared:

> The Owl Drug Co. bankruptcy was the product of the conspiracy originated in San Francisco. . . . The intent of the conspiracy was to take a solvent company through the forms of bankruptcy without interruption of its business in the meanwhile, discharge its burdens and, at the conclusion, leave it in the hands of its original owners. The facts demonstrate the execution of the agreement and the complete realization of its purpose.
>
> The conspiracy was joined by William Woodburn, and the other members of the Wingfield group just prior to the filing of the petition in voluntary bankruptcy. Judge Norcross lent his aid to the scheme with knowledge of the facts and the intent of the unlawful agreement. He, however, permitted his court to be used to lend a legal color to the illegal arrangement.
>
> . . . The Owl Drug Co., going through bankruptcy after the stage had properly been set and using the processes of the bankruptcy court, known to the judge, to retire its preferred stock, scale down its leases,

pay off a mere percentage of its general claims, and wind up after bankruptcy owned by the previous owners, doing business under a slightly changed name, with the same officers and managers—a fraud of a most pronounced character which allows a debtor to divest himself of his burdens and retain his property.[25]

It is interesting that the only issue considered by the subcommittee in the hearings on Norcross's nomination was the judge's handing of the Owl Drug bankruptcy proceedings, a matter on which he was quite vulnerable. McCarran himself was careful to take only a cautious part in the public hearings, but Neblett was allowed a perfectly free hand in developing his case, and it all went into the printed record.

McCarran was too astute to come out irrevocably against the appointment, which would have meant breaking his earlier commitment to Woodburn. Instead he adopted a strategy of delay, which was calculated to have the same effect. Hearings were postponed, and a final vote was never called, until eventually the Seventy-Third Congress just ran out.[26] Finally, in January, 1935, Judge Norcross requested that his name be withdrawn from consideration for the circuit court as a "bitter fight" was expected over his confirmation.[27] Since Norcross had prudently retained his position as judge of the District Court of Nevada, there was now no vacancy on that level, and William Woodburn was not considered. The vacancy on the circuit court was not filled by a Nevadan.

In 1933, Pittman succeeded in getting a longtime friend, Robert Douglass, appointed as Internal Revenue Collector of Nevada. Initially McCarran believed that the appointment was a most unfortunate one, and he used his later familiar tactic of threatening to go to the Senate floor to fight the matter. However, he offered to compromise, if given the right to name all of Douglass's subordinates. The price, although high, was met by Pittman and Douglass. As McCarran wrote a friend, "My communication to Douglas [*sic*] was in substance that I would withdraw my opposition providing I should name his office force. To this he assented." In another letter he argued ingeniously that he was merely insisting "upon protecting Douglass by putting around him people who were capable of handling the work." The final result was that McCarran had the political fealty of the whole crew of the Internal Revenue Service in the state of Nevada.[28]

He adopted the same strategy, with similar results, in his battles with Pittman over the choice of a U.S. Marshal. Pittman got his way on the main appointment while McCarran, after much threatening, hired the deputies. Then, while the U.S. Marshal could be working for Pittman, the deputies could send reports to McCarran. It was like having a private intelligence service. Pittman wrote a friend with much exasperation, "Upon the elimination of MacSherry by McCarran's objection we agreed on Zed Ray. McCarran said he had already pledged two deputy jobs no matter who is appointed Marshal. It seems to be a habit of his, pledging jobs." McCarran subsequently named "practically every deputy" in the Marshal's office. Pittman maintained that he found these habits of the junior senator "not very pleasant."[29]

McCarran was also able to have his men appointed to responsible positions in the state government. Harvey Dickerson, one of McCarran's deputy U.S. Marshals, wrote the senator that he was having some success in trying to group some of the legislators "into a solid machine for the furtherance of your ideals and principles." Apparently the position of Deputy U.S. Marshal gave plenty of free time for political organizing. Governor Richard Kirman, at one point, told a friend of Pittman's that "Pat wants every job in the state."[30]

McCarran's position on the Appropriations Committee was a great aid in controlling state patronage, as he had a say over federal appropriations for highways. Therefore, he could demand and get, from Governor Kirman, the appointments of Robert Allen as highway engineer, and his close associate, Alfred M. Smith, as state engineer. These two kept the senator apprised of the latest political developments in the state,[31] and were to become valuable adjuncts to the developing McCarran organization.

Ultimately, however, McCarran's most important patronage appointment was that of the Reno postmaster. It was the custom that a United States Senator of the party in control of the national administration had the prerogative of choosing the postmaster of his own home city, and McCarran was fortunate enough to be a resident of the state's largest and most important city. In 1936, when Reno postmaster William Kinnikin suddenly died, McCarran nominated labor leader Pete Petersen for the position.[32] Born in 1895 in Denmark, Petersen had come to the United States in 1915. His trade was that of a baker. In 1932, he caught McCarran's eye by his assiduous efforts in McCarran's behalf. Despite his never having worked a day

in the Post Office, Petersen was confirmed by the Senate and became
McCarran's most important political henchman in the state; McCarran's enemies were to call him the senator's "hatchet man." From
his vantage point in the Reno post office, Petersen over the years
wrote gossipy, informative letters on state politics to McCarran
(these have fortunately been preserved). He always helped plan the
senator's political strategy, invariably gave practical, valued advice,
and became a warm, personal friend. No political appointee of
McCarran's ever served him better, or more loyally.

McCarran's never-ending patronage battles with Pittman were
reasonably successful. His position on both Judiciary and Appropriations gave him strong leverage for a freshman senator, and he did not
hesitate to threaten, even to Key Pittman, that he would go to the
Senate floor and declare a candidate who refused to meet his terms
"personally obnoxious." McCarran's personal papers indicate that
he spent a major portion of his time on matters of patronage. By skill,
more than a little ruthlessness, and the stomach for a good, old-
fashioned patronage fight, he forged a considerable machine. Because of that machine he was far stronger in the state in 1936 than
he had been in 1932.

In McCarran's estimation, patronage meant survival. He never
could have enough of it. Because of this attitude, his enemies characterized him as a "political hog." One U.S. Marshal, who served
during World War II, described the political realities of being a
McCarran appointee:

> What did I do to keep Senator McCarran happy beside acting as his
> chauffeur? Well, that's about all. As a matter of fact, that's about all
> I was called upon to do. There was no requests for much other activity.
> You would be expected to get out and campaign, and campaign hard
> come election time, hard enough that you kept your skirts clean, but
> yet get the necessary number of votes. You'd be called upon to assist
> with the organization of precinct meetings, and that sort of thing prior
> to election. But that's about all.[33]

McCarran did not do as well with those patronage appointments
not requiring Senate confirmation. In those cases he could not use
his leverage on the Judiciary Committee. His generally independent
stance, though helping him among the people of Nevada, certainly
gained no points from the Roosevelt administration. By contrast
Pittman was a loyal party supporter and had a warm, personal

relationship with the President. His advice was genuinely valued in national councils, and he was appreciated for serving his party unselfishly over the years.[34] Consequently, Pittman insisted upon and obtained tight control of the patronage derived from federal relief projects, and McCarran was not allowed to intrude upon the senior senator's bailiwick.

From 1933 through 1934, the state government of Nevada was Republican. Consequently Cecil W. Creel, a Republican and director of the Cooperative Extension Service of the University of Nevada, was in charge of state relief operations. Senator Pittman's strong opposition to Creel brought about his replacement by Frank Upman, Jr., in 1934. McCarran had also opposed Creel, but was angered by Upman's appointment, which was made without consulting him; Upman had lived in Nevada only since 1929. After McCarran vociferously objected in the press, Pittman coolly advised his colleague, through a telegram sent to the newspapers, "to refrain from annoying" the administration and "to get behind Hopkins and Upman and assist in granting relief to the people of Nevada." Pittman supported Upman because Upman would take orders from him; but the appointment was unpopular throughout the state. Pittman later admitted that Upman had been "fought bitterly, not only by Republican politicians but by a powerful faction in the Democratic party." A similar exchange ensued when Pittman was instrumental in the appointment of George Friedhoff as federal housing administrator and coordinator of federal recovery agencies in the state, again without consulting McCarran and over his public objection.[35]

Since Pittman had the ears of Roosevelt and Hopkins, and McCarran did not, McCarran's only recourse was to append amendments to various relief bills, requiring all relief directors receiving $5,000 or more to be confirmed by the Senate. Jealous of its prerogatives, the Senate twice passed these amendments, but the House always dropped them.[36]

On the surface, Pittman and McCarran were cordial enough. In fact there was a certain similarity in their characters; both were sensitive, nervous, brilliant men. In general, during McCarran's first term, McCarran was considerably more adroit than Pittman with patronage. He usually came up with better men, and was much the more ruthless of the two in pushing his nominees. Only on relief projects did Pittman have full sway on appointments, and then he selected men who hurt him more in the state than helped him. After McCarran's reelection in 1938, and coincident with Pittman's deteriorating strength from excessive drinking, McCarran was in a position to become the dominant force among Nevada Democrats.

Senator Key Pittman came up for reelection in 1934. Although there is no direct evidence in the McCarran papers to support the allegation, Pittman was always convinced that McCarran was behind a deep conspiracy to force his retirement from public life. For the first time since 1916, when McCarran himself had been the antagonist, Pittman was confronted with potentially serious opposition within the Democratic primary. H. R. Cooke, his rival, had started in politics at the same time as McCarran. They had been the close friends and cohorts in the 1902 Nevada Assembly. Later, Cooke had become a prominent Reno attorney. Although not as close as formerly, Cooke from time to time corresponded with McCarran on the political and financial situation in Nevada. Like McCarran, Cooke was a strong antagonist of George Wingfield. In 1934, he campaigned on the main issue that Pittman was tied too closely to Wingfield, a charge that Pittman always denied. Thus it was natural for Pittman to believe that Cooke and McCarran had some sort of alliance.

Pittman wrote his brother, Vail, before Cooke announced, that McCarran was "seeking an opportunity to support somebody in opposition to me in the primaries." He added resignedly that it was "almost impossible" to get along with the junior senator.[37] Pittman also took the trouble to denouce McCarran in a letter to President Roosevelt, a move not exactly calculated to enhance McCarran's standing in the party:

> An insidious fight has been conducted against me for months. . . .
> The insidious fight has been secretly led in a very secret way by my
> distinguished colleague. He appears, however, now to be coming out
> into the open. Personal letters are being written—and frequently over
> official titles—to members of his organizations. None of these letters,
> of course, reach the public.[38]

McCarran, if guilty of the charge, was able to cover his tracks. Publicly he maintained a facade of neutrality, but there was probably some substance to Pittman's suspicions. It should be noted that this was a period of serious infighting between the two over patronage, and McCarran's previous and later record certainly indicates that attempting to defeat the party-regular candidate was not foreign to his nature. McCarran obviously was aware that it would be difficult, if not impossible, to achieve primacy in the party organization while the senior senator was still around. He had written Joseph McDonald that the party needed new leadership and had told at least one associate that he believed Pittman would lose.[39]

But Cooke, as the realistic McCarran surely knew, was too weak a candidate to successfully take on a man who had the regular organization working in his behalf, plus the claim of twenty-one years of seniority in the Senate. The senior senator soundly trounced his challenger in the Democratic primary, by a vote of 13,474 to 4,334. But the 1934 primary did give the McCarran forces considerable hope for the future. Gray Mashburn, McCarran's law partner, won the Democratic nomination for state attorney general; and Richard Kirman, a prominent Reno banker who was deeply antagonistic to George Wingfield, and not unfriendly to McCarran, although independent of him, narrowly defeated party regular Harley Harmon for the gubernatorial nomination.

In the fall, Pittman handily won by a two-to-one margin over the Republican candidate, George Malone. Pittman was again convinced that McCarran was trying to undercut him, indeed that McCarran secretly supported Malone and was responsible for a scurrilous article in *Plain Talk,* which appeared a few days before the election and pictured Pittman in the pay of the Wall Street silver interests. But public relations between the two men did not quite reach the breaking point; McCarran even once sat on the same platform with Pittman and publicly supported his reelection.[40]

Kirman easily won the governorship. His election was an important milestone in Nevada history, as it marked the end of the Wingfield domination in Carson City. Mashburn became the state's attorney general, which put an effective political ally of McCarran's in a high position in the state capital. Despite Pittman's triumph, the election was also a success for McCarran.

It is customary for a state's fellow senator to escort his colleague to the vice-president's chair for the oath of office. This was to be Pittman's fifth term. McCarran wrote Pittman, however, that because of "illness" he could not attend to this duty. Pittman replied with a cold note ("My dear senator") thanking McCarran for his "courtesy" in notifying him. The illness, if any, was a quick one, as McCarran was able to answer the roll call the following Monday, January 7, 1935.[41]

In 1936, there were no important elections in Nevada except for
the House seat, and that was in James Scrugham's pocket. McCarran
campaigned indefatigably through the west for the Roosevelt-Garner
ticket. He was undoubtedly tooling up for his own reelection campaign two years later. Most observers foresaw a close race; McCarran
had made striking inroads in the party organization, but the Pittman
forces still controlled more jobs than did the McCarran forces.

McCarran faced mounting personal problems during his first Senate term. Several of these problems had public ramifications: his
chronic money troubles and some serious health problems.

The money troubles had their roots many years earlier, and reflected an inability on McCarran's part to live comfortably on his
salary. Speculation in his earlier years, frequent political campaigns,
a growing family, and maintenance of an affleunt standard of living
took all he could make and more. The upshot was a propensity to
avoid or delay the payment of bills. The McCarran papers are filled
with examples.

McCarran generally could hold off his creditors with an aplomb
born of long experience; he would pay "the next month," or the bills
had "slipped my mind." One Nevadan who worked for a Sparks
service station in the 1920s related how McCarran would occasionally come by and fill his big Cadillac with Gasoline, and then "just
airily wave and say, 'Charge it to Pat McCarran,' and drive on."
After that he would not show up again for a matter of months. In
later years, after he had accrued power, he could rage at collectors
who dared present bills. But such cavalier practices took their toll
on his political career, and he developed a bad financial reputation
around the state.[42]

Although his Senate salary was a seemingly adequate $10,000, he
found it extremely difficult to remain solvent. The depression had
unsettled his finances when clients proved unable to pay for his
services. His eldest daughter remembered how, by 1932, "he often
paced the floor of his office in anguished worry over the state of his
finances." McCarran was consequently forced to sell property at a
considerable loss, and forfeited several life insurance policies for his
children. His 1932 campaign expenses also proved burdensome.[43] By
necessity his home was remortgaged. At the time of his election
McCarran owed Reno's First National Bank of Nevada the full sum
on a note for $15,000. For at least a two-year period, as records in

the McCarran papers attest, he refused, despite many plaintive and then threatening notes, to pay on either the principal or interest, or even to answer the dunning letters. The bank's president, Richard Kirman, was elected governor in 1934.[44]

In later years, McCarran's wealthier friends, such as Norm Biltz, paid many of his bills and supplied him with clothes and other gifts. Hotels provided his room and food without charge. McCarran was thus relieved of some of the financial burden that plagued his earlier years.[45]

Health problems also intruded at this period in his life. McCarran, who had always been a robust if overweight man (he weighed 235 pounds at 5'7"), suffered his first serious illness on December 17, 1935, in Chicago, when he was suddenly afflicted with what the newspapers called a "stomach ailment" and rushed to the hospital. This may have been a result of the combination of tension and his sedentary existence. The stomach ailment was a bleeding ulcer, which apparently also affected his heart. He was, by later testimony, desperately ill. When he got out of the hospital, in February, 1936, he returned to Washington, D.C., briefly attended a few Senate sessions, suffered another collapse, and was ordered back to bed, this time out of Washington. Dr. George W. Calver, the Senate physician, made the following statement to the press:

> Senator McCarran has recently been sent home to recuperate from a heart condition caused by overwork and his failure to keep up to his proper physical standards by exercise and fresh air. His condition is not serious but will become so unless he follows strictly the routine which has been imposed on him.[46]

So in March 1936, with the Senate in session, McCarran returned to Nevada to convalesce during several months at his in-laws' ranch in Clover Valley, eighteen miles south of Wells. He was put on a stringent diet, exercised by riding the range in his beloved desert, and remained out of communication with his office. While at the ranch he was forced, at least temporarily, to give up drinking and smoking. "The doctors won't let me smoke," he grumbled to newspapermen later, "I'm lost without a cigar. And eat? Listen, I eat a diet of nothing three times a day." He lost forty pounds, and observers commented on the improvement in his appearance. He even maintained, when he returned to Washington, that he had now learned to be philosophical about the "petty annoyances" of politics.

In all, McCarran was out of commission for approximately nine months and missed the entire second session of the Seventy-Fourth Congress, to the detriment of his legislation.[47]

However, with his particular personality, McCarran could hardly avoid controversy and all the nervous irritations that afflict a sensitive politician. The arduous nature of the close fight in 1937 over Roosevelt's plan to "pack" the Supreme Court was to affect his health adversely. On July 10, when he made a major speech on the Senate floor attacking the President's plan, he did so defying doctor's orders. Joseph Alsop wrote later that "he was ill and showed it, yet talked on vehemently and intensely for hours." McCarran portrayed himself in the most melodramatic terms as a member of the "battalion of death," and acting contrary to doctor's orders. The speech got a huge press notice.[48]

This was not simply melodrama. His health, strained by the excesses of too much work too soon, rapidly declined. In the middle of August, 1937, he began to hemorrhage again, and his wife thought, as she later wrote, that he was going to die. He was rushed to the Navy Hospital, where the doctors diagnosed a leaking blood vessel in his intestinal tract. Once again McCarran was forced to give up all Senate business, and he remained in the hospital for a month. He wrote cheerfully to his daughter: "It has been a wonderful rest —complete in every respect. I have done some reading but mainly resting and sleeping. I could have a parade of visitors, but there is a 'no visitors' sign on the door and only a select few can get in." Even by December, 1937, Mrs. McCarran noted she was worried about his health, and he still had a ringing in his head. But the senator showed steady improvement and his ulcer did not afflict him again, although he was forced to be relatively careful about his diet.[49]

Despite these personal problems, on both national and state levels McCarran's first four years as senator were successful. He had attracted wide national publicity, most of it favorable, and had put together an independent and respected record. In Nevada he had placed many political allies in key positions. The foundation was a sturdy one. In fact it was strong enough by 1938 that he could contest for leadership of the Democratic party within his state.

CHAPTER 5

PARTY PRIMACY

FROM 1937 to 1939, Senator McCarran broke with the Roosevelt administration, earned reelection, and gained primacy within the Nevada Democratic party. The senator's national prestige, particularly among the large eastern newspapers was never higher, before or after. Afterward, his personality and his positions on foreign policy, silver, and internal security, would erode this prestige, although not his power, outside of his home state.

McCarran's record on national issues, upon which this respect was based, was a solid one. More than anyone else, McCarran was responsible for the drafting and passage of the landmark bill establishing a Civil Aeronautics Authority (CAA) to oversee the civil aviation industry. McCarran had been the first important legislator to call for the regulation of civil aviation by a single authority, with powers similar to those of the Interstate Commerce Commission over railroads. The bill, passed in 1938, is probably his greatest, although not his most famous, legislative achievement. Although Senator Harry Truman later took chief credit for the legislation in his memoirs, contemporary statements and evidence clearly establish McCarran as the primary author and champion.[1]

Another national issue with much deeper implications for internal Nevada politics was President Roosevelt's attempt to appoint additional federal judges and to increase the size of the United States Supreme Court to a possible fifteen members. This battle earned McCarran a national reputation and made him virtually unbeatable in his home state.

At first it did not seem that way. Roosevelt's record-breaking electoral and popular majority in the 1936 election, and his carrying

75

with him an enormously lopsided Democratic Senate and House, made him appear invincible. At first McCarran came out rather unequivocally in favor of the President's plan to change the judiciary.[2] After closer examination of the plan, however, he began to worry about its implications for the courts and its potential for increasing executive power. Hedging, McCarran shifted to a neutral stance. Ultimately, at a late but crucial juncture, he came out against the President's plan. Because of his membership on the Judiciary Committee which considered the proposal, his wavering made him an unknown quantity and greatly heightened his influence.

A determining factor in McCarran's thinking was the fact that his mail from Nevada ran heavily against the proposal. He soon realized there might be political profit from breaking with the President, which buttressed his initial inclination to dissent. A friendly letter from Nevada Republican Party National Committeeman Lester D. Summerfield, hinted that what would be lost in Democratic support might be made up by Republican support. "I do not have the slightest doubt," Summerfield wrote, "that opposition of the plan will be the soundest politics."[3]

While Congress was considering the proposal, McCarran returned to Nevada to sound out sentiment. Mainly he listened. During his trip he was accompanied by a young Reno attorney, Gordon Rice. According to McCarran's daughter, "the two argued every step of the way about the proposed changes in the Court, Rice against the President's position, McCarran defending it." The senator was attempting to gauge how people thought. He soon learned that the weight of opinion in Nevada ran strongly against the President's plan. This discovery became vital to the making of his own decision.[4]

Not until April 26, 1937, did the senator announce his opposition. On May 10, he addressed a Philadelphia audience and explained his viewpoint. Nevada was flooded with 20,000 copies of this speech, almost one for every voter.[5] The reaction within the state was overwhelmingly favorable. Summerfield asserted that the senator was rendering "his greatest service to the common people." Because of the announcement McCarran gained, for the first time, significant Republican support within Nevada. He also received enthusiastic editorial backing from the state's major newspapers.[6] At the same time, McCarran was quite careful to not directly attack the President, and so did not alienate the great mass of Democratic voters.

One of the senator's chief worries in staking his independent position was that the administration might deprive him of his patronage and those other favors so convenient to a senator. By contrast, Senator Pittman, also a member of the Judiciary Committee, had gone down the line for the President. What would be the attitude of the administration toward McCarran's reelection, toward political jobs under his control, toward WPA money to Nevada, toward needed federal projects—to a whole host of such bread-and-butter, sensitive issues? Would the administration give Pittman all the credit for any favors given Nevada? As McCarran certainly realized, the President was not above using such tactics to get his way. In fact, Roosevelt had already told James Farley that judicial appointments might be held up in those states where the delegation refused to go along, and Senator Wheeler of Montana, for one, found himself getting the silent treatment. Wheeler even had his tax returns audited.

Thus McCarran was probably not too surprised when, on May 16, Farley replied to newspapermen who asked how the court battle was going by excoriating Senators McCarran and O'Mahoney of Wyoming for their perfidy. Farley's attack, although off-the-record, was far too juicy to be ignored by the journalists. As the newspapers quoted Farley (and he did not deny the statement), the Postmaster General had said, "When Senator O'Mahoney comes round for help on a sugar bill, his conscience won't be bothering him then, will it? Neither will Senator McCarran's when he wants something for his state. It's all in the point of view."[7]

Senator McCarran chose to regard these remarks as a threat, and they were universally so regarded by the press and by McCarran's colleagues. Farley had committed a grievous error, as he now forced McCarran to become much more adamant in his opposition, less amenable to compromise. McCarran was not the type to be pushed around by threats, anyway, and Farley's statement actually helped McCarran in Nevada. Realizing this, the Postmaster General's own *post mortem* of the situation was: "It taught me a powerful lesson in holding my tongue."[8]

The debate on the Judiciary Reorganization Act began on the Senate floor on July 6. Senator Wheeler opened for the opposition on July 9. On July 10, McCarran made his first major speech on the Senate floor since 1935, attacking the President's plan. He was ill at the time, and "showed it" according to one reporter; he was still recovering from the dangerous illness from which he had nearly died the previous year. A full house of senators and visiting House members came to listen. The galleries were packed.[9]

Perhaps because of his illness, McCarran delivered his speech in a high-pitched voice that "frequently trembled." It was given without notes and this showed in its organization. The speech, unusual for the senator, was meandering and repetitious, but it was vehement and highly effective. Its intensely emotional quality gave it great vitality. McCarran was often interrupted by questions from sympathetic listeners. Despite its weaknesses this was probably McCarran's most celebrated speech ever to be delivered in the Senate.

The importance of the speech was emphasized, and the interest in it heightened, by McCarran's repeated references to the state of his health, expressed in the most melodramatic terms. "This is the first time for a year and a half," the senator thundered, "that I have attempted to deliver a speech of any magnitude, and I am delivering it now contrary to a doctor's orders, but I think the cause is worth while. I think the cause is worthy of any man's life." In words quoted around Nevada and the nation he declared, "I think this cause in which we have enlisted, and in which I say without hesitancy we constitute a batallion of death, to the end that the Constitution of the United States shall prevail, is worthy of the effort."[10]

The only section of the speech where McCarran permitted himself the luxury of personal attack was directed at the Postmaster General. Farley's statement to reporters on May 16 had elevated McCarran to high ground and the senator was able to adopt an attitude of injured innocence. In a highly emotional passage, universally quoted in the press, McCarran declared:

> I wish Mr. Farley, the Postmaster General, were listening today. I know he made a terrible mistake; but, mistake though it may be, it was a dagger driven into my heart. It was driven home to a voting population of 42,000, which is all the voting population there is in my home state. But every man and woman knows Mr. Farley's candidate there,[11] and when he said that when I asked for something for my humble state there would be a different viewpoint, he wrote my death warrant, and he knew it, and I may be today delivering my valedictory by reason of a mandate of Mr. Farley.[12]

Once he mentioned his "humble state," the senator really warmed up to the subject:

> I do not know that 42,000 votes mean much. I do not know that three votes in the electoral college mean much. I do not know that a little

state where hearts and homes and hearth fires constitute a haven for the toiler means much. I only know that principle lives where desert lands put forth their bloom. I only know that human hearts are just as red and just as fresh in desert lands as they are where verdure grows.[13]

Obviously this speech was delivered at a time of high emotion for the speaker. Although it now seems extravagant, its impact on contemporaries was sensational; it may not have swayed the mind of fellow senators but it received huge press coverage and a most sympathetic hearing. The usually staid *New York Times* devoted five columns of space to the speech. The *Washington Post* applauded the effort even while describing it as "sometimes a little oratorical."[14]

The speech, and in fact McCarran's whole position on the court issue, produced tremendous political benefits in Nevada. The *Nevada State Journal* trumpeted on its front page: "MCCARRAN IN DEATH BATTALION—SENATOR READY TO GIVE LIFE TO DEFEND CONSTITUTION." The *Elko Free Press* declared editorially, "His was a brilliant speech which will go a long way toward placing him in favor with the people of this state for the coming election. . . . We do not agree with Senator McCarran when he says he might be making his valedictory."[15]

Private letters from Nevada reinforced the idea that McCarran had done the politically expedient thing. A Pioche attorney wrote the senator, "I am of the opinion you are now stronger in this county than ever before which, if correct, means extraordinarily strong." E. M. Steninger, editor of the *Elko Free Press* notified the senator, "Those that I have contacted are from every walk in life, ranchers, laborers, merchants, business men and so forth; and their reaction leads me to believe that I must reiterate what I told you before—you are a foxy politician." Al Cahlan, powerful editor of the *Las Vegas Review-Journal* made much the same point: "Many who have been hitherto luke-warm, Pat, are rallying to your support in outstanding style." Peter Petersen, canny postmaster at Reno, ended on a more personal note:

It is with a great deal of pride on my part to tell you how gratifying it is to know that we here in Nevada have at least one Senator who has the courage to speak his mind and not follow the direction laid down by the powers in Washington. You can rest assured that the thinking people of Nevada are justly proud of your stand on this Bill. You have made yourself hundreds of friends at home . . .

> I read that the strain on you is terrific. For that reason I would at
> this time like to warn you to take care of your health. I would not like
> anything to happen to you.[16]

McCarran's anti-court stand, more than anything else, made his
reelection in Nevada inevitable. Because of his fight against the
administration, he picked up enough Republican support to make his
constituency in Nevada far more bipartisan than it had previously
been. The only cloud on his political horizon was that he had to win
the Democratic primary before facing any Republican in 1938. But
his popularity in the state had never been higher.

Despite his unprecedented popularity, McCarran faced some immediate problems before he could be completely sure of his election.
For one thing there was Farley's implied threat to cut McCarran's
access to patronage appointments. If this came about, it would mean
that credit for whatever federal aid and projects were made available
to the state would be given exclusively to Senator Pittman. This was
precisely what was happening, for example, to Senator Wheeler of
Montana. Farley was not the chief proponent of such a policy, but
his name was the one identified with it. As McCarran well knew,
the policy emanated from the President himself. And as it turned
out, the threat was a very real one for the junior senator from
Nevada.

Thus McCarran well knew that he had to secure his own flanks.
People who held appointments directly or indirectly responsible to
him (and his position on the judiciary and appropriations committees
gave him great leverage) were made to toe the line. Walter Baring,
a zealous supporter of Senator Pittman and the administration and
later U.S. Representative for twenty years, found this out the hard
way. In 1937, as a young politician just starting out, he held the two
positions of Washoe County Democratic Central Committee Chairman and deputy internal revenue collector. During the summer of
that year, fired up by the court fight, the inexperienced Baring wrote
a letter to the *Las Vegas Review-Journal,* a newspaper close to
McCarran, accurately asserting that many newspaper articles purporting to cover McCarran were in fact written in the senator's own
office. Furthermore, "the people of Nevada sent representatives to
Washington to back Roosevelt and his policies. McCarran has not
done this." Instead of printing the letter, the newspaper forwarded

a copy of it to the senator. This was probably done by Al Cahlan, the paper's editor and a prominent politician in his own right. Because of these criticisms of McCarran, Baring was forced to quit as chairman of the Washoe Country Democratic Central Committee and was suspended as deputy internal revenue collector for a thirty-day period. The ostensible reason was for "undue political activity." Baring would have lost the latter job as well if Senator Pittman had not personally intervened to save him. The story, prominently featured in the Nevada press, was intended to serve as an object lesson to other federal officeholders in the state.[17]

Certainly President Roosevelt, for his part, desired McCarran's defeat, as the senator well knew. Even though McCarran had supported the great majority of New Deal legislation, that was not enough. The court fight, and McCarran's independence, rankled the President too much. James Farley, whose natural instincts were to avoid intraparty fights, received a foretaste of what was on the President's mind on January 27, 1938, when he learned "that the President's hate for members of the party who had opposed him on the Court fight had not cooled by the lapse of time, but glowed as fierce as ever under the ashes of the past six months." At that time Roosevelt told his postmaster general that he was going to interfere in the Democratic party's primaries and, according to Farley, "expressed himself confident that the people would support him by defeating his opponents, adding that he might, like the schoolmaster, have to apply the political birch to teach refractory members of the party the three R's—Regularity, Right, and Reason." In a series of conferences in late April and early May, the President specifically mentioned that McCarran was one of the senators he wished to see defeated, even though Farley had warned the President there was no chance for that.[18]

But what Democrat in Nevada could be persuaded to run against McCarran? Not that the Senator lacked party enemies, but Senator Pittman had given no one direct encouragement, and had even privately declared to friends who mentioned possible candidates that he would keep hands off the race. Pittman doubtlessly considered his own interest, but he was also a stalwart party loyalist who had never previously interfered in other people's primary fights, and he declared that he was not going to begin now. He also suspected that McCarran was unbeatable anyway. Thus he wrote Jack Robbins, the Elko party leader, in April, 1937, "Well, personally, Pat and I get along all right together. We can't agree on appointees because Pat's idea of an agreement is that everybody has got to agree with him. That's just dispositional, that's all." Two months later, after McCarran had declared himself on the court plan, he wrote Governor Kirman:

> I have no intention of fighting Pat McCarran for renomination unless he does some acts that force the fight. . . . Unfortunately McCarran [is] of a very suspicious nature and exceedingly sensitive. . . . I said that for some reason he feels that I am a bitter enemy of his. I have never spoken in any way except kindly of McCarran.[19]

If Pittman was not going to encourage anyone else in the party to run, it was difficult for anyone who had political strength to challenge the junior senator. Certainly William Boyle disliked McCarran enough, but he sensed his own political weakness and aspired to the office of U.S. Attorney instead. William McKnight, who was a man of great popularity in Nevada, and who harbored bitterness at McCarran for blackballing him for the U.S. Attorney job in 1934, decided not to make the race. James Scrugham refused to leave a safe House seat for a very chancy race against the incumbent senator. Perhaps the most popular Democrat of all was Governor Richard Kirman; but despite all sorts of blandishments, he refused to make a race against McCarran, and in fact refused to run even for sure reelection as governor. Being 61 years of age, he simply yearned for a speedy retirement from public life.[20]

This left only a few weak candidates within the Democratic fold who might be willing to tackle the junior senator in the primary. Hence realistic anti-McCarran Democrats began to realize that if McCarran were to be defeated it would have to be by a Republican. Several urged former Senator Tasker Oddie, the strongest Republican in the state, to come out of retirement and make the race.

The most prominent Democrat eventually to challenge McCarran for the Democratic nomination was Albert Hilliard, who announced his candidacy in May, 1938. Hilliard was a Reno resident, ten years an attorney, and virually unknown in the rest of the state. To make up for that formidable weakness, Hilliard swore absolute fealty to anything proposed by the President. Thus, according to Hilliard's strategy, the race would be McCarran versus Roosevelt instead of McCarran versus a virtual unknown:

My campaign will be one hundred per cent for Roosevelt, including of course, his bill to reform the Judiciary, the reorganization bill, wages and hours legislation, with no pussy footing on any of those or other Rooseveltian policies. In other words, I will run as a strictly New Deal Democrat.[21]

McCarran refused to play along with this strategy. On June 16, 1938, he officially announced his candidacy for a second term. "It has been my privilege," the senator stated at the time, "to have served in cooperation with a great progressive national administration and to have supported every social and economic reform offered under the constitution for the uplift of the people."[22] He consistently refused in his own campaign to criticize the President directly and underplayed his own opposition to the administration. In fact, McCarran tended to avoid national issues altogether, including even his own important bill setting up the Civil Aeronautics Authority. Instead his campaign focused on local needs, listing the pork barrel projects he had provided for the state. He came down especially hard on silver: "As a friend of silver, I do not propose to relinquish my efforts for remonetization." One campaign brochure gave the senator full credit for the increase in silver prices and in mineral production in Nevada from 1932 to 1937.[23]

Hilliard's candidacy was weakened not only by McCarran's refusal to criticize the President, and his emphasis on local issues, but also because most leading Democrats in the state, headed by Senator Pittman, refused to support him. Hilliard, while on a visit to Washington, D.C., directly solicited the senior senator's support. But Pittman, probably to Hilliard's astonishment, refused to join the cause, and made it clear that ever since he had been in public life, he had always taken "no part whatever in any other Democrat's primary campaign." When Hilliard brought up McCarran's name, the senator "told him that it applied to McCarran the same as it did to anyone else." Perhaps taking their cue from Pittman, no major Democrats in the state publicly campaigned for or even endorsed Hilliard.[24]

Franklin Roosevelt had announced plans to visit the west in July, 1938, and part of his itinerary was over the Southern Pacific Railway route through northern Nevada. Here was the opportunity for Presidential intervention if it were to be made. In other states, Roosevelt had already endorsed candidates who were running against senators who had defied him on the court issue. In Nevada, however, Roosevelt decided against a public endorsement of Hilliard, because the word he had received from everyone from Farley on down was that McCarran could not be beaten by the challenger.

Not being privy to this information, McCarran was understandably nervous as he joined the Presidential train in Ogden, Utah, for the trip west. He told friends, as he sat in the dining car, that he would consider it a personal victory if he received no worse than "silent treatment" at the hands of Mr. Roosevelt. The train's first stop in Nevada was at Carlin, a small railroad town in Elko County, in the state's northeastern corner. There Al Hilliard joined the train.

Hilliard accompanied the President to the rear platform. Only after the President commenced speaking did McCarran made his entrance on the platform. Someone shouted, "Hello, Pat" and the crowd began applauding. The President stopped speaking, smiled, and shook hands with the senator. He then continued.[25] Robert Douglass, the Internal Revenue Collector for Nevada, wrote his close friend Pittman to apprise him of developments:

> Over at Carlin, the other guy [McCarran] had someone to shout "Hello Pat" after the President had started to speak, and then with a set stage, several ignoramuses cheered and naturally interrupted the President so his talk there was cut extremely short on that account— which was quite noticeable.[26]

Throughout the train ride across northern Nevada, accompanied by McCarran and Hilliard, and later by Representative Scrugham and Governor Kirman, the President complimented the state administration "from the governor on down" for its cooperation with the national administration. In Sparks he spoke of "my friend Al Hilliard." The most he could say of McCarran was to refer to him as "the Senator."[27]

Afterward, Roosevelt wrote his son, James, that McCarran had been treated with "due courtesy," which means in effect he received the silent treatment.[28] But there was no open endorsement of Hilliard. Most analysts agreed that the jaunt was a plus for McCarran since he had clearly upstaged the president in Carlin. The furthest Roosevelt went to support Hilliard's candidacy was allegedly to tell Hilliard (and we have only Hilliard's word for this, although it seems to have been in character for the President) that whatever influence McCarran had ever had in Washington was gone. Hilliard quoted the President as saying, "Senator McCarran has consistently and stubbornly refused to play ball. That is why I am against him, and that is why I wish you the best of luck in your campaign." However, that was not public support, even though it was widely leaked to the press.

Yet the President did have other, more subtle ways of undermining the senator. In June, 1938, the Democratic party of Nevada received the astonishing news that the United States Attorney for Nevada, Edward Carville, would not be reappointed to a second term in that post. Carville, who had originally been appointed in 1934 at McCarran's instigation, had built an enviable record as a fearless federal attorney. He had a high number of successful prosecutions to his credit, including a victory in the trial of James McKay and Bill Graham on mail fraud charges which sent the two to federal penitentiary. McKay and Graham had been close associates of Wingfield and controlled some of the leading gambling houses of western Nevada. According to Assistant United States Attorney Brien McMahon (later United States Senator from Connecticut), this marked "the conclusion of a long-drawn-out contest between the bosses of Reno's underworld and the Federal Government." Al Cahlan, the Las Vegas editor, pointed out that "the battling Elkoite will have no part of the finagling which was an integral part of the machine. Carville has struck a lot of dynamite under the Reno politicos and they don't like it." McCarran had endorsed Carville for reappointment in the strongest possible terms, but Pittman had refused to join in the recommendation, affecting a public guise of neutrality.[29]

Instead, on July 6, the administration nominated William S. Boyle to the post. McCarran later claimed that he had been assured that Carville would be kept on. The nomination of Boyle was a heavy blow to the senator. Almost a year later McCarran testified, "I do not know that I should go into what the feelings were. I think it best to leave that out."

The beauty of the appointment was that since the Senate was not meeting at the time, Boyle could begin his term immediately as an interim appointee, and would have almost a year in the office before the Senate could act on the appointment. As everyone knew, Boyle was close to Postmaster General James Farley and it was generally accepted that he was Farley's appointment. Everyone of course remembered Farley's famous "threat" against McCarran at the time of the court fight. McCarran then received word that Marvin McIn-

tyre had told someone when the presidential train was in Reno on
July 13, that Carville had been replaced "to take a slap at Pat." No
one could deny that. It was also generally accepted in Nevada that
Key Pittman had acquiesced in what amounted to the firing of
Carville. Pittman, declaring his neutrality, told reporters that he had
declined to endorse any candidate for the position, but that he would
support Boyle's appointment. McCarran, among many, believed
Pittman's complicity went far deeper than that.[30]

It did. Pittman was lying. It is apparent from a perusal of Pittman's papers that he had been behind the appointment from the very
beginning—although it was undoubtedly also an idea shared by Farley—and that he had buoyed up Boyle's hopes about his chances for
Senate confirmation. Since Pittman, like McCarran, was on the Judiciary Committee, he was confident that he could whisk the whole
thing through. As early as February, 1937, even before McCarran
had announced his opposition to the President's court plan, Pittman
had carefully laid plans for supplanting Carville with Boyle. In a
letter to Boyle, Pittman told the aspirant:

> I am quite friendly with Judge Carville, but I am more friendly with
> you. Again, I feel that you would give more satisfactory service than
> Judge Carville. I am going to take this matter up quietly with the
> Attorney General and with Farley. In the meantime, of course, this
> matter must remain quiet.
>
> I do not know whether Judge McCarran would oppose your appoint-
> ment or not. I feel satisfied, however, that if you were appointed you
> would be confirmed without regard to opposition.[31]

In his later confirmation hearings, Boyle insisted that he had
supported McCarran in the 1938 elections. Yet, a letter from Boyle
to Pittman in the summer of 1938 demonstrates the falseness of that
assertion, as McCarran was well aware. It also proves that Pittman,
despite his official neutrality in the primary, knew all along what
Boyle was up to and acquiesced in it:

> I will start to harmonize all the groups for 1940. I have done pretty
> well so far. There appears little personal objection to me, if any.
>
> We must get Oddie to run. We can put him over. Our Democra-
> tic line up is hopeless. I tried so hard to get Dick Kirman to run. If I
> have to take the stump against the present crop I will have little
> trouble.
>
> Keep out of the matter. I will bear the brunt of any attacks upon the
> President or you.[32]

Obviously Boyle thought he could bring about McCarran's defeat in the general election through Oddie's Republican candidacy. He had unsuccessfully attempted to bring Governor Kirman in the race against the junior senator. The letter demonstrates Boyle's arrogance, and, what is more dangerous for an ambitious politician, his complacency.

But Carville refused to play the role allotted to him. When Peter Petersen heard of the sacking of Carville, he got hold of McCarran, and the two together talked Carville into running for governor of Nevada. Carville was at first reluctant, but eventually agreed to run. According to the newspapers, he was an underdog, since the regular party organization was backing Harley Harmon for the post; but it promised to be a lively contest. McCarran, of course, threw all his resources behind Carville's candidacy. The attempted Roosevelt-Farley-Boyle-Pittman humiliation of McCarran might still be turned into political gain.

McCarran's own primary campaign went well. He received endorsements from the American Federation of Labor, the Railway Brotherhoods, the American Legion, the National Grange, and the American Livestock Association. His careful attention to the needs of special groups had paid off well in the 1938 campaign.[33]

Thus the senator's primary victory over Hilliard was hardly a surprise, although the dimensions of the victory were. This was partly because many Republicans had registered as Democrats to vote for McCarran (the Democratic vote outnumbered the Republican vote 3 to 1), but it also attested to his popularity among the Democratic rank and file, and to Hilliard's weakness as a candidate. McCarran was popular in Nevada *because* of his independence of the White House, not in spite of it. He carried every county in the state, with 17,921 votes. Hilliard received only 5,329 votes and a third candidate, John E. Worden, 857. More surprising was that McCarran's ally, Edward Carville, soundly defeated Harley Harmon for the Democratic gubernatorial nomination, 12,279 to 9,558. A third candidate, Charles L. Richards, gained only 2,428 votes. In a victory statement, McCarran thanked Nevadans "for a splendid response to a call that demanded independence of thought." He added, "I will sustain and support the executive of the nation as I have sustained him in the past when he was right. I will oppose him when he is wrong. I will be true to my oath to uphold and defend the Constitution."[34]

At the Democratic state convention held in September, 1938, the McCarran faction, in conjunction with Carville's friends, gained dominance in the Democratic party. Eighty-five percent of those named to the state central committee were McCarran-picked men. One newspaper editor commented:

> Senator McCarran was among the first to present his smiling counte-nance at the state convention and he had reason to smile, judging from the enthusiastic greeting he received on every hand. It was a McCarran convention, pure and simple, and emphasized the fact that the demo-crats of Nevada resented any action tending to select their representa-tive in congress, and it seemed to me that the attempted "purge" unified the party as nothing else could have done.[35]

McCarran's opponent in the general election was the same man he had narrowly defeated in 1932, Tasker Oddie. Oddie ran a gentle-manly campaign, but it was not his year; he was 68 years old, and seemed too much a voice from the past. Most of the newspapers in the state, with the important exception of the consistently Republi-can *Reno Evening Gazette,* although giving Oddie high praise for previous performance, supported McCarran. Even James Farley sent an open letter to all the Democrats of Nevada, urging McCarran's election.[36]

The result was never really in doubt. McCarran defeated Oddie handily enough, by 27,406 votes to 19,078, which was a 58.8 percent majority. Carville defeated Republican candidate John A. Fulton by a rather greater margin, 28,528 to 17,586.

Because of the events of 1938, observers of the Nevada political scene agreed that McCarran and Carville now controlled the Demo-cratic party machinery in Nevada. McCarran was universally recog-nized as the senior partner in the coalition, but much depended on the two men sticking together. Senator Pittman, for one, found that he was now without influence in the state administration, his advice no longer sought or valued. In a complaint to a political lieutenant, he bitterly blamed the whole debacle on James Farley:

> Unfortunately, I was not in a position to advise confidentially with Governor Carville. He undoubtedly believes that I could have caused his retention as United States Attorney. It is immaterial that he is mistaken in this matter. . . . The facts are that the Department of Justice determined irrevocably not to have Judge Carville reappointed. It was based partially on the grounds that he had not been and was not an active supporter of the President and his New Deal. . . . Of course you know that Boyle was Jim Farley's appointee. Jim had insisted that

he be appointed when Roosevelt came in, and he never abandoned his intention of having Boyle appointed United States Attorney.[37]

McCarran had a score of his own to settle with Pittman. As a first priority, he was now planning how he could prevent Senate confirmation of Boyle. This could test Pittman's and McCarran's relative strength in the Senate and in Nevada.

After his reelection, McCarran apparently had some initial doubts as to the political propriety of challenging the appointment of William S. Boyle to the position of United States Attorney. His main concern was that he might just make a martyr out of Boyle. In discussing the matter with Pete Petersen, the Reno postmaster advised him that the nomination should be fought "primarily because the people of the State of Nevada are watching with keen interest and if they don't stop him they will be in a position that you have lost your grip in Washington." Basically, Petersen's argument was that McCarran's prestige and credibility were at stake. However he added that if Boyle were willing to come to terms with the Senator, McCarran should withdraw his opposition.[38] Two days later, Petersen advanced a slightly different argument:

> We all agree that if possible it will be best for you to oppose Bill Boyle. I don't believe you have anything to worry about as far as making a martyr out of Boyle. His friends are few and far between and the ones that would be sore about his being removed are already your enemies. For that reason I don't believe there is anything to lose, and perhaps a lot to gain.[39]

However, McCarran did not publicly disclose his intentions until a Judiciary subcommittee, consisting of six senators, convened to consider the nomination on April 19, 1939. Key Pittman was the subcommittee chairman and McCarran was a member.

When the committee did meet, McCarran immediately expressed his dismay and bitterness over the nomination. One of his unstated reasons was that the nominee had refused to negotiate with him. McCarran's diatribes were initially aimed at Senator Pittman and it did not take him long to expose the fundamental weakness of the senior senator's position. McCarran demanded, "Mr. Chairman, before you proceed on that, I am going to ask the chairman of the committee, as senior senator from Nevada, whether he ever recommended the nominee. I would like to have an answer on that." Pittman replied, in an exasperated manner, "I did not. May I say what happened? We might just as well settle it and be done with it, so there may be no misunderstanding about my position in the matter." Senator Pittman phrased his remarks guardedly and he was careful not to disclose the encouragement he had given all along to Boyle. He declared he had never brought up Boyle's name (which, as noted, was straining the truth), but that since Boyle now held the office, he supported the appointment, as Boyle was "entirely qualified." The weakness of Boyle's position was that one senator from Nevada was determinedly fighting the appointment while the other did not dare express his own complicity in its making.[40]

William Boyle was then put on the stand (McCarran refused to say hello to him) and stated that he had long supported McCarran's candidacies for the Senate, that he had encouraged McCarran to run in 1932, and that he voted for McCarran in both the primary and general elections of 1938: "At the time the argument came up with relation to the Supreme Court, I never failed to tell the audience that there were two sides to every argument, and because Senators disagreed, they should not be militated against."[41] This assertion, however, is contrary to the tenor of Boyle's private letters to Pittman, previously quoted, written during the campaign.

McCarran naturally wished to know, since Pittman disclaimed credit for the appointment, who originally instigated it. He received an answer of sorts from Joseph B. Keenan, former assistant Attorney General, who was personnel officer in the Department of Justice, during June and July of 1938. McCarran's great experience as a trial lawyer proved useful at this time:

Senator MCCARRAN. Going through the file, let me ask: Was Mr. Boyle recommended by either Senator or any Member of the congressional delegation from Nevada?

Mr. KEENAN. No. I know that Senator Pittman states that he did not desire to take any part in the appointment, and in a longer letter that I recall it indicates that several people came to see him while he was in Nevada, regarding this appointment, and that he decided to endorse nobody. . . .

Senator PITTMAN. Did you consider Boyle's appointment a better appointment than Carville's?

Mr. KEENAN. I hadn't got to that. That record was searched, and as reports were made to me, there was no question whatsoever but what Mr.

Boyle was distinctly superior, and an abler man, and so known in his own community, and had an excellent record at the bar; and we felt he would be an abler man at the bar than Judge Carville. . . .

Senator PITTMAN. Somebody did talk to you about Boyle, did he not?

Mr. KEENAN. Yes.

Senator MCCARRAN. May I ask a question there?

Mr. KEENAN. Yes.

Senator MCCARRAN. Who?

Mr. KEENAN. My best recollection is that it was the Chairman of the Democratic National Committee [Farley]?

Senator MCCARRAN. In other words, this is the appointment of the Chairman of the Democratic National Committee?

Mr. KEENAN. I saw a long—

Senator MCCARRAN. I do not want that. Won't you answer the question?

Mr. KEENAN. I would say that it was the nomination of the President of the United States today.

Senator MCCARRAN. Oh, you are just dodging the question, are you not?

Mr. KEENAN. Well—

Senator MCCARRAN (interposing). I admire your smile when you say it. I rather like your smile.

Mr. KEENAN. Well, if you want to put in the record that I am smiling, I am answering questions to the best of my ability.[42]

Toward the end of the subcommittee's first session, McCarran for the first time used the phrase "personally obnoxious" in his condemnation of Boyle.[43] At Senator Norris's insistence he promised to give the subcommittee substantiation for the charge at later sessions.

McCarran's argument was not basically that Boyle was "personally obnoxious" as the phrase is usually interpreted. Instead he maintained that Carville had compiled an unusually excellent record as United States Attorney, and that his replacement by Boyle, without the recommendation of either senator (he was using Pittman's statement for his own purposes), was a direct slap by the administration at McCarran. The senator failed really to substantiate the charge that Boyle had opposed him in the 1938 primary, although he knew perfectly well that it was true. The only proof McCarran offered was a telegram from Governor Carville stating that he had asked Boyle in June, 1938, how he stood toward McCarran's election: "He answered me that he and Senator McCarran were enemies and had nothing in common whatsoever."[44] The rhetoric was flamboyant; at one point McCarran thundered that the appointment "gave comfort to the enemies of the United States."[45] But the case against Boyle really came down to the point that Senate prerogatives had not been attended to, and that it was an outright attempt to humiliate McCarran:

> The nominee has lent himself to a combination to take a slap at the junior Senator from Nevada and to demonstrate that whatever influence the junior Senator had in Washington had gone, and to demonstrate that he, the junior Senator from Nevada, had made it impossible to help the State of Nevada through the Federal authorities.[46]

McCarran's case, as Pittman went on to demonstrate, was strong only if one interprets "personally obnoxious" to cover a situation where an administration had acted vindictively toward a senator. McCarran had failed to establish that Boyle had worked against him; he knew it, but except for Carville's statement—and Carville was an interested party whose statement did not quite address itself to the specific point—he had no proof of it. McCarran, who was susceptible to dark moods when he allowed himself to be, knew that his case was not the best, as he confided to Petersen:

> I am terribly put out about the Boyle matter. I looked for some real collaboration and I didn't get any. I put in the strongest case I knew how, but I am not at all sure it was strong enough to win. If I could have relied on some who made statements to me I would have been all right, but when I came to rely on them they fell down miserably, so what with falling down and getting up I had to go along as best I could in the fight. If I had it to do over again I would not engage in it at all. This was my judgment from the very beginning that I was making a martyr and an actively bitter enemy out of Boyle. Fellows who wouldn't look at him before will walk around the block now to see what he looks like.[47]

McCarran also became angry at Governor Carville, for whom he had fought so hard, when on May 5, 1939, the governor irritably declared, "I'm being caught in the crossfire of this controversy and I'm getting tired of it." This convinced McCarran that if the fight were lost, it would be because the governor really had not backed him up.[48]

But McCarran also had several advantages, including his fiery presentation and a shrewd bid for the Senate's protection of its precious prerogatives. He also had the priceless advantage of leftover resentment at Jim Farley stemming from the court fight. By contrast

Pittman's defense seemed weak and tired. Although Pittman pointed out many of the shortcomings of McCarran's case rather accurately, he was defensive in spirit. And Pittman's case was further hampered because he had not officially recommended Boyle; all he could say was that Boyle was a good man, that he had supported McCarran in 1938, and that his record in the office so far had been satisfactory.[49]

In the end the fight was not even close. The Judiciary subcommittee voted 4 to 2 against Boyle's nomination.[50] Those senators who had opposed the President on the court fight supported McCarran on this one; those senators who backed the President supported Boyle. The following month the Judiciary Committee voted 13 to 5 to disapprove the nomination.[51]

On June 29, 1939, the matter went to the floor of the Senate and both McCarran and Pittman made short statements. The vote was a stunning defeat for the supposedly popular Pittman. Three senators rose from their seats in favor of Boyle's appointment (Pittman, Hatch of New Mexico, Murray of Montana), and an estimated 25 to 30 senators rose to express their opposition to the appointment. Boyle was thereupon ousted from office, and became an embittered enemy of McCarran.[52]

Even though the appointment of a United States Attorney may seem to be a minor affair, the fracas was an extremely important milestone in McCarran's career. It expressed, of course, the resentment of many senators toward Farley's heavy-handed intervention into the court controversy the previous year. The foundation for Boyle's defeat had been laid in the court fight. In reviewing McCarran's rise to primacy in the Nevada Democratic party, one cannot avoid the ironic conclusion that Jim Farley and ultimately Franklin Roosevelt, had given the senator a healthy nudge toward that primacy.

McCarran was now the preeminent leader of the Democratic party of Nevada. All indications were that the junior senator from Nevada had more prestige and real power among his Senate colleagues than did the state's senior senator. Yet political problems remained. Since McCarran was essentially a lone-wolf operator, continued cooperation with Governor Carville was chancy. Already the fight over Boyle hinted of a future rift. Enemies still abounded among Nevada Democrats. And McCarran's relationship with the Roosevelt administration, never an easy one, would suffer as foreign policy issues assumed increased importance and the world slid toward war.

CHAPTER 6

A NARROW SURVIVAL

SENATOR MCCARRAN'S second term was marked by a diminution of his national prestige and an augmentation of his power. In Nevada, there was a break with Governor Carville, and a bitterly fought and narrowly survived bid for reelection.

Seniority and the resultant chairmanships increased his power in the United States Senate. In 1941 he became chairman of the District of Columbia Committee, although this was not one of his chief interests. More important, in 1944 he became chairman of the Judiciary Committee, which considered approximately 40 percent of all Senate legislation.

But his increasingly sharp disagreement with President Roosevelt's policies and his excessively parochial views tarnished his prestige nationally, and even in Nevada. His break with Roosevelt was intensified by his profound opposition to the President's foreign policy. From 1939 to 1941, McCarran consistently and vocally fought what he thought was Roosevelt's drift toward war. Fundamentally, McCarran was more anti-communist than anti-Nazi. He was also suspicious of the broadened executive powers brought about by Roosevelt's foreign policy. There is evidence that this consistent opposition on McCarran's part hurt him even in Nevada, or so thought such an astute observer as Pete Petersen.[1]

On domestic issues, he was perceived as parochial—quite a change from his first term. During World War II, after Key Pittman's death, he became the acknowledged leader of the silver bloc in the Senate. His never-faltering efforts, including the use of the filibuster, to force unnecessary government stockpiling of silver during World War II, brought him some of the worst notices of his career.[2] His imaginative scheme to use federal power to bring about a decentralization of American industry for the benefit of the south and west was denounced by Massachusetts Governor Leverett Saltonstall as "a plan characteristic of Hitler."[3]

McCarran's difficulties were exacerbated by Nevada's political volatility. World War II brought explosive changes for the state. Because of the availability of cheap electric power from Boulder Dam, the giant $150-million Basic Magnesium, Inc. (BMI) plant was built outside Las Vegas in 1941, to produce vital finished magnesium for defense. This plant brought in thousands of workers, most of them Democrats, and with it a troubling jurisdictional dispute between the AFL and the CIO as to which would represent those workers. The implications for Nevada politics, and for McCarran, were momentous.

The McCarran-Carville coalition, which had so successfully gained control of the Nevada Democrats in 1938, was doomed to a temporary existence. McCarran's personality made a breakup inevitable. Strains in the relationship of the two men were apparent almost from the beginning. For one thing, Carville wished to be his own man as governor; despite a temporizing facade he was a very independent operator. McCarran, on the other hand, could not readily work with any politician except in terms of opposition or domination, and he found out early that Carville could not easily be dominated, in spite of his surface geniality. Carville had received a greater majority in 1938 than had McCarran. This may have contributed to his independence, and it certainly increased McCarran's sensitivity.[4]

The split began insidiously, with McCarran wanting to direct all of Carville's appointments and Carville insisting on being his own man. Pete Petersen, who was McCarran's liaison with the governor, soon wrote the senator that Carville was not acting precisely according to plan. It is probable that Petersen, deeply suspicious of Carville himself, helped fan McCarran's mistrust.

Even before Carville's inauguration, Petersen warned the senator "our mutual friend, Governor Carville, has an excellent chance of going to the dogs politically," because he was taking advice from the "old gang." "I don't mind telling you it doesn't look at all good to me."[5] McCarran confidentially replied to the Reno postmaster that the governor was certainly a bit slow, "he apparently fails to catch on to political tricks."[6] In turn Petersen replied, "I believe that one of his biggest troubles is that he has had practically no experience whatever in hiring or firing men."[7] By June, 1939, Petersen, who knew how to play on the senator's fears, declared of Carville, "I am afraid that he has gone haywire and that things in general have gone to his head."[8] Both men had become condescending in their private remarks about the governor.

Once McCarran even attempted to suggest the person who should be Carville's secretary, since, in Petersen's words, "he is easily led."[9] Whenever Carville made an appointment, copious correspondence from the senator ensued. McCarran lost his respect for the governor early. By early 1940, McCarran was deeply offended by what he thought was Carville's offhand disregard of many of his patronage suggestions. A letter to the governor expressed McCarran's resentment:

> I note you say, "Your letter is being transferred to Mr. Berning of the highway department. . . ."
> Would you kindly tell me if you care to have me write to you further in making recommendations for those who are so gracious as to write me for my endorsement. If my letters are to be referred to Mr. Berning, I may as well desist from writing.
> I am awaiting advice from you.[10]

Carville replied as tactfully as possible, although not sufficient to soothe the senator, maintaining that taking McCarran's suggestions "in so many instances shows better than anything that I do recognize your recommendations." "I have often wished," the governor added, "that you and I could talk things over more and even though we may not always agree we certainly would have a better understanding." In an oblique criticism of Pete Petersen's attempts at promoting agreement, Carville ended, "When we get several other people's view points mixed with ours it does not make for harmony."[11]

McCarran's gradual cooling toward Carville had its influence on his relationship with Pittman. Key Pittman was to come up for reelection in 1940, for a record sixth term as a Nevada senator. At first he believed that McCarran was grooming the governor to challenge him in the 1940 Democratic primary. This belief was also often voiced in the press. And since Pittman had not often visited the state, nor followed the advice of his political lieutenants, it was generally thought that he might be vulnerable to a Carville candidacy.[12]

What happened was quite different. Carville apparently never ever planned to challenge the formidable Senator Pittman, and McCarran, increasingly exasperated by the governor, never encouraged him to do so. One journalist, Denver Dickerson, who wrote the statewide syndicated "Salmagundi" column, was more prescient than most when he hazarded the prediction that "1940 will see the cementing of the Democratic party bringing both the so-called factions under one unified banner."[13] Although no formal bargain appears to have been made, McCarran promised not to field any candidate against Pittman. In return Pittman would not fight the McCarran-Carville domination of the party machinery. Pittman was quite willing to refuse to fight for trusting subordinates in order to guarantee his own reelection (although he said it was to ensure party unity), and McCarran in turn was willing to sacrifice Carville's advancement for the same good cause. The interests of both senators were well served.

Pittman witnessed the defeat of his supporters in the county and state conventions with equanimity. He lifted not a finger in their behalf. As long as McCarran and Carville did not oppose him in the primary they were welcome to the state organizations: "I have no desire to control the Washoe County Convention nor the State Convention."[14] Pete Petersen, always looking to the future, wrote McCarran that the McCarran-Carville forces had completely routed the opposition and laid "the foundation of a good organization for the years to come, if of course, the Honorable E.P. Carville will learn to play ball. If not, it is going to be a little harder to accomplish what we are after."[15]

Pittman, on his part, mildly bawled out William Boyle for fighting the McCarran-Carville combine in the Washoe County convention: "I deeply appreciate your friendship, but I seek harmony in the Democratic Party above all things."[16] He wrote his brother Vail more honestly:

> I am sorry to see Boyle taking such an active part in everything. There is no doubt that he is like a red rag before a wild bull. . . . I am satisfied that Carville is entirely out of the picture, and that it is McCarran's intention that I shall be nominated without opposition.[17]

Evidently, McCarran believed in 1940 that a reconciliation with Pittman was of higher priority than mending any differences with Carville. By now Carville was, in Pete Petersen's words, "the little boy," and in McCarran's, "the high muckamuck." "I am not so crazy about building the Governor up any more," the senator wrote.[18] At the 1940 Democratic National Convention in Chicago, the Nevada delegation was dominated by McCarran forces. Pittman received a seat only at McCarran's sufferance. Pittman and McCarran coolly divided the prestigious positions between them. Pittman was made chairman of the delegation and McCarran was put on the platform committee. When Carville, backed by Representative James Scrugham, vociferously objected that he had not been consulted about the arrangement and that he wanted the chairmanship for himself, McCarran told Pittman "to hell with it" and Carville was left out in the cold entirely. Incidentally, McCarran, who abhorred the concept of a third term, voted with most of the delegation for James Farley for president, an ironic action considering his previous relationship with Farley. Pittman voted for President Roosevelt.[19]

It was too late, however, for the reconciliation to have much meaning. Pittman's heavy drinking, combined with the burdens of running for reelection, exacted a fatal toll. Relations between McCarran and Pittman proved to be harmonious during the campaign,[20] but Petersen warned McCarran shortly before election day that Pittman was drinking heavily:

> Of course, Senator Key Pittman is touring the State and it looks more or less good for him; but if he continues to try to drink the entire supply of John Barleycorn and keeps making a fool out of himself, no one can tell what will happen. . . . I am informed that he is still taking on plenty of whiskey. At the same time Sam Platt is hammering away, turning out great crowds wherever he has appeared, and if it were not for the fact that he is a Jew, no one knows what could happen in November.
>
> He [Pittman] has been drunk practically every day he has been in the State of Nevada, and last Monday night he appeared at a Democratic rally in Sparks, at which time he had to hold himself up in order to stand.[21]

Only a day before the election, Petersen forecast Pittman's early demise: "It is generally conceded that the Honorable Senior Senator will pass out of the picture in the near future; or, in plain English, he will kick the bucket."[22] On November 5, Pittman was reelected to his sixth term by a heavy majority; he won the race by a greater percentage margin than McCarran would ever receive. By November 10, he was dead.

For twenty-eight years, Pittman had proved an able senator. He had had close ties with the Roosevelt administration. Despite what had been asserted by several historians, the evidence is that his greatest interests were in national and foreign affairs rather than his state's own problems. Except in election years he rarely visited Nevada, and he was far more willing than McCarran to compromise on the silver issue. By 1940, weakened by excessive drinking and older than his years, he had measurably relaxed his grip, and allowed his dominance in the Nevada Democratic party to pass to McCarran and Carville. He had refused to fight the junior senator on key issues. But alone among Nevada senators, Pittman had earned McCarran's respect. Now that McCarran was the senior senator, he was never again to accord this respect to any Nevada colleague.

Senator Pittman's death forced Governor Carville to name a successor to serve until the 1942 election, and Carville was greatly worried by the responsibility. McCarran, who certainly never dreaded decision making, could not quite understand this side of the governor's temperament. "You saw what a complete wreck he was," McCarran wrote Petersen of Carville's mood when he finally made his choice, "and the next day he was thoroughly sick. He very candidly told me that when he had to make up his mind on these things he did get sick, and I believe he is telling the truth. I pity the fellow."[23]

McCarran, of course, insisted on being consulted on the appointment, but to his dismay Carville rejected the proffered advice. Carville's final choice was the thirty-five-year-old Speaker of the Assembly, Berkeley Bunker, a close friend and ally of the governor's, but a man lacking political experience and prestige. Bunker did have the advantage of residing in Clark County and of being a prominent Mormon, both of which supposedly offset McCarran's Reno residence and Roman Catholicism. But more experienced Clark County leaders such as Ed Clark and Al Cahlan, who believed they had won their spurs through long, devoted service to the party, felt betrayed by the choice. Rumor had it that Carville would have liked to have chosen himself, but his wife resisted. Also embittered was Vail Pittman, Key's younger brother and publisher of the *Ely Daily Times*, who apparently thought the job should be kept in the family. After the announcement, Vail went to the *Reno Evening Gazette* office, his face scarlet and his voice shaky. As remembered by John Sanford, Pittman sputtered that it was a "sacrilege" and a "slur on the memory" of Key that he, Vail, was not chosen. Vail was not to forget the slight and would attempt his revenge against McCarran in the future.[24] In general, Carville's choice of Bunker created resentment throughout the state party.

Despite what many thought, McCarran was not responsible for the appointment; but, ready to make the best of things, he did initially go along with it. Postmaster Petersen put things in proper perspective, at least for McCarran, when he wrote the new senior senator, "Everybody is of the opinion that if Berkeley will listen to you everything is going to be all right; and I feel sure that he will do that." McCarran and Bunker started on an affable note, traveling together on the train from Las Vegas to Washington, D.C. McCarran thought well of Bunker: "The young fellow is certainly breaking in nicely here. . . . He is certainly a pleasant young fellow to work with."[25]

But from the very beginning McCarran attempted to dominate Bunker as he had Carville. Petersen recounts an incident just after he and McCarran heard about Bunker's appointment:

> So going home that night, the roads between here and Carson City was terribly icy that night. First thing Senator McCarran said to me, "Now, we got to find a good secretary for Berkely Bunker.
> I says, "Well, who do you have in mind?" "Well," he says, "I have in mind somebody that'll keep me advised of what goes on in his office."[26]

Accordingly, McCarran recommended Florine Maher as Bunker's secretary and Bunker gratefully accepted the recommendation. Florine Maher was the sister-in-law of Carville's secretary, Alice Maher, but it must be noted that she did *not* keep McCarran clued in as to what transpired in Bunker's office, much to McCarran's dismay.[27]

As was inevitable, Bunker and McCarran were soon at odds. Bunker promptly announced that since he had been appointed to replace Key Pittman, he would attempt to follow the late senator's philosophy on foreign policy, an announcement not calculated to endear him to McCarran.[28] This meant that Bunker would pursue a pro-administration course at a time when McCarran was violently opposed to the President's foreign policy, which he was convinced was leading the nation into a bloodbath. When Petersen learned of Bunker's statement the postmaster could only comment "inasmuch as it looks like the boy wants to regulate his own affairs I guess it is far best to just let him keep on and perhaps before it is over he may learn a few lessons."[29] Bunker did not change. He firmly supported the President (who invited him in for several conferences) on lend-lease and other vital legislation. McCarran was furious. When Bunker voted for the President on the legislation to repeal the Neutrality Acts, McCarran wrote heatedly:

> We passed the damnable war bill last night by a vote of 50 to 37. As per usual Little Boy Blue was "Johnnie-at-the-rat-hole." I often wonder what that bird thinks about. I have come to the conclusion that he hasn't much to think about, I have come to the conclusion that he hasn't much to think with, so he shouldn't be blamed too much. At least I always believe in applying a full measure of charity.[30]

Encouraged by Petersen (who was now calling Bunker "junior" and "little boy" in his letters),[31] McCarran constantly derided Bunker's intelligence, because he was frustrated by Bunker's independence:

> The Junior Senator has not done me the courtesy to call since he has returned to Washington. . . . I can't quite figure out that boy's mental operations. I don't know in what channel his mind runs, and not being able to figure it out, I can say nothing.[32]

McCarran's growing dislike of Senator Bunker was also transferred to Governor Carville, since Bunker continued his close association with Carville and had been, after all, Carville's appointee. In McCarran's mind the blame for the seemingly disastrous appointment accrued to the man who had made it. More than any other incident, the appointment of Bunker soured McCarran on Carville, although the disillusionment had been ongoing since 1938. Even though McCarran's reaction to Bunker's appointment was a delayed one, his bitterness and anger were sincere.

It did not take McCarran long to decide that he would not enjoy his junior colleague's company in the U.S. Senate for any extended period of time. But who could be groomed to take on Bunker in the 1942 Democratic primary? And who would prove strong enough to defeat the rapidly ascending Bunker?

James Scrugham, born in 1880, had been Nevada's governor from 1923 through 1926 and its lone congressional representative after 1933. By 1942 he had begun to gain some seniority in the House and headed the subcommittee on naval appropriations. Although 62 years old and not in the best of health, he was to run for Bunker's seat. Scrugham would probably have been better off in the House of Representatives. From a local standpoint, the position of representative is as responsible as senator and seniority, influence, contacts, and power were his if he remained in the House. But, inveigled by friends and ambition, Scrugham decided there was more prestige to be had in the Senate.

Scrugham had been part of the Wingfield machine and a certain personal animosity remained between him and McCarran. In fact, at a Washington party in early 1941, Scrugham and McCarran almost came to blows. The argument was occasioned by a difference over patronage, and, not surprisingly, over McCarran's penchant for claiming credit for all good things that happened to Nevada. As reported in a Reno newpaper:

> The encounter came close to being a physical engagement, it is claimed, but friends stepped in, quieted the bristling legislative warriors and attempted to pour soothing oil on the troubled waters. But Scrugham did not remain at the Nevada party, leaving McCarran somewhat pale and shaken, to hold forth on his own. . . . At any rate, according to those who had ringside seats at the affair, the two Nevada legislators met in the crowded Washington banquet room. There were profane words, some violent personal epithets, and then came several irritating shoves—shoves such as precede fistic combats between two small boys. However, friends stepped in and Scrugham left the party.[33]

It would appear that Scrugham got the best of the argument, at least if we can believe his own version:

> What precipitated the matter was McCarran's effort to block the appointment of Henry Chretian as a field deputy, and his persistent claiming credit for everything done in Nevada. I took the occasion of the Nevada party on the 20th to show up his practices. I called him a "fat four flushing faker," and told him that I would smash him in the jaw if I heard any more of his meddling with my patronage recommendations. This seems to be the only way to deal with the man, as he has become almost unbearable in his arrogance.[34]

Encouraged by various party members, James Scrugham challenged Bunker in the 1942 primary. Although it must have pained

McCarran to do so, he decided to support Scrugham. He disliked the congressman, but he was anxious to get rid of Bunker. When Scrugham made his announcement, McCarran phoned Pete Petersen and told the faithful Postmaster "he was going to support Jim Scrugham with everything he had."[35] He figured that Scrugham, because of his experience in Nevada politics, would have no trouble beating Bunker. Petersen, on the other hand, was more cautious and advised McCarran to remain out of the race entirely.[36] The result was that McCarran merely adopted a position of benevolent neutrality, saying nothing publicly, but encouraging his friends in the state to support Scrugham. He decided not to be too public about his support since his own term was ending in 1944, and he faced a possibly tough re-election fight.[37] Believing, however, that Scrugham would win easily, McCarran decided to effect a quiet reconciliation:

> I want to make clear my plan. I think nothing should be left undone that can be done to bring about at the proper time a consolidation between Scrugham and myself. I don't believe this is the proper moment. I think it can be so worked around that the advance will come from Scrugham's side.
> . . . I don't want to have it said that I took a hand that would in anywise aid Bunker.[38]

Despite McCarran's tacit support, the results were amazingly close. Bunker campaigned vigorously and effectively. Scrugham defeated the junior senator in the 1942 Democratic primary by only 11,461 to 10,315 votes, and was subsequently easily elected in the November election. McCarran sent Scrugham a warm letter of congratulations and promised to campaign for him in the general election. In return, Scrugham promised to cooperate with McCarran.[39]

So McCarran had his revenge on Bunker. He and Scrugham for the most part did cooperate in the Senate, but Scrugham was gravely ill and ineffectual until his death in 1945. The election was quite detrimental to the interests of the state, because Bunker had the youth and ability to have made a long, distinguished career as senator. Certainly he would have been more effective than the ailing Scrugham. In effect, for two years McCarran was the only senator Nevada had, an arrangement which he doubtless found rather comfortable.

By 1938 the McCarran and Carville forces had gained primacy in the Democratic party machinery. McCarran's second term as a senator witnessed his separation from Carville and his steadily increasing personal power within the state party organization. One of the keys to this power was his consistent, unfailing devotion to patronage details and his blatant insistence that jobholders responsible to him must show their gratitude by cooperating and working for his political advancement. Pete Petersen, Reno postmaster, was his closest, most loyal adviser on patronage matters.

One of the problems faced by McCarran and Petersen was the Hatch Act of 1939. This bill, authored by Senator Carl Hatch of New Mexico, prohibited political activity by federal employees. In Nevada the act was a dead letter from the beginning. In Denver Dickerson's words, Senator Hatch would have had a nervous breakdown within two weeks if he had ever visited the state. For its part, the Roosevelt administration chose to look the other way. The most obvious example of a person to whom the Hatch Act did not seem to apply was, of course, Reno Postmaster Pete Petersen, who was McCarran's triggerman to the day the senator died.

When Federal Marshal Les Kofoed, in 1946, refused to campaign for an individual whom McCarran supported, he learned a lesson which cost him his job:

> He [McCarran] called me and told me that I must be active in the campaign. I told him that I understood the Hatch Act prohibited that, and he said, "Well, you know how far you can go on that. . . ."
> . . . However, little did I dream that he wouldn't give me the privilege of resigning. And I thought that there might be further discussion of it. There wasn't however. Out of a clear sky, shortly thereafter, when I was out of town on another business trip. I received a call from the chief deputy at Carson City that a new Marshall had been appointed, that I had better come home and turn in my key.[40]

McCarran not only disregarded the spirit and letter of the Hatch Act, he believed that merit systems and civil service generally were of little worth. He advised Governor Carville of his feelings: "I note that you have been considering the establishment of a merit system. It would seem that the present confusion would convince you that a merit system in any state is a complete flop, creating only turmoil."[41] His real desire was to control the patronage of the state of Nevada, which was, of course, a chief reason he eventually broke with Governor Carville. When Carville first assumed office, he offered, as a friendly gesture to McCarran, to appoint Pete Petersen state warden. Senator McCarran thought this might just provide an opportunity to enhance his own power:

> If the Governor will give you the appointment of Superintendent of the State Police and ex officio warden of the Penitentiary, with absolute power in your hands to organize and carry on the work of the State Police of the State of Nevada; to employ and dismiss whomsoever you will in the organization; and if the Governor will confer upon you the unequivocal right to employ all officers and attendants and employees in and about the Penitentiary of which you will be Warden; and if the Governor will confer upon you the right and power to reorganize the economic and financial structure of that institution—then in my judgment that you may, with propriety, accept the appointment and assume the responsibility.[42]

But this would have meant the transfer by Carville of certain of his prerogatives to Petersen, a man attuned to McCarran's political interests, not the governor's. As Petersen freely admitted:

> My only reason for ever even entertaining the idea of accepting the Wardenship was that I had the idea in mind that it might place us in a position to give many fellows jobs who otherwise would not be taken care of; also, to perhaps get control of the State Police.[43]

Not only did McCarran dabble in state patronage matters, he also intervened in municipal affairs. In return for McCarran's support of Reno Mayor August Frolich, McCarran and Petersen were allowed a large say as to who would be the city engineer and the chief of police in Reno. "My conversation with Frolich today," the postmaster wrote McCarran, "indicated that we are going to have splendid cooperation from him at all times." Such contacts were encouraged by the senator.[44]

McCarran and Petersen not only thought big, they also thought small. No position was too insignificant for their full attention. Part of Petersen's usefulness to the senator is that he took time to apprise the senator of *everything:*

> I have sent in the necessary papers nominating Charles Bacon as a janitor in this post office. This is the young fellow you may recall that Eva recommended. I made his appointment November 16th. I don't

know if it will be necessary for you to take this matter up with the Fourth Assistant; but in order to be sure the appointment will go through and expedite approval, it might be well for you to take it up.[45]

Senator Pittman's death left the door open for an enormous augmentation of McCarran's power. When Pittman died, McCarran lost little time in attempting to gain power over the federal-relief patronage in Nevada. He did succeed in having Gilbert Ross, an old enemy, fired as WPA chief in the state.[46] Unfortunately, federal relief activities ended with World War II, so that source of patronage ceased to exist.

Two offices which McCarran came to control after Pittman's death were U.S. Marshal and Internal Revenue Collector. Both victories, however, necessitated some smart infighting with Senator Bunker.

Taking over the marshal's office was complicated. The term of Frank Middleton, who had been a close friend and political adviser to Pittman, was to end June 30, 1942. Soon after Pittman's death, desiring Middleton's immediate removal, McCarran decided that his nominee for the position would be James Whalen, a machinist formerly from Ely. Of course this was after Whalen had been told of certain political realities. In a written statement, Whalen assured the senator that on political matters, McCarran was to have full control of the marshal's office:

> I believe it is your job to lay the foundation for an effective organization in the state and my job to keep it functioning in that manner after we get it organized.
>
> The appointment of the Deputy's as suggested by Pete meets with my approval and I can assure you that if any change is necessary later, your counsel will guide my actions.[47]

But a snag developed when Senator Bunker supported Middleton's candidacy for reappointment. Middleton also had key administration backing. McCarran was furious. "In other words," he confided to Petersen, "my colleague did what I told you he might do, doublecrossed me in the matter."[48] Strongly pressured by McCarran, however, Bunker eventually changed his mind about Middleton and joined with McCarren in recommending Whalen. Whalen's nomination was held up at the last moment by national party chairman Ed Flynn, who had a ranch in Nevada and many political contacts in the Silver State.[49] The pugnacious McCarran, by now second in seniority on the Judiciary Committee, was not afraid to fight it out with the powerful Flynn:

> The Marshalship seems to be tied up somewhere. I understand the Chairman of the National Committee, Mr. Flynn, has his foot on the wire. I have returned the compliment, as a pet of his was nominated to be Judge of North Dakota. I had that tied up; so it is a case of tie versus tie. I don't know who will come out first and it doesn't make much difference anyway. He has been sticking his nose into other states and going against recommendations of other Senators and carrying the matter to the White House. There is going to be a showdown soon, and it might as well be now.[50]

Probably McCarran would have won this fight, except that an FBI investigation of Whalen made the whole question academic. It revealed that Whalen had certain unsavory blotches on his record, including a history of writing bad checks.[51] Meanwhile, Middleton continued as marshal. Not until May, 1942, were Bunker and McCarran able to agree that Les Kofoed of Lovelock would be an appropriate nominee for Federal Marshal.[52]

The Department of Justice went to the trouble of telling McCarran "in no uncertain terms" that he was not to meddle with the deputy marshals; they were not removable except for cause. But the ingenious McCarran did not let that warning deter him, he suggested that life for certain deputies could be made so unpleasant that "they might not care to remain as deputies." The proper procedure was this: "What I want is for you to get in touch with him [Kofoed] and show him, if you can, how he can rearrange those deputies so I can get rid of some of them. McCarter should be moved. He is a bad actor ... He is no friend." Kofoed did become the federal marshal, and the evidence is that the deputies proved loyal to the senior senator.[53]

McCarran had a more bitter tangle with Senator Bunker over the position of Internal Revenue Collector. This job had been held by Bob Douglass since 1933. Douglass had been a longtime friend of Senator Pittman's and also had ties with Representative Scrugham. He had always been one of McCarran's most implacable enemies, so it would have been natural for McCarran to force his removal. The initiative for removing Douglass, however, came from Senator Bunker, who demanded that Douglass be fired on the grounds that he had violated the Hatch Act.[54] Bunker was doubtless fearful that Douglass's close relationship to Scrugham might be used against him in his imminent stiff battle for reelection.

The fact that it was Bunker who was demanding Douglass's ouster put the matter in an entirely different perspective for McCarran. If he could save Douglass's job, he might strengthen his own patronage position by placing Douglass in his debt and exacting certain promises from him. No doubt McCarran also welcomed a chance to humiliate Bunker. Surely Douglass was pragmatic enough to listen to political reason: "I believe Douglass will listen very attentively to reason, and he is just enough of a politician to play ball when he is scared. By handling Douglass right, we can bring Scrugham into the picture as an out-and-out candidate." The whole incident could therefore "be a golden opportunity to take Douglass in under my wing and make a valuable ally of him."[55]

It is not surprising that Douglass made a special trip to Washington, to confer with the senior senator. He promised full fealty in return for keeping his job. Petersen had predicted: "I am sure he would agree to make the changes in personnel that you wanted him to."[56] The bargain was made and Douglass kept his position, much to Bunker's embarrassment. A year later, McCarran could note with great satisfaction that every suggestion he made to Douglass regarding appointments had been carried out. In his upcoming fight for reelection in 1944, he was absolutely "convinced that the entire crowd at the Internal Revenue Office are going along with me to the best of their ability."[57] It might be noted that when the Internal Revenue scandals broke during Truman's second administration, press attention focused on the Nevada office of the agency, and specifically on Bob Douglass, who was accused of selling worthless mining stock at high prices in exchange for tax favors to purchasers.[58]

By 1943, McCarran was the leading politician in Nevada even without Carville's support. In the fall of that year, he wrote, for Petersen's benefit, an assessment of just how he stood in relation to federal patronage in Nevada. His conclusion was that he stood very well indeed. The U.S. Marshal's office had his "manifest confidence." The senator found himself "working well" with the Office of Internal Revenue. The Office of Price Administration was at least "neutral." The U.S. District Attorney's office presented a more complex story. Tom Craven, who was district attorney while Miles Pike went off to war, was not pro-McCarran, but other than that, the senator stated that he was "entirely content."[59]

Thus when McCarran came up for reelection in 1944, he had obviously consolidated his power among federal officeholders in Nevada. They became important supporters of his campaign. He was the strongest Nevada Politician. Yet, McCarran was too fractious an individual to be a really first-rate political boss. He had come up in a rough school, and his single-minded emphasis on personal loyalty was so intense and blatant that it irritated many within the party. Often he created fights and enemies needlessly. Many applauded his independent cussedness, but others were shocked by his selfishness. And as he grew older, those characteristics were becoming more and more obvious.

Pat McCarran would be 68 years of age when he ran for reelection in 1944. In two Senate terms he had received more than his share of honors and recognition. He had reached a position of primacy within the Nevada Democratic party. Despite these achievements the senator's mood had a dark side. Although in vigorous health, he must have been aware of his advancing years, and the little time which remained to him to accomplish what he wished to do. Most uncharacteristically, he mused to Petersen about whether he should retire from the political arena:

> It may surprise you, but I am seriously turning over in my mind the matter of whether or not I would be a candidate to succeed myself. Some things have happened recently, and are continuing to happen, that make me feel that I cannot, in justice to myself, carry on here much longer. Mind you, I have not made up my mind on the matter, but nevertheless, I am seriously thinking.[60]

Perhaps these moments of introspection were atypical. But it is true that, by 1943, McCarran's national and local reputation, as distinct from his power, had declined. World War II was probably the period when McCarran experienced his lowest public prestige nationally. For the first time since he became senator, business groups and conservatives tended to unite against him because of his obsessive defense of silver, which struck many easterners in particular as selfish. Locally, journalist Denver Dickerson wrote, perhaps wishfully, that one of the state's "topical conversations" was "McCarran's waning power,"—this because of his prewar isolationism. Dickerson also asserted that McCarran could be "duck soup for some hopeful in next year's battle."[61]

McCarran did little to increase his popularity in Nevada when, in June, 1943, he introduced a bill which provided that any overpopulation of deer, elk, and other game animals could be reduced by killing for consumption and for market. This infuriated many sportsmen's groups, and McCarran's reasons for introducing the legislation remain unclear, although perhaps certain livestock interests had suggested it to him. *Field & Stream,* the sportsmen's magazine, called it "loosely worded and dangerous . . . it plays right into the hands of those interests who wish to see a reduction in Wildlife population where it conflicts with the welfare of domestic animals." More to the point, Pete Petersen warned the senator that there could be unfortunate political repercussions; a "bit of a wind storm" was brewing in the state over the issue.[62]

This issue had an enormous adverse impact in Nevada, which has thousands of hunters. The senator backed down and attempted to excuse himself, declaring that he had introduced the bill in order to "stir up discussion" and to awaken "people to the danger of the loss of state's rights," Paradoxically, however, his bill could only have increased the powers of the federal bureaucracy. Eventually McCarran solemnly promised not to allow his own bill out of committee. Petersen declared many years later that this bill, so seemingly insignificant, was the single "biggest trouble" McCarran had to face in 1944.[63] He was probably right.

McCarran was plainly worried about his reelection chances, although his own brutality toward political competitors had caused the problem in the first place. Speculation, including his own, was that he would have major opposition in the 1944 Democratic primary, and the opponent would be one of three men: Governor Edward Carville, Berkeley Bunker, or Lieutenant Governor Vail Pittman. Any of the three would be formidable. All had been treated ruthlessly by McCarran. Carville, who had been elected to a second term as governor in 1942, was still antagonistic to McCarran. Bunker had been narrowly defeated in 1942 and had gotten along wretchedly with McCarran in the Senate. It was well known that he retained his political ambition, and as the 1942 campaign proved, he was an excellent campaigner. Vail Pittman must have remembered his brother's difficulties with McCarran, and he remained bitter about not having been appointed Senator in 1941. He became lieutenant governor in 1942, outpolling the combined vote of five opponents in the Democratic primary, and running at the head of the ticket in the final election. Any of these three men could count on the support of those segments of the party that had traditionally rallied around Key Pittman and who resented, for one reason or another, McCarran's policies.

Governor Carville would probably have been the strongest of the three candidates; he certainly was the one whose possible candidacy most worried McCarran. The senator believed his one bargaining card with Carville was that the governor presumably desired a federal judgeship above anything else. The very idea was abhorrent to McCarran, partly because of his antagonism toward Carville, but also because if Carville were to become a federal judge, Lieutenant Governor Pittman would automatically be the new governor. "No one need believe that I will be coerced into any appointment," McCarran thundered. However in the fall of 1943, McCarran and Scrugham submitted to the U.S. Attorney General Carville's name "for consideration for appointment" to the United States Ninth Circuit Court of Appeals. Both McCarran and Scrugham must have been sounding out the governor's intentions; they assuredly wished him out of the way, either for 1944 or 1946. But the enigmatic Carville refused to be considered for the appointment. The governor delayed in announcing his own noncandidacy for McCarran's seat until April, 1944, which certainly contributed to McCarran's growing irritation with him.[64] It is possible that Carville had initially planned to challenge McCarran in 1944, with an excellent chance of winning, but his candidacy was precluded by ill health at the time. Bunker decided to run for the House of Representatives in 1944 (he was successful), which left Vail Pittman as McCarran's natural opponent. And Vail Pittman took a long time to make up his mind.

In January, 1944, when Senator Van Nuys of Indiana suddenly died, McCarran became the chairman of the powerful Senate Judiciary Committee. This greatly aided his fortunes in Nevada. Now McCarran could convincingly tell the voters of Nevada that he had real power in the nation's capital, a crucial point in a state so vulnerable to federal pressure. Before, when McCarran was merely chairman of the District of Columbia Committee, Nevadans could see little advantage in his position. The benefits to be derived from reelecting the chairman of one of the Senate's preeminent committees was obvious to almost everyone, however.

By mid-1944, astute observers could detect an upswing in McCarran's fortunes. Certain politicians, although having little affection for McCarran, made a cold-blooded assessment that he was going to win, and decided to support him despite past differences. Thus Senator Scrugham let it be known he would vote for McCarran, although he did not take an active part in the primary. Tom Miller, Scrucham's closest adviser, acted successfully as the intermediary between the two men. More interesting, considering previous relations, was that George Thatcher, who had been so close to Wingfield and Key Pittman, gave his influential support to the senator. Thatcher refused to be put on any public committees, but he helped raise money and gave advice to the McCarran campaign, acting as a sort of senior inside adviser. Early in the campaign, Petersen wrote McCarran that "place on the corner of Second and Virginia Streets" (Thatcher and Woodburn) had attempted to discourage Pittman from running. These experienced professionals cast in with McCarran because they had decided he would win, and that accommodation was desirable.[65]

McCarran also put together an effective campaign organization. Eva Adams was his official campaign manager. Pete Petersen, because of his postmaster duties, was prevented from assuming any official role but managed, despite the Hatch Act, to be right at the center of the organization. As postmaster, Petersen had registered aliens during the war: "We registered something in the neighborhood of about 6,000 foreigners here in Reno." These aliens became important to McCarran's campaign. Petersen, an immigrant himself, worked well with them: "I had done favors for an awful lot of people, foreigners, because they had confidence in me, and they came around. . . . A lot of these people helped in the campaign."[66]

Another noteworthy fact about McCarran's campaign organization is that Norman Biltz and John Mueller, both important Republicans, volunteered their services. Biltz had been close to Wingfield, and Mueller was perhaps the most important lobbyist before the Nevada State Senate. Both had many influential financial contacts. Biltz in particular raised money. According to Petersen, Biltz "knew so many people with money, and money is a very important thing in campaigns. So he was a sort of finance chairman. Only thing I know, whenever we needed any money, I would tell him how much we needed, and he would come up with it."[67] Since McCarran had assiduously cultivated a wide spectrum of business and labor interests during his twelve years in the Senate, and Biltz had many contacts among those Republicans who thought McCarran's defeat might mean CIO domination in the state, obtaining money was presumably not difficult. The most authoritative estimate is that the election cost the McCarran forces approximately $80,000, about $4 for each voter in the Democratic primary. This compares with approximately $10,000 to $15,000 that Charles Russell and Walter Baring spent in their respective races for the House of Representatives in 1946 and 1948.[68]

McCarran's campaign was oriented to local issues and emphasized his power and experience in the Senate. His campaign ads portrayed him as the one individual who could do the most for Nevada, and played up his devotion to silver, to mining, and to the state's development. A "Postcard for McCarran" which was widely distributed stressed many of the pertinent themes:

> I'm for Pat McCarran because his record of accomplishment for Nevada and Nevadans has earned the support of all of us; because he is one of the best friends labor has in Congress; because his seniority and ability have won for Nevada a position of leadership in the Senate which must not be sacrificed; because he has been neither an easy "yes-man" nor an obstinate "no-man," voting his conscience in the light of the wishes of the majority of Nevadans, but never placing personal or political advantage above the interests of his country, his state, and the West as a whole. Because I love Nevada as Pat McCarran loves it, I'm for Pat McCarran.[69]

Of necessity, McCarran ran hard. In early June, 1944, opponents of McCarran, who had worked diligently and organized on the precinct level, took control of the Clark County Democratic convention. McCarran's allies, the Ed Cark-Al Cahlan-Archie Grant combine, were overconfident and surprised by the extent of the opposition. They lost badly. This convention enthusiastically endorsed a fourth term for President Roosevelt, but refused to endorse McCarran. The importance of this rejection is clear from the fact that for the first time, Democratic party registration in Clark County (but not total registration) surpassed that in Washoe County.[70]

The Democratic state convention, held later in the month in Reno, was a hectic affair. There was controversy over a resolution "commending," but not supporting, McCarran's senate activities, coupled with a like commendation for Senator Scrugham. The Clark County delegation, along with delegates from the CIO-dominated copper region of White Pine County, voted heavily against the resolution. Representatives from Washoe and the cow counties voted substantially in McCarran's favor. The vote was public; it is possible that if there had been a secret ballot, more delegates would have voted against the resolution, watered down as it was. The resolution "commending" McCarran passed by only 110½ to 91½ ballots.[71]

Still Pittman delayed his decision, which weakened any possible opposition movement. Significant convention roll-call votes passed without any candidate for McCarran's opponents to field against him. Even without such an announced candidate, the large vote against McCarran in both the Clark County and state conventions amply demonstrated the senator's unpopularity within the party. McCarran was well aware of how many people were out to get him.

> It looks as though I may have some serious opposition in the primary. The C.I.O. has set out to find a candidate to run against me, and they are flirting with the Lt.-Governor, Pittman; so I may have to put on my sword and buckle, but I have never been very lucky in having anything handed to me. I generally have to fight my way for whatever I get. It doesn't seem to make a continental bit of difference how hard I work, or how much I accomplish; when it comes to getting something for myself, I have to take on the battle—but I approach it without fear and with a hellish determination.[72]

McCarran's CIO reference indicates the importance that organized labor played in the 1944 campaign. Like the Democratic party, organized labor in Nevada was hotly divided on McCarran, even though the senator had long cultivated its vote. In fact McCarran's prolabor record could hardly have been more consistent. Consequently both the national AFL and the railway unions endorsed McCarran for reelection. Labor newspapers put out special editions extolling McCarran's many virtues, to be circulated in Nevada. In a strong letter to the president of the Nevada State Federation of Labor, AFL President William Green stated: "There is no member of the United States congress in either house, past or present, who has rendered the high type of service to labor which has been rendered by Senator McCarran."[73]

But the CIO, which had strength among the copper workers in Ely, and which was trying to organize the Basic Magnesium workers, bitterly opposed the senior senator. In some ways the 1944 race took on certain attributes of a CIO-AFL intramural squabble. CIO opposition to McCarran was based on his isolationist record and his refusal to support so many aspects of the President's program. To the CIO, more was at stake than the senator's labor record; consistent and undeviating support of Roosevelt's foreign and domestic policy was also essential. Its publications simplistically characterized McCarran as a "reactionary."

But even the AFL had trouble keeping its own organizations in line. William Green sent national AFL organizer Joseph J. Ozanic to Nevada to pressure the various labor groups in behalf of the McCarran candidacy. The Reno Central Trades and Labor Council (AFL), however, refused to endorse the senator. At the end of July, when the Nevada State Federation of Labor met in Ely, Ozanic and Pete Petersen, who was a member of the baker's union, lobbied strongly in behalf of a McCarran endorsement. They succeeded in getting one, but the result was somewhat less than impressive. A resolution "commending" the Senator and "recommending his renomination" was passed by 46 votes to 19, 40 delegates being absent or boycotting the vote. An anti-McCarran figure, Frank J. Bacigalupi, was reelected president of the State Federation.[74]

Not until July 29 did Pittman announce his candidacy, and he filed on August 6, less than a month before the primary.[75] If he had announced earlier, he might have waged a stronger fight. Pittman's campaign focused on national issues, probably a mistake in Nevada. According to Pittman, the chief issue was McCarran's isolationist record before World War II:

> Look what has happened in Guam the last few days. We have lost hundreds of men out there in the total and all essential effort to retake the island—but Senator McCarran resisted every effort in Congress to fortify Guam so the Japs could not take it.
>
> Look what the Russians are doing—McCarran opposed lend lease for them.
>
> These and many other things have caused Nevada citizens—with their sons, brothers and fathers in the service—to think, and to think deeply. They believe that McCarran, perhaps unwittingly, has opposed almost every fundamental war demand that will hasten the day of victory for us.[76]

The campaign soon got heated—and dirty. McCarran supporters accused the Pittman camp of indulging in a one-sided mudslinging campaign, while Pittman's supporters alleged that McCarran's campaign used unfair tactics. Both appraisals were correct, although the McCarran tactics were probably the rougher.

William Boyle, obviously bitterly remembering the past, declared in a radio speech that "after Manila and Pearl Harbor had been bombed by the Japs, Senator McCarran failed to show up in the senate and vote for war against the Axis. He dogged it."[77] This refers to the fact that McCarran, because of the sudden Pearl Harbor attack, and since Congress was not in session, was in Nevada and could not make it back to Washington in time.

For their part, the senator's supporters tried to pin a CIO label on Pittman. At a time when there was much resentment of the CIO role in Democratic politics, the voters were led to believe that the profoundly conservative Pittman was a pawn of dangerously radical groups. President Roosevelt's famous "Clear it with Sidney" statement (referring to Sidney Hillman, head of the CIO Political Action Committee and his supposed veto power at the 1944 Democratic national convention) became a prime Republican campaign issue. There were many who believed the PAC was communist-supported. On June 21, 1944, a public letter was sent from a CIO-PAC official to the International Union of Mine, Mill and Smelter Workers of Nevada, bitterly castigating McCarran for his opposition to much of the Roosevelt program. Predictably, McCarran supporters professed to be shocked and resentful of this outside CIO interference in Nevada politics.[78] On July 19, 1944, a full page advertisement in the *Nevada State Journal* asked:

> WHO WILL RULE NEVADA?
> THE PEOPLE OR THE C.I.O.?
> THE C.I.O'S CAMPAIGN IS UNDER WAY.
> WHO WILL BE THE C.I.O. CANDIDATE?

McCarran's groundwork had been laid. When Vail Pittman did make his announcement of candidacy later in the month, he had to make considerable effort to deny that he was the candidate of the CIO. He also denied that the CIO was financing his campaign,[79] but these denials merely put him on the defensive. There is no direct evidence that the CIO pressured Pittman to become a candidate. Probably it contributed money in one form or another to his campaign, but Pittman ran for reasons that had little to do with the CIO.

Ostensibly damaging charges were made again by the McCarran people only a week before the election. Some of McCarran's Capitol

Hill friends had done some digging. The House Un-American Activities Committee, which was then under the chairmanship of Martin Dies, decided to investigate the political activities of the CIO in California. The committee then ordered Western Union to turn over all telegrams charged to or paid for by the CIO-PAC committee in California. Some results of the investigation were leaked to the *Salt Lake Tribune,* and then copied in huge political ads paid for by the McCarran forces in all Nevada newspapers:

> The first shot of the CIO in the Nevada senatorial race was fired by Mrs. Helen Gahagan Douglas.
> The drive against McCarran by the political action committee is said to be chiefly directed by George B. Roberts of Los Angeles, who is director of the CIO political action committee for District 13, which includes California and Nevada. All the telegrams gathered in by the Dies Committee were charged to his office, including one sent by Mrs. Douglas. But for the fact that her telegram had been paid for by the CIO, PAC, what she had to say about the Nevada senatorial contest might have established only that she was butting in.
> Her [Mrs. Douglas's] telegram, dated Los Angeles, June 27, 1944, addressed to U.S. Sen. Claude Pepper of Florida, senate office building, Washington, reads: "If at all possible please prevail upon Vail Pittman to run against McCarran in Nevada. Everything is in his favor and he is the most electible."
> What gives this telegram significance is the fact that in the lower left corner it bears this charge memorandum: T U 8193 R, B, George Roberts, 112 W. 9th St.
> Roberts, to whom the telegram was charged, is director of the CIO political action committee for District 13, and his office is in Room 620, Rives-Strong Bldg., 112 W. 5th St. Los Angeles.[80]

These supposedly damning revelations were heavily used by McCarran in the campaign's final week. In the closing days, Pittman announced in full-page advertisements that the PAC had not contributed a cent toward his effort. Actually, despite all the insinuations, there was nothing particularly incriminating about the evidence. But people were led to believe otherwise, to fear that Nevada was somehow in danger of becoming a CIO fief if McCarran were defeated. The issue was a false one.

The election resulted in a narrow McCarran victory. The *Chicago Tribune* put matters into proper perspective, at least according to its lights, by emblazoning on its front page: M'CARRAN BEATS CIO

CANDIDATE IN NEVADA RACE. The AFL periodical, *Labor,* trumpeted: M'CARRAN VICTOR: CIO LIES FAIL TO BEAT PROGRESSIVE.[81]

The final tabulated vote was 11,152 (52.9 percent) for McCarran and 9.911 (47.1 percent) for Pittman. The distribution of the count was illuminating. Washoe County, McCarran's home area, voted 3,018 to 2,541 in favor of Pittman. Reno and Sparks both voted for the Ely publisher; and Sparks, despite the strength of the railroad unions there, went for Pittman by a comfortable margin. Vail Pittman also did strongly in his home area of White Pine County, defeating McCarran there by 1,226 to 732 votes. This reflected not only on his Ely residence but the fact the CIO copper workers supported the recommendation of their union leaders. It was Clark County that elected McCarran; against all expectations, McCarran defeated Pittman there by a 3,892 to 2,369 margin. The rest of the state had voted narrowly in Pittman's favor.[82]

The key to McCarran's victory therefore was Clark County. His victory extended to Las Vegas, Henderson, and Boulder City, and covered various social groups. Perhaps one reason for this surprising outcome was that the leading Clark County Democrats, alerted by their defeat at the county convention in June, 1944, worked that much harder to turn out the vote for McCarran in September. Certainly there was considerable appreciation for McCarran's efforts to gain federal aid for southern Nevada. The American Federation of Labor lent its powerful support among BMI workers, and the endorsement of Al Cahlan's widely read *Las Vegas Review-Journal* probably was helpful. In addition, after the ballots were counted it became apparent that black voters in Las Vegas had chosen McCarran, although Pittman had expected their votes. Later there were charges that black voters had been paid to vote for the senior senator, and even that busloads of blacks had been imported from Los Angeles. Vail Pittman privately wrote, "Every means was used to obtain the desired result." Some of these charges may have had some foundation. Normal Biltz's laconic explanation given many years later, that "We found a way to get the Negro vote," hardly settled the question.[83]

Pittman had undoubtedly taken the black vote too much for granted; he was, after all Mississippi-born, and retained a pronounced Southern accent.[84] In retrospect, it is difficult to see how it was in the interest of blacks to vote for him, although he was greatly annoyed when they did not. Furthermore, since McCarran was chairman of the important Senate Judiciary Committee, he was in an ideal position to do something about black rights. Pittman was not. Finally one must remember that the black vote was hardly large enough singlehandedly to have affected the outcome. Pittman probably put his finger on the major reason for McCarran's victory when he stated:

> McCarran had a pet project in nearly every town in the state: Housing projects, sewage systems, airfields, power projects, school houses, and heavens knows what all. . . . People remember the little personal favors and the things that help them financially, but they forget the things done that are more remote but more vital.[85]

McCarran had so much going for him—the chairmanship of the Senate Judiciary Committee, and a single-minded devotion to Nevada's interests—that the closeness of the vote probably attests to his personal unpopularity among the registered Democratic voters. His victory testifies to the respect he had won from Nevadans, not to the affection he had gained. If Pittman had announced earlier, had waged a stronger campaign, and if the CIO issue had not come up, McCarran could very well have been defeated.

Both Pittman and McCarran remained enemies; the election left many angry scars. McCarran privately wrote, "The primary fight was really a bitter one, and the nastiest I have ever seen in this section of the country, and I was confronted by one of the most vicious smear campaigns that I have ever seen in America." Pittman's concession statement did not mention McCarran's name or that he would support him—merely that he would "accept with good grace the will of the voters of Nevada."[86]

Once having gained the Democratic nomination, the final election was comparatively easy, since McCarran had considerable Republican support. His opponent was George Malone, an engineer who had run again Key Pittman in 1934. McCarran's victory was comfortable, he gained 30,595 votes to Malone's 21,816. His 8,779 vote margin was considerably greater than Roosevelt's 5,012 majority, but less than Berkeley Bunker's 13,552 margin in winning a seat in the House of Representatives. McCarran carried Clark County by well over 2 to 1, and even managed to win Republican Washoe County by a safe margin. On the other hand, White Pine County, with its large CIO-influenced vote, went for Malone, even though Roosevelt carried the county 2 to 1. It is interesting that the most pro-Roosevelt precincts in White Pine County were also for Malone.[87]

The 1944 election campaign had two vitally important ramifications for McCarran:

First, his bitterness against Vail Pittman and those elements in the party who had supported Pittman did not subside with his victory. On the contrary, it remained and grew. McCarran determined to thwart Pittman's ambition wherever possible, also the ambitions of those Democrats such as Edward Carville who had stayed on the sidelines during the campaign. McCarran was now in a strong enough position to settle some of the old political scores. The 1944 election thus intensified certain long-run divisions within the Nevada Democratic party. McCarran would neither forget nor forgive, a purge would be necessary.

Second, the CIO-PAC issue also did not fade away. After McCarran's primary victory, important allegations concerning communist influences within the CIO were made. Later the charge was spread by the Hearst press, the American Federation of Labor, and certain elements within the House Un-American Activities committee among others.[88] *Labor,* the AFL organ, declared:

> Senator McCarran should have carried the Democratic primary without opposition. He would have scored the triumph he deserved, if it hadn't been for the utterly unscrupulous fight made against him by Sidney Hillman and his Communist-controlled C.I.O. Political Committee.
>
> Never in the history of Nevada and seldom in the history of any other state has such a torrent of falsehood and misrepresentation been devoted against an outstanding public character, whose life, public and private, has always been an open book.
>
> McCarran's unscrupulous foes lost the primary, but they succeeded in deceiving many intellectual voters. . . .
>
> Having secured a candidate, the Communists proceeded to develop their campaign. Apparently, they had money to burn. They sent into Nevada thirty-five or forty paid "agents." These men and women had been given a course of training in Los Angeles. They had been schooled to make all kinds of fantastic charges against McCarran. . . .
>
> In any number of Nevada towns, they went from house to house telling these tales to everyone who would listen. . . . In addition, the C.I.O. bought any amount of radio time and flooded the newspapers with "ads," all packed with falsehoods about McCarran.[89]

These allegations were hotly denied by everyone in the Pittman campaign. Yet, in McCarran's suspicious mind, they festered and grew. Convinced of the innate justice of his own ideas, it seemed more plausible to attribute opposition to communist influence than to admit that there may have been valid political issues at stake. The House Committee on Un-American Activities did some investigating of the "subversive aspects" of the PAC. It is indicative of McCarran's feelings about the CIO and communism that his Senate Internal Security Subcommittee, in the early 1950s, launched a full scale investigation of communist influences on the International Union of Mine, Mill, and Smelter Workers. In 1944 it was the only important CIO union in Nevada, and an implacable enemy of the senior senator.

CHAPTER 7

OFFICE OPERATIONS: LINCHPIN OF POWER

THE CHIEF REASON McCarran was reelected three times was that he succeeded in convincing the voters of Nevada of his deep commitment to them and the state. National issues had little to do with it. "The voters of Nevada," the *Nevada State Journal* asserted, "don't give a hoot how he votes on most of the national bills that have no direct connection with Nevada, but they do want someone in Washington to whom they can turn when they need help on local problems and even personal problems. There has never been," added the newspaper, "a senator in the history of the state who has paid as close attention to the needs of the state."[1]

The senator solicited problems. Anyone caught in a jam with the bureaucracy—the Bureau of Land Management, Social Security, or the Veterans Administration, for example—could just write the senator and he would help. He became a type of ombudsman, telling listeners to one radio broadcast, "When your community has any kind of problem, let me know about it, whether or not you think I can help." He was proud of the help he could give. "I thank God," he declared, "that he has seen fit to place me in a position where I have been able to aid my many friends and neighbors in Nevada." His whole office was geared to the needs of his constituents. No problem was too small for him, and his seat on the Senate Appropriations Committee put him in an ideal position to lobby for airports, school aid, highways, or whatever else was needed.[2]

Several examples will demonstrate the scope of McCarran's interest in his constituents' needs, and his willingness to take extra trouble to solve their problems. Once an old prospector in Tuscarora wrote to McCarran, seeking help. Soon afterward, Norman Biltz, who was staying on a ranch near Winnemucca, received a telephone call from the senator in Washington. "You got any wood on that ranch?" McCarran asked. "What do you mean wood?" "I mean firewood." "Hell ... I guess so." "Well, do me a favor ... there's a miner up Tuscarora Canyon who broke his chopping arm and can't get in his winter wood. Would you take up a couple loads for him?" Biltz did and never forgot the incident.[3]

Another example of McCarran's intercession on behalf of a constituent occurred when old friends discovered that their son had stolen 150 volumes from the Library of Congress and had mutilated hundreds more. The frantic parents called on McCarran for assistance, and the senator devoted considerable personal time and attention to the matter. He interceded with the Library of Congress (which went along with the settlement most unwillingly), with U.S. District Attorney Ed Curran ("a very warm friend of mine. I have his confirmation up on two different occasions when he has been appointed to his present office"), and even with J. Edgar Hoover. In his correspondence with the boy's parents, the senator was consistently understanding and sympathetic, an experienced man of the world not unduly shocked by the sometimes disturbing aberrations of human character.[4]

The case of Joseph McDonald, editor of the *Nevada State Journal,* provided a prominent example of the senator's intervention and assistance. McDonald had long been a good friend to McCarran. At the time of Pearl Harbor, one of his two sons, Joe, Jr., was stationed on Wake Island. Wake was attacked by Japanese landing forces on December 11, 1941, a landing repulsed by the Americans. But a second Japanese force attacked on December 23 and this time stormed the island. The McDonalds were officially notified by the Navy Department that their son had been killed in the action.[5]

The initial grief, however, soon changed to some hope that their son was alive. In February, 1942, the navy acknowledged that it had made a grievous error, that in fact there had been two Joseph McDonalds stationed on Wake Island, and it was the other Joe McDonald from Cody, Wyoming, who had been killed.[6] Soon the International Red Cross notified the McDonalds that Joe, Jr., was indeed alive, a prisoner of the Japanese in Shanghai.[7]

Senator McCarran was involved in the case from the beginning. He had known Joe, Jr., since boyhood and expressed his special gratitude the soldier was alive. He wrote the happy parents:

> Every one of us here was just delighted at this absolute definite information about him. He had been on my mind many, many times, and I can't

tell you how happy I feel and how glad I am that my feeling that night
when I looked at his picture, on that occasion when you were so kind
as to have me for dinner, has been verified. I refer to that deep conviction that he was still alive.[8]

But the senator did not let the matter rest at that. Instead he
attempted the seemingly impossible task of securing Joe's release by
the Japanese. He began by seeking information about the prisoner's
status, even consulting the Vatican. More promisingly, he attempted
to have Joe declared a UP correspondent (he had done some stringer
work on Wake Island), which would have enhanced his chances for
exchange. The senator kept at the effort, which reflected not only his
usual practice, but deep emotional involvement as well. Eva Adams,
his secretary, wrote the father, "He speaks of young Joe so often . . .
the Senator seems to feel very close to him." For the senator's part,
he only promised, "We will keep plugging away." He even sent
telegrams to the young man in China as regularly as possible, "We
are leaving no stone unturned in your behalf. Keep your chin up and
take good care."[9]

At one point, McCarran believed he had actually been successful.
"In strictest confidence," he wrote McDonald, Sr., "I have had a
talk with a party who has been trying to help me in the State Department, and Joe's name is on the list of those who are supposed to
come out on the next boat." But he advised initial caution: "This is
the deepest, darkest secret I have ever given you, and you must
not mention it to anyone."[10] Unfortunately, this news was premature; McCarran had no control over the Japanese and the arrangement fell through. Joe, Jr., remained in the prison camp through
August, 1945. But McCarran never did stop trying to arrange his
release.

After the war, Joe, Jr., worked in McCarran's office. And there
were certain political dividends for all the senator's efforts. Joseph
McDonald, Sr., who had been pro-McCarran all along, made the
Nevada State Journal into an undeviating McCarran organ.

McCarran was not unmindful of the necessity of keeping his constituents advised of these efforts on their behalf. His chief vehicle for
this purpose was the press releases to state newspapers. These releases were written so newspapers could print them verbatim. Many
of the smaller newspapers did so, presenting them as news items.
McCarran also inundated individuals and newspapers with telegrams to apprise them of his work on their behalf.

A typical McCarran wire would begin "I am happy to advise of success in securing . . ." and then would go on to tell just what made the senator happy.[11] The senator's office kept up a constant flow of propaganda and information. The *Reno Evening Gazette,* not McCarran's most devoted press supporter, once solemnly announced that "Senator McCarran who usually shows the way among Nevada officials in obtaining publicity in the state press, hasn't sent more than fifteen or twenty releases in the last 30 days and many have been wondering why."[12] Generally the press releases presented the senator as a man of constant activity, with a finger in every pie, always exerting himself to the limit to help his state and his constituents. No man could have been quite so busy as McCarran was made out to be, and supporting the image was in itself a full-time, self-perpetuating industry. Even when McCarran was hospitalized for considerable periods, that did not staunch the flow of releases.

The press of Nevada reacted to the senator in different ways. Most of the small-town newspapers slavishly printed the press releases, and, doubtless grateful for the filler, consistently supported him. The *Las Vegas Review-Journal,* under the leadership of Al Cahlan, was a steadfast editorial friend. The *Nevada State Journal,* under Joe McDonald's helm, could not have been more supportive of the senator. McDonald lacked critical independence, he allowed McCarran to do too many favors for him (both his sons worked in the senator's office). But he was naturally grateful for what the senator had done while his son was in prison camp. "I was often accused of making the newspaper into a mouthpiece for McCarran," McDonald later told an interviewer. "Well, I did as best I could." For his part the senator knew to perfection just how to play to McDonald's vanity in his correspondence with the editor.[13]

Under the editorial guidance of John Sanford, however, the *Reno Evening Gazette* was usually critical of the senator. It also at this time enjoyed the state's largest circulation. The *Gazette* was ardently conservative (some critics said "neanderthal") Republican in its principles, and Sanford marched to nobody's drum, except perhaps Bob Taft's. Many people thought he was "cranky," an image he cultivated with delight, but no one questioned his integrity or his independence. Denver Dickerson, writer of the statewide "Salamagundi" column, and also the owner of various small newspaper enterprises, took many perceptive potshots at the senator, but in 1952 he accepted a State Department job under McCarran's auspices.[14] The *Ely Daily Times,* under the ownership of Vail Pittman, was a predictable foe, and at times the *Boulder News* presented problems for the senator. But only after 1950, when the *Las Vegas Sun* made its debut, did Nevada get a journal which was willing to fight the senator by hard-hitting, montraditional, ungentlemanly tactics. Generally the Nevada press was more supportive than otherwise.

The senator and his staff read the papers quite closely, and favorable or unfavorable editorials earned letters from Eva Adams or the senator himself.[15] All Nevada newspapers were clipped for every reference to the senator, until, in 1952, the staff stopped doing this for the infuriating *Sun.* McCarran's own favorite newspaper, not surprisingly, was his hometown, consistently devoted *Nevada State Journal.*[16]

If McCarran labored assiduously to put his own efforts in the best possible light, the unpleasant corollary was the assumed necessity to demean any efforts by his colleagues. After Pittman's death, McCarran's referred to his senatorial colleagues as "Junior." Full credit for any achievement for the state was to be given only to the senior senator, never shared. Belittling private remarks were the norm. This attitude naturally impeded an easy relationship with the man who happened to be "Junior" at the moment. It also necessitated some fancy footwork at times. In 1942, Denver Dickerson reported how McCarran successfully stole some credit away from Senator Bunker and Representative Scrugham:

> Senator McCarran stole the show from the remainder of the Nevada delegation this week by announcing the approval of the $12,000,000 army air base in Lemmon Valley. Representative Scrugham and Senator Bunker were both in Las Vegas so the senior senator had the stage all to himself.
>
> With the artistry of an Edwin Booth, Senator McCarran called a meeting of Reno business and civic leaders, leaving Las Vegas Monday and driving all night to get to the scene of the spectacular episode.
>
> When the group was assembled the senator made his dramatic announcement pausing in the right places for effect, and rounding it out with a blood-pulsating accolade to his native Reno and his native state. The Reno radio station gave the senator time to announce it to the air listeners, while the Republican *Reno Evening Gazette* in a story NOT written by the regular political reporter, ran a McCarran autobiography on the obvious political gesture.
>
> Needless to say, Scrugham and Bunker are not too happy at having their thunder stolen. Scrugham is particularly rankled in view of the fact that he was equally responsible in securing the base.[17]

McCarran's insatiable desire to be given sole credit for every benefit to the state led him to some questionable actions. In World War II, for example, the senator was prepared to leak allegedly confidential defense information prematurely, in order to serve his own political interests. A letter to the editor of the *Lovelock Review Miner* provided some interesting wartime news:

> I want to give you the following information because I think you will be greatly interested in it, in addition to the fact that you might want to keep it in mind with the thought of future activity.
>
> I cannot emphasize too much the importance of your keeping this absolutely confidential. It must not, under any circumstances, be published in the press, nor must it be made known to anyone other than yourself. I have every confidence that you will keep this matter entirely in the back of your mind until such time comes as we can announce it publicly.

So why tell Paul Gardner, publisher of a weekly newspaper with 1,000 circulation? Even stranger, McCarran also sent the identical "absolutely confidential" information to interested editors and business leaders in Winnemucca and Reno, giving each one the impression they were in on some deep, dark secret. McCarran finished each of the letters with as many details as he could supply:

> The War Department has gone forward at my request and made wide plans and engaged in extensive activities, looking to the establishment of an aerial gunnery range in the Black Rock Desert country in Humboldt County, Nevada.
>
> This will involve the securing of some 5,800 acres of land to be used by the Army in activities connected with the aerial gunnery range program.
>
> Appraisals have been made of land in this region as of March 7th, and within the next two or three weeks I look forward to completion of details and final approval by the War Department officials in charge, at which time we can advise interested parties of the project and make the news public.
>
> Until this time, however, I must again ask you not to say anything about this matter; but I know you will rejoice with me that I have been finally successful in getting some army activity into some of the wide open spaces of Nevada. I will give you details of the project at an early date.[18]

The letter points out McCarran's indispensable role in obtaining this federal project. This confidential news may have been divulged in order to flatter editors, making them feel they had privileged information, courtesy of McCarran, of course. Sending this information also enabled McCarran to get a publicity jump on the competition—Nevada's other senator and representative. Yet the final phrase in the letter's first paragraph is puzzling—"that you might want to keep it in mind with the thought of future activity." Perhaps this meant that if his friends, the people obtaining the news, were to profit financially from the confidential information, McCarran would look the other way—anything to further the development of Nevada and its citizens.

McCarran's staff was acknowledged as one of the finest in the senate. In his later years, he had more staff members available to him than normal, because of his chairmanships of the Judiciary Committee and of the Appropriations subcommittee on State, Justice, and Commerce. Because of the senator's varying duties, the functions of the individual staff members tended to get mixed up. Views of the senator's staff varied. Robert Allen, a vehemently anti-McCarran reporter, once wrote that the senator had turned "the Judiciary Committee setup into a patronage pigsty, crawling with hatchet men and incompetents." But Alfred Steinberg more accurately assessed the staff's capability when he said it operated "perhaps the finest intelligence service on Capitol Hill."[19]

In September, 1939, McCarran's personal secretary, Hazel Smith, announced her impending marriage and her decision to retire from the office staff. Smith had aided the senator in getting established in Washington. A charming and able woman, she was admired by all who knew her. Many believe that she was of no small importance in establishing and maintaining McCarran's initial success as a senator.

In December, 1939, Eva Adams succeeded her as McCarran's secretary. Born in 1908, in the then mining town of Wonder, Nevada, Adams was a graduate of the University of Nevada. She had taught at Las Vegas High School and studied journalism at Columbia University, where she received a master's degree in English. She then served for several years as an instructor in English at the University of Nevada.

In 1946, Eva Adams was promoted from personal secretary to administrative assistant. She became the first woman president of the Senate Secretaries Association, taught a course in "Administrative Operations for Congressional Assistants," and found time to earn a law degree.[20] At a time when achievement by women was difficult in Washington, Adams was able to go far. Indeed, her contacts eventually came to rival those of the senator. Norm Biltz, who knew both of them well, once stated that Adams had more power on Capitol Hill than did Senator McCarran himself. "I'd choose her," he said, "above Senator McCarran because she had that smooth way of getting the job done, and ruffling the fewest number of feathers.[21]

Adams commanded deep respect and admiration from all for her intellect, ability, and loyalty, but some who knew her well said that underneath a sweet exterior she could be a tough operator. Most were quite guarded in their appraisal. Along with Pete Peterson and Norman Biltz, she was McCarran's closest associate and confidante in his later years. And she saw McCarran far more frequently than the other two.

Adams was an able, forceful woman teamed up with an aging, but vigorous, often bitter and vindictive senator. The combination could be lethal. McCarran was a brilliant, nervous man who relied upon Adams for emotional and intellectual support. As the years passed by she grew more and more protective of McCarran.

McCarran would come into his office at 8:30 or 9:00 A.M. never later than 9:15. Jay Sourwine, one of the senator's chief staff members, would pick him up, and they would drive in together. The staff was expected to be present by 9:00.

Eva Adams was in charge of mail sorting. Perhaps a hundred letters would come in during a typical day, consisting of all types of requests, ranging from important correspondence to schoolchildren asking for a flag. Adams would apportion all the mail, and a staff member would handle perhaps 8 or 10 letters a day. The office was run on the basis that every letter had to be answered within 24 hours, even if all the staff member could do was acknowledge the letter and promise a later answer. Indicative of the office's efficiency was its filing system, acknowledged by some as the finest in the Senate Office Building.[22]

Many of the senator's speeches were written by Sourwine, who also served as an expert on drafting legislation. A brilliant, vehemently anticommunist thinker, Sourwine was particularly close to the senator on internal security matters. The thoughts in McCarran's speeches, however, were universally acknowledged as the senator's. It was Sourwine's function to translate McCarran's ideas into words. Sourwine never claimed to be anything more than the technician for someone who lacked the necessary time to compose speeches himself. Also helpful in writing speeches were Chet Smith and other staff members.[23]

Every staff member who was interviewed declared that McCarran was himself an extremely hard worker, who knew exactly how to use his staff. Correspondence, committee hearings, conferences, and floor debates filled his day. He rarely left for home before 5:00 P.M. Since he did not socialize much and had no hobbies, he immersed himself in work while not at the office. Much of his evening would be spent on the phone, often to Nevada. He went to bed early, 9:00 P.M. or so, and often rose as early as 4:00 A.M. The senator was known to call staff members as early as 5:00 or 6:00 A.M. to check on a problem, either forgetful of time or possibly just to keep them on their toes.[24]

To a certain degree, McCarran allowed opposition from those staff members who had earned his trust. Both Jay Sourwine and Eva Adams have stated that he invited disagreement from them; in fact they were specifically instructed to oppose him. However, the senator did not believe in complete popular democracy, and staff members in a less exalted position than Sourwine and Adams tended to keep opposition positions to themselves.

The composition of the senator's staff had immense political significance in Nevada, largely because Nevada had no law school. Lawyers held an unusually important place in Nevada life and politics, partly because of the state's easy divorce laws. Yet any ambitious young man in the state who wished to enter the legal profession had to go elsewhere for his training.

In the nineteenth century, Nevada's Senator William Stewart had initiated the practice of bringing deserving, ambitious young men to Washington, D.C., and finding them government jobs to help pay their way through law school. Key Pittman continued this practice, but it was Senator McCarran who first used it as a systematic way of building up his own political strength in the state. Many young men from Nevada were put through law school—George Washington, Georgetown, American, Catholic, National, or Southeastern— by McCarran's patronage. In return for studying the law, they worked in McCarran's office or on one of his committees, served as elevator operators, capital policemen, clerks, assistants, or what not. And McCarran checked on their grades. For the most part these men returned to Nevada, began practicing law there, and became vital cogs in the senator's machine. The web reached into almost all of

Nevada's counties, and there was an obvious attempt at geographical distribution.[25]

The list of Nevadans who at one time or another served as "McCarran's boys"—as they were popularly called—reads like a who's who of Nevada politicians, although not all of the "boys" actually went into politics, and some never returned from Washington, D.C. Among "McCarran's boys" were: Alan Bible, attorney general of Nevada, 1942–50, and U.S. Senator, 1954–74; Harvey Dickerson, attorney general of Nevada, 1963–70; Grant Sawyer, governor of Nevada, 1959–66; John Laxalt (brother of Paul Laxalt, governor, 1967–70, U.S. Senator, 1975–); and Jon Collins, Nevada Supreme Court justice, 1967–70. Even Charles Russell, governor, 1951–58, obtained employment in Washington through McCarran, after his defeat for the House of Representatives in 1948. Others, mostly prominent lawyers, who worked for McCarran include: Chester Smith, Joseph T. McDonnell, Joseph McDonald, Jr., Bob McDonald, Clark Guild, Jr., James Johnson, Ralph Denton, Virgil Wedge, Les Leggett, C. E. ("Dutch") Horton, Calvin Corey, Gordon Rice and James Archer, who went to dental school at Georgetown. It was not absolutely necessary to become a lawyer to work for McCarran.[26]

Doubtless attracted by his personal magnetism and his paternal interest in their well-being, these young men believed in the senator's policies. The senator commanded and obtained instant loyalty, and the young men remained loyal even after leaving the office. *Time Magazine,* in its obituary on the senator, quoted one of McCarran's boys as saying, "What the hell. McCarran took me off the street when my belly had wrinkles in it. He fed me and clothed me and put me through law school and helped me get started in practice. What kind of jerk would I be to turn on him now."[27]

Thus the office staff and its efficient procedures became a prime ingredient of McCarran's appeal in Nevada, as well as the nucleus of his formidable machine. The procedures were set up to make every Nevadan believe the senator was personally interested in him or her, therefore the constant flow of press releases and the quick attention to correspondence and constituents' problems. It was all highly effective.

Pat McCarran, 1916.
(Nevada Historical Society, Reno)

A meeting of old political foes at the national capitol in the 1930s. Ray
Baker and Senators Patrick McCarran and Key Pittman.
(Nevada Historical Society, Reno)

Pat McCarran, relaxed from a hunting trip, 1950.
(Nevada Historical Society, Reno)

Harry Truman, Vail Pittman, and Pat McCarran campaigning in Reno,
September 22, 1948.
(Special Collections, Getchell Library,
University of Nevada, Reno)

Pat and Harriet McCarran, fiftieth wedding anniversary, 1953.
(Nevada Historical Society, Reno)

Pat McCarran, 1942.
(Nevada Historical Society, Reno)

Senator McCarran with one of his favorite foreign leaders,
Generalissimo Francisco Franco of Spain, 1949.
(Nevada Historical Society, Reno)

from *The Herblock Book* (Beacon Press, 1952)

Senator McCarran's internal security investigations earned strong criticism in the press and had political consequences in Nevada. Herblock's caricatures of McCarran were models for his later studies of Joseph McCarthy and Richard Nixon.

CHAPTER 8

THE NEW BIPARTISAN COALITION

BY THE TIME Patrick McCarran finished his third term in the Senate, he had become one of the most powerful members of that body. This was particularly true in 1949-50, when the Democrats organized the Senate and McCarran thus chaired the Judiciary Committee. It was also the period when he became the butt of some of Herbert Block's (Herblock) most cruel cartoons in the *Washington Post*, depicting him as fat, slovenly, and unshaven, a precursor of Herblock's later, famous, unshaven McCarthy and Nixon. Senator McCarran was listed in 1950 by *Time Magazine* as one of the ten most "expendable" United States senators—"pompous, vindictive, and power grabbing."[1]

McCarran's interests, and the controversy surrounding him, had shifted to foreign-policy issues. Until after President Truman's reelection in 1948, he basically hewed to the prevailing bipartisan foreign policy, voting for the UN charter in 1943, supporting aid to Great Britain in 1946, and voting for aid to Greece and Turkey and the Marshall Plan in 1947. This support for the administration ceased in 1949, when McCarran vociferously argued for more aid to the Chinese Nationalist government and aid to Franco's Spain. He did his best to stop the influx of postwar refugees from Europe, and in 1950, his name was on the McCarran Internal Security Act, requiring the registration of all communist and communist-front organizations.

On domestic issues, his impact was less important. True to his labor orientation, he voted against the Taft-Hartley Act of 1947. After World War II he was a hard-driving proponent of the "All American Flag Line," a federally chartered airline which would have had sole responsibility for all American passenger aviation overseas. Although the idea did not pass, he was more successful as the author of the 1946 Airport Act, which promised federal aid for airport development.

In Nevada during these years, he became the undisputed political boss. One of the first activities of his new senatorial term in 1945, however, was the necessity of dealing with an attempt by the Roosevelt administration to remove him from the scene. In February, 1945, the district judge of Nevada, Frank Norcross, having served seventeen years on the federal bench, announced his long-anticipated retirement, effective June 30. The Justice Department informally asked Senator McCarran if he would care to take the position. In many ways this was an attractive offer; McCarran could finish out his days on the bench and avoid many of the more obnoxious details of politics. He told reporters he was seriously considering the offer. The motives of the Roosevelt administration are obvious, it wanted McCarran out of the Senate.[2]

It is doubtful that the senator was too seriously tempted. Although he was now 68, he had just been elected to a third term, and he retained in overflowing measure his zest for political power. In a letter to Norman Biltz, Senator McCarran indicated that he was worried about the danger "to future democratic existence" represented by the Henry Wallace wing of the Democratic party. He pointed out his anxiety over the welfare of his state and his belief that he would leave stranded those supporters who had worked so hard to elect him: "the political field in Nevada is not encouraging, when one considers what might happen under certain contingencies." Implicit throughout the Senator's letter was the idea that he was indispensable where he was. Thus, at the end of February, McCarran issued a public statement that he wished to remain in the Senate.[3]

McCarran and Senator James Scrugham—now gravely ill in a hospital—selected Roger Foley as Norcross's replacement. Foley was a comparative unknown and had not figured prominently in the speculation over the position, but McCarran had his reasons: "We —Jim Scrugham and I—were determined to appoint someone who could not create a vacancy in some office. We didn't care to have Judge Carville troubled by having to appoint anyone."[4] Judge Foley was nominated by the administration (McCarran being head of the Judiciary Committee) and was later to have a major, although not entirely beneficial, influence on McCarran's political happiness.

On June 23, 1945, Senator James Scrugham died. This provided a unique opportunity for McCarran's foes within the state. Governor Carville resigned his office, putting Lieutenant Governor Vail Pittman into the state's highest position. In turn, Pittman appointed Carville to fill Scrugham's term through 1946. Needless to say, McCarran was not consulted, and he found the whole arrangement completely distasteful.

But there would be ample opportunity to properly punish Carville. When Carville went to the Senate, McCarran saw to it that he was given the worst possible committee assignments. This, of course, was in marked contrast to the way McCarran was treated by Key Pittman and others when he initially went to the Senate. So Carville received an assignment on Post Office and Post Roads ("because it is dead as the dodo, and one man runs it"), on Mines and Mining, on Indian Affairs, and on Banking and Currency. Carville had desired an appointment on the important Finance Committee, but McCarran made sure his wishes were not gratified. The senior senator's motives were entirely selfish:

> So—I have succeeded in my project of getting Carville away from Finance Committee. The Committee on Finance is the Committee to which the nomination for Collector of Internal Revenue goes. I thought perhaps one of these mornings, I might wake up and find a resignation on my hands from Douglass. Then the battle royal might be on, and I didn't quite want to go up against a member of the Committee to which any nomination might be sent. So—now you have the history of what happened.[5]

This not entirely disagreeable task accomplished, McCarran set about arranging Carville's final political destruction. One of McCarran's characteristics as a senator is that he could not keep out of other people's political races. In 1946, his intervention was especially heavy-handed, and left considerable resentment within the Nevada Democratic party, although it enhanced McCarran's power, if not his popularity.

Someone had to be found to challenge Carville in the 1946 senatorial race. McCarran found a willing accomplice in representative Berkeley Bunker. It did not matter that the conservative Carville had a senatorial voting record rather similar to McCarran's and that Bunker was far more liberal. It did not even matter that McCarran had intensely disliked Bunker during his 1941-42 stint as U.S. Senator and had worked against him in 1942. McCarran saw the situation in simple terms: Carville had to be gotten rid of, and it would take someone of Bunker's popularity to defeat him. McCarran did not particularly like Bunker, but he was out to destroy Carville.

To accomplish this end, McCarran went out of his way to be helpful to Bunker, who was serving his first term in the House. In the end, McCarran, "very aggressive and very forceful," asked Bunker to run against Carville. In a meeting in Las Vegas, attended by various powerful associates, Bunker made the commitment. Nothing was asked from Bunker except a pledge that he would remain in the race until the end.[6]

McCarran never formally endorsed Bunker, but there was no doubt as to whom he supported. In January, 1946, in a public gathering, McCarran lifted his glass and proposed a toast "to the next Senator from Nevada, Berkeley Bunker." In August, just before the primary, McCarran told an audience about Bunker's "inestimable assistance" in the House: "He is a fine boy with a great future." During the campaign Bunker's ads played up the association, praising McCarran to the hilt, and asking the voters to elect a junior senator who "Will Work With Pat McCarran as a Teammate." More important, the McCarran organization (including Bob Douglass, who had previously been Bunker's strong enemy) was given orders to work hard for Bunker. Lieutenants who refused to go along with the request, such as Marshal Les Kofoed, were summarily fired. In the September primary, Bunker defeated Carville, 13,354 votes to 10,826.[7]

But McCarran's political vengeance was only half satisfied in 1946. McCarran could not find a strong and willing candidate to challenge Vail Pittman. He had started his search early, and had written several people in 1945 that it would be necessary to groom someone to run against Pittman for governor.[8] Overtures were made to Attorney General Alan Bible, a law partner in McCarran's office, but Bible hesitated. In the meantime, Pittman consolidated his position as governor. "I think Pittman would be a push-over for somebody," McCarran wrote Petersen, "but the bird has all of the gambling element now lined up in his corner." Some of McCarran's associates insisted that he could not oppose Carville and Pittman at the same time, so McCarran acquiesced to Pittman's nomination; revenge would simply have to wait.[9]

The final election in 1946 saw many surprises. Pittman easily won the Nevada governorship by a margin of 7,408 votes over perfunctory Republican opposition. But George W. Malone, the Republican candidate, in his third run for the office, defeated Bunker by 5,248 votes, effectively ending Bunker's political career. McCarran and his organization had worked actively for Bunker, but Bunker's challenge of Carville had caused so much bitterness within the party that Carville's supporters in turn worked for Malone.[10] Although 1946 was generally a Republican year throughout the nation, Democrats did succeed in sweeping most of the local races in Nevada.

Another surprise, even to the candidate, was the election to the House of Republican Charles Russell, an Ely publisher, by a strong margin over Malcolm McEachin. McCarran undoubtedly all along preferred Russell, whom he characterized as a "fine" man. His friendliness with Russell dated from 1944, when McCarran could not get his advertisements and literature into the *Ely Times,* owned by Vail Pittman, and went instead to the weekly *Ely Record,* owned by Russell. McCarran did not publicly intervene in this race, but a number of his friends quietly worked in Russell's behalf. McEachin had been a friend of Key and Vail Pittman, which made McCarran singularly unenthusiastic about his candidacy.[11]

Despite Bunker's defeat, McCarran's position in the party was bolstered by the 1946 election. Carville's defeat had destroyed him as a serious political rival. Bunker's loss also proved an advantage, since it removed Bunker as a major force in Nevada politics and meant that Nevada would have only one Democratic senator. Thus all federal patronage from a Democratic administration would go exclusively through McCarran's hands. McCarran was now more powerful than ever within his state.

The problem, however, was that the anti-McCarran forces were able to solidify behind Governor Vail Pittman. They had someone to rally around. McCarran had obvious primacy within the party, but complete domination still eluded him, as it would until the day of his death. To obviate this, McCarran's friendliness with Russell's candidacy demonstrated his increasing willingness to make contacts and alliances with Nevada Republicans. A new bipartisan coalition, somewhat like the old Wingfield bipartisan coalition which McCarran had so resented, seemed to be developing.

Malone and McCarran were to be Senate colleagues until McCarran's death in 1954. McCarran did not particularly respect Malone, but neither, for that matter, did the Washington press corps or many of his fellow senators. A common story in Washington and in Nevada went that the easiest way to clear the Senate chamber was for "Molly" Malone to open his mouth. He had a habit, one observer noted, of saying "to close my remarks" and then going on for another thirty or forty minutes.[12] Pete Petersen believed that McCarran did not dislike Malone, it was just that "he didn't think that Malone had very much on the ball."[13] McCarran's later support for "junior," as he occasionally referred to Malone in his correspondence, was simple political expediency, not high regard.

McCarran's relationship with Governor Vail Pittman—crucial to his leadership of the Democratic party—predictably worsened after 1946. Pittman's independent political base made it unnecessary for him to serve McCarran's interests. Much of the problem, as with Carville and many others, was over appointments; even though Senator McCarran consistently refused to visit the governor when he was in Carson City, he curiously desired some control over the governor's appointments.[14] According to McCarran, Governor Pittman was "the most perfect word breaker that I have ever known." Petersen did nothing to discourage these feelings; according to the Reno postmaster, the governor was "thoroughly unreliable and untrustworthy," a "palooka." Petersen's advice to McCarran was "the best kind of politics we can play from now on out is to belittle Pittman whenever we can."[15]

In 1948, McCarran kept out of most of the races. Although he was privately unenthusiastic, he supported Truman in the Democratic convention and national election. Even though there was no gubernatorial or senatorial race in Nevada that year, the senator did not feel his political organization should let down its guard; otherwise the Pittman forces could take over. "We just must get the Washoe delegation, so that we can handle it," he warned Petersen. "If it requires a little money to do it, I think we can raise it. We should control every single precinct in Washoe County."[16] The only upset in the election of 1948 was the narrow defeat of Representative Charles Russell by Democrat Walter Baring. The chief reason for this appears to have been Russell's vote in favor of the Taft-Hartley Labor Act (McCarran voted against it), which infuriated Nevada labor leaders. Russell's removal from the House, however, opened up some intriguing possibilities for future attempts at other offices. Although defeated, he appeared to be the best available Republican vote getter.

In 1950, McCarran's chief problem was to get himself reelected for a fourth term. Contrary to his previous practice, he announced his candidacy two years early.[17] The reason was to dispel doubts that he might retire because of age (he would be 74 in 1950) or poor health (he suffered a near-fatal heart attack in 1947). Not surprisingly, he made sure that his personal organization would be as strong and smooth running as possible. Control of the party was absolutely essential in his thinking, and he was not overly particular about the means used for that control:

> I think something should be done toward controlling the precincts, especially the two precincts, one occupied by Carville and the other by Hilliard. I don't want them to get a single delegate out of either of those places. I don't want those two birds to have a chance to show their noses in the State Convention, or any of their friends. This can be done if we just get the matter arranged as to a favorable place to hold the mass meetings and then have our friends so organized that they will fill the places plumb full so that nobody else can get in and then have the motions all ready to put over and adjourn P.D.Q. with all the delegates nominated and elected. It may be necessary to rent five, ten or twenty busses so as to have them loaded up and take them to the respective mass meetings where they can take over. We want to do this thing and do it right.[18]

Petersen convinced McCarran that some of these excessive measures might be self-defeating. The means actually used were strong enough. Despite strong opposition, the McCarran forces did succeed in gaining control of the Washoe County, Clark County, and state conventions. The Washoe County Convention in particular was bitter and packed. "Of course we had dozens of good loyal people," Peterson wrote McCarran, "and I am proud to say that 14 of our delegates and proxies were carried by the wives of post office employees." A few roughhouse tactics were deemed necessary to gain the day: "It was of course unfortunate for Mr. Pittman that his temporary chairman, Mr. Benson Tapscott, never got close to the platform."[19] The Republican, and usually accurate, *Reno Evening Gazette,* described the Washoe Democratic convention this way:

> Virgil Wedge, Reno city attorney, was named temporary chairman on a voice vote taken in a terrific uproar. He was nominated by Ben Maffi, whose motion was seconded by Dinny Hill.
> Before the Pittman forces could gather themselves, Cleary had leaped to his feet to move that nominations be closed. Despite vociferous objections from the opposition, Chairman Leggett[20] ruled that Cleary's motion had been carried by voice vote and Wedge took over the chair.

After an uproarious five minutes during which Pittman delegates stamped, shouted, and beat their chairs on the floor, Wedge declared a recess.[21]

The Clark County and state conventions were calmer, with the McCarran group in full control. Regrettably, all this was unnecessary, but McCarran believed that if he let his guard down even a little, a chain of circumstances might occur that would lead to his eventual defeat. He ascribed his own motives to others. Conciliation was not in his makeup.

Another tactic used by McCarran and his supporters in the 1950 election was to frame the opposition by accusing it of being the tool of outside groups. This device, as noted, had been used effectively in 1944. Because of McCarran's strenuous opposition to any liberalized displaced persons legislation, the strategy was to make it appear that the opposition was heavily financed by "New York" (the words "Jewish" and "Zionist" were occasionally used and usually meant) money. Peterson, for one, thought this was clever strategy:

> My idea of the thing was to emphasize the fact that the Jews were after you. I don't think that particular race is too well thought of in this state. . . . It may not be a bad idea to create the impression that there are certain Jews after you for their own selfish purposes.[22]

In 1944, the CIO was blamed for seeking to dominate Nevada, now it was to be the Jews. McCarran did not disagree with these tactics, but he thought they could be refined a bit. After expressing his doubt that there was actually much "Jew money" coming into Nevada, he suggested his own idea: "What we want them to do is to send the money on and get it into the hands of our own friends, and we'll use their money for my election. I think we should get the work started on this plan."[23]

Sympathetic columnists spread the canard that outside money was pouring into Nevada. Hearst columnist George Sokolsky wrote that the "Committee on National Affairs" in New York was attempting to raise money to elect liberal senators, and to defeat men such as McCarran. In a statement inserted in the *Congressional Record,* Senator James Eastland charged that "outside" groups were attempting to defeat the senior senator from Nevada. In Eastland's words, "The Communists and Communist-front groups . . . are determined to get McCarran." The *Nevada State Journal,* under the always friendly editorial guidance of Joe McDonald, also tried to pin the New York-financed label on McCarran's enemies: "All of which discloses that Nevada can expect a New York invasion, backed by money, to determine the kind of Senator we want."[24]

It is true that there was some outside money and intervention in Nevada politics, which is entirely normal and legal, but it appears to have been of meager proportions. The Americans for Democratic Action (ADA) attempted to enlist labor support for a challenge to McCarran; the ADA found out that the AFL and the Machinists Union had already endorsed the senator. Even the CIO was not prepared to fight. As an ADA representative was told, "Senator McCarran voted right on the Taft-Hartley Act; and unfortunately, that seemed to be the only criterion with the labor unions."[25] The threatened flood of money was really a trickle. The Committee on National Affairs officially gave a total of $5,500 to the anti-McCarran forces. Apparently that was all, as they were by all evidence badly financed.[26]

McCarran's only announced opponent in the Democratic primary was a relatively unknown politician, the 34-year-old chairman of the Clark County Commission, George E. Franklin, Jr. Franklin declared that he had announced only because of the roughhouse tactics used by the McCarran forces at the various state and county conventions.[27] But Franklin rarely left Clark County, and he posed no real threat to McCarran, who did not even bother to return to Nevada to campaign. National issues were not prominently mentioned, even though this was a period when Senator McCarran was intensely controversial nationally. Probably the most potent argument used against the senator was his age. Petersen recognized this and suggested, in a letter to Eva Adams, that nothing should be done (such as having a birthday celebration) "to call to the people's attention that the Senator will be 74 years of age."[28] Despite all the rumors of Zionist money flooding the state, Franklin's campaign soon ran out of gas . . . and money. McCarran walloped Franklin in the September primary by 23,102 to 8,461.

McCarran was probably unbeatable in 1950; certainly no one of any political stature was willing to take him on. During the summer of 1950, a private in-depth interview of 326 Nevada voters in Clark and Washoe Counties was conducted by Research Services, Inc., of Denver, in behalf of prospective Republican candidate William Wright. The survey found that McCarran was highly popular in Nevada. An astonishing 71 percent of the respondents were fairly or highly favorable to the senator, and only 15 percent had fairly or highly unfavorable opinions of him. Fourteen percent were "totally uninformed." The chief arguments for McCarran were general, non-specific ones such as "He's a good man, wonderful, etc.," mentioned by 58 percent of the people. A sizable 35 percent mentioned, "He has helped Nevada." On the debit side, 13 percent of the total group pointed out that McCarran was "to much of a politican . . . plays politics too much," and 10 percent mentioned he was "too old, senile." Surprisingly, national issues were hardly mentioned, either for or against the senator, which confirms that senatorial races in Nevada tended to be waged on purely local issues. The conclusions of the study were that McCarran was probably unbeatable, but that a smart opponent would capitalize on his overattention to politics and his age. Wright decided not to run.[29]

In the final election, McCarran easily defeated his Republican opponent, George E. Marshall of Las Vegas, who was a comparative unknown. McCarran received 35,829 votes (58.0 percent) and Marshall 25,933 (42.0 percent), for a majority of 9,896. The senator barely carried Washoe County (51.7 percent), took Clark County by a strong margin (57.6 percent), and completely swamped Marshall in the rest of the state (62.9 percent).

Since McCarran's energies were hardly occupied by his own race, he had ample opportunity to fiddle in other contests, and perhaps pay his respects to Pittman. Although he toyed with the idea of urging Alan Bible to challenge the governor, nothing much came from it.[30] Perhaps the invariably cautious Bible believed he stood too great a possibility of being defeated by the incumbent Pittman. Perhaps McCarran realized that a greater menace for Pittman might be the candidacy of a strong Republican, someone like Charles Russell.

When Charles Russell served in the House of Representatives from 1947 to 1949, he and McCarran had gotten along well together. Clark Guild, Russell's brother-in-law, had worked for McCarran and then went to Russell's office, so there was a liaison between the two offices.[31]

After his defeat in the 1948 election, Charles Russell returned to Washington to close his office, while the lame-duck Republican Eightieth Congress was still in existence. Ed Converse, president of Bonanza Airlines, suggested to Senator Styles Bridges, then chairman of the Joint Committee on Foreign Cooperation, that Russell might like to be a member of its investigating unit. Russell had family obligations and no available job in sight. Bridges replied that he would appoint Russell if the latter could get McCarran's approval, since McCarran would be the chairman in a few weeks when the Eighty-First Congress met. McCarran said he would be happy to have Russell. Bridges made the actual appointment, but with McCarran's complete agreement.[32]

In attempting to find a candidate sufficiently popular to defeat Pittman, some of McCarran's close associates thought of the still politically ambitious Russell. Russell was initially approached by Norman Biltz and Ed Converse (both Republicans and both close to McCarran) to run for governor. McCarran undoubtedly was aware of the overtures, and at the least did not disapprove of them. For his part, the senator suggested to Russell in the spring of 1950, that perhaps he would like to return to Nevada and make a swing around the state, ostensibly to see the strength of the opposition to McCarran's candidacy. Russell correctly interpreted this as an implied go-ahead to sound out sentiment about his own possible candidacy.[33]

Russell visited Nevada in April, 1950 to test public sentiment. While there, he received a financial pledge from Biltz. Everything looked propitious. Returning to Washington, Russell gave McCarran a full report. As he wrote Biltz:

> On returning I talked with the Senator and he stated he would not be opposed to my running either for governor or for congress. I frankly told him that I would not consider running at all if he felt it would react against his own candidacy.[34]

Not only was McCarran "not opposed," he lent Russell much of his campaign organization. Appearances, however, had to be kept up. McCarran never officially endorsed Russell. In fact, he even sent a "confidential" letter to Norm Biltz and Pete Petersen, disclaiming any interest in Russell's candidacy, and solemnly stating that he had urged Russell not to make the race: "I tried to keep him from running."[35] This letter was a complete subterfuge, and was intended to be shown to the labor people, who disliked Russell because of his vote on the Taft-Hartley Act. It was meant to cover the senator's tracks, and was written at Petersen's suggestion:

> In our conversation we agreed that you would send me a letter to the effect that Charlie Russell's filing was none of your affair; and that you had nothing to do with it. I would like to get that letter as early as possible so as to be able to straighten out the Laboring boys as soon as possible. . . . P.S. don't post date the letter.[36]

Duplicity was thus the order of the day. McCarran publicly denied any backing of Russell. Eva Adams later declared, "Russell never realized how much the senator did for him in 1950. The whole thing could have blown up in the senator's face, since he was going out on a limb for Russell."[37] Biltz and Wallie Warren, a Reno publicist, helped organize things. In Biltz's words:

> We came back and we hired Wallie Warren to handle the campaign, and started to put it together. I'm guilty I guess, of using some of the McCarran organization, which he never accused me of, but I think he knew it. I don't think he was too unhappy about it.... He never authorized me to use it, but see, we had an organization, the McCarran organization, and we had in those days about 1,800 people. Dead loyal people. You could just depend on them one hundred percent. It covered the state.[38]

As the returns came in, the only worry that McCarran and Biltz had was that it appeared for a few hours that Russell might get even more votes than McCarran. "This upset Mrs. McCarran very much," recalled Biltz, "not so much the Senator. She was furious." In the end McCarran received 200 more votes than Russell. Pittman had received his just desserts. "This was the bipartisan machine. And it was very interesting," Biltz said many years later. The day after the election, McCarran went to Russell and told him, according to Biltz's account, "Now, Charlie, you're governor and you're a Republican. I'm a Democrat, but any way in the world I can help you, you just send the word, and I'll do anything whatever in the world I can to advise you or help you." Then McCarran added, in words the full significance of which Russell would soon realize, "And there might be times when I'm going to ask favors."[39]

By the election of 1950, McCarran reached the apogee of his power in Nevada at the same time that he was at the height of his career in Washington, D.C. He had gained reelection to the U.S. Senate for the fourth time. All federal patronage in Nevada was now concentrated in his hands. He had close and sympathetic ties with the state's financial leaders. He now had a seemingly cooperative ally in the governor's office. With the help of Norm Biltz and others, he had created a powerful bipartisan machine. And he had crushed and demoralized his foes within the party.

The machine and its electoral victories were supported in great part by federal officeholders in the state. In one letter, Pete Petersen, after naming the long list of federal employees working for McCarran's reelection, stated his pride in how well they had labored for the senator's interests: "My honest belief is that the Federal employees have shown more enthusiasm, and have done more work than I have ever seen before, and will continue up to the last minute, and will definitely not take anything for granted."[40]

The principal architect of this organization, with federal office-holders working in McCarran's behalf, was, of course, the senator himself. Once McCarran wrote Petersen exactly what to tell a newly-appointed Chief Field Deputy for the Internal Revenue Service:

> Now, Pete, what I want you to do is to have an interview with this gentleman and tell him, for the love of Mike, to get around over the State. That's his duty and that's where he can do the greatest good . . . and then bear down on the fact that neither the Hatch Act nor the Civil Service Act nor any other Act prevents a Federal employee from criticizing, abusing, maltreating, mis-using, or otherwise maligning a public official such as a U.S. Senator, and as he moves around over the State he can with propriety, tell the people how really good I am—if he thinks I am good. Then when he catches some poor devil a little off his foot as regards taxes, go easy with him and make it known that he is going easy because he is a good friend of Pat McCarran. We must be "at our father's business."[41]

The quote is revealing in that it indicates the senator would not take offense if the Internal Revenue Service were to give tax breaks to his friends. In such a moral climate, it would be quite easy to do the reverse to McCarran's enemies, although there is no documentation of such advice.

Clearly, McCarran willingly suffered incompetence among federal employees so long as he had their loyalty. The criterion for satisfactory performance remained political faithfulness. Thus many federal employees and people dependent on federal contracts in the Nevada of 1950 were second-rate. Statewide rumor had it that many of McCarran's friends with lucrative federal contracts or appointments were making illicit money from their positions. For example, Robert Douglass, Internal Revenue Collector for Nevada and by now McCarran's close political ally, was forced out of his position in 1950 for conniving in the sale of worthless mining stock in return for protecting buyers from income-tax prosecution.[42] There is no evidence that McCarran himself shared in this type of activity; on the contrary the accumulation of wealth did not seem to interest him particularly. He was careless, as he always had been, about his finances, and he died a man of comparatively modest means.

Federal jobs and contracts were used to reward friends and punish enemies. It was widely reported in 1952 that when contracts were handed out on the housing project for Nellis Air Force Base near Las Vegas, it was McCarran who was in charge of their distribution. He was quoted in the press as declaring, "Joe Cleary will get the insurance on the housing or there will be no housing project."[43]

No such friendliness extended to enemies. In 1952, Vail Pittman told Drew Pearson that McCarran had "even refused to let some of Pittman's old friends get jobs. Companies that wanted to hire them were afraid of having their taxes investigated too thoroughly by Internal Revenue."[44] This allegation is difficult to document, although it was widely believed. It can be documented that close associates of Pittman were deprived of positions with the federal government. When the Nevada district Office of Price Stabilization was set up during the Korean War, Forrest Bibb, an associate of Pittman's, was initially selected to head the office, after being assured that it was a nonpolitical position. McCarran objected to the appointment, and Bibb was told he would have to resign. People who did manage to get jobs with the Office of Price Stabilization included Verner Adams (father of Eva) and Wallie Warren, who had done yeoman service in the election of 1950.[45] Enemies were eliminated. Morry Zenoff, the anti-McCarran publisher of the *Boulder City News,* had a written contract with the Nellis Air Force Base to publish a weekly base paper. The profits from that would offset his losses from the Boulder City paper. In Zenoff's words, McCarran, "peeved to a boiling point because I had dared criticize some of his Washington maneuvers concerning Nevada," sent a letter to Air Force Secretary Stuart Symington "demanding that Symington suspend the air force publication at once." Symington apologetically complied, and the contract was eventually awarded to someone more friendly to McCarran.[46]

Quite consistently, McCarran opposed any proposed legislation, by the Truman administration or others, that would reduce the number of appointive positions in the executive branch or extend civil service. This, to his way of thinking, would only reduce his power. In fact he wished the boundaries of civil service considerably reduced. He concisely stated his position to his good political friend, the U.S. Marshal for Nevada:

I am enclosing a bill which I introduced some days ago, and which I hope to get through—it is for the purpose of taking the deputy marshals out of the category of Civil Service status. To my mind, it is a damned outrage to have a marshal who has to carry a heavy responsibility burdened with men who are foisted upon him because they can pass a Civil Service examination. The United States Marshal, above all people in the world, should be permitted to select his own deputies, on whom he can rely, and in whom he can have confidence. It was a little skullduggery that brought deputy marshals under Civil Service and I hope to clear away the cobwebs in this respect.[47]

McCarran was one of only 17 senators to vote against a Truman plan to revamp the Bureau of Internal Revenue, by removing virtually all top officials of the bureau from the realm of political appointment and bringing them under civil service.[48] Newspaper reports of unprecedented corruption in the IRS (including the Douglass case) had forced a reluctant Truman administration to advance this plan. McCarran was more successful in defeating a bill that would have vested the sole appointive power over U.S. marshals in the attorney general, and taken away the confirmation right from the U.S. Senate. After a passionate appeal from McCarran on the Senate floor, the proposal was voted down.[49]

By 1950, McCarran's political prospects had never looked better on the surface. Yet, though the senator was reelected for a fourth term, portents for decline of his organization existed. Nevada was undergoing explosive growth, particularly in its southern portion; and it was difficult for one man, or even one organization, to keep tabs on all the newcomers, who were unused to the old ways of political operation. The leader of this most personal of machines was 74, and not in the best of health. Also important, the senator lacked a temperament that might have conciliated opposition and absorbed it; rather, his instincts were to crush his enemies, which he could not quite do. All of these factors, as well as some unsuspected problems, could result in the decline of the seemingly invincible McCarran machine. That decline was not far in the future.

CHAPTER 9

A WANING OF POWER

AFTER 1950, Patrick McCarran continued to be an immensely powerful senator. His national influence was such that the *Washington Post,* which hardly approved, declared in July, 1952, "It sums up the character of this congress to state an unquestionable fact: that its most important member was Patrick A. McCarran."[1]

His most famous legislation in this period was the McCarran-Walter Immigration Act of 1952, vetoed by President Truman, but passed over his veto. This act continued, with modifications, the previous quota system, with its bias in favor of immigration from northern and western Europe. For the first time, however, it did allow American citizenship for Japanese and other Asian immigrants, who had previously been forbidden such citizenship.

It was, perhaps, McCarran's role as an ally of Senator Joseph McCarthy that gained him his greatest notoriety. Much more legal-minded and precise than McCarthy, and also more strategically situated in the Senate because of his position on the Judiciary Committee, McCarran was better able to imprint, or force, his ideas on the federal bureaucracy. He was more effective than the Wisconsin senator, just not as famous. The attacks on the Institute of Pacific Relations which resulted in its eventual demise, the hounding and "disgrace" of those old China hands who had predicted the victory of the Communists over the Nationalists—men such as John Carter Vincent, John Paton Davies, Jr., and John Stewart Service—and the government prosecution of Owen Lattimore, owed their impetus to him. Had he lived long enough, McCarran would have voted against the censure of Senator McCarthy, and he might have carried several other Democratic senators with him. As it was, his death and the censure of McCarthy, coming within three months of each other,

147

marked a watershed. After that the Judiciary Committee would focus more on civil-rights problems, and much less on internal communism.

After 1953, McCarran's national importance diminished as the Republicans organized the Senate. In Nevada, his reputation went through a like period of power, controversy, and diminution. At the end of 1950, McCarran was at the apex of his power within Nevada. But the state was rapidly changing, probably more than he realized. From 1940 to 1950, Nevada's population increased from 110,247 people to 160,083, a 45.2 percent gain, fourth among the states. This rate of increase was accelerating and meant that it would be increasingly difficult to keep close tabs on individual voters. Thousands of potential voters were streaming in, people to whom the name McCarran meant little or nothing.

The increase, however, was confined to two counties. From 1940 to 1950, Washoe County's population rose from 32,476 people to 50,202; Reno, its largest city, increased from 21,317 to 32,497, and Sparks, Reno's sister community, grew from 5,318 to 8,203. But it was the southern portion of the state that gained by far the largest number of newcomers. Clark County soared from 16,414 people in 1940 to 48,289 in 1950, and its largest city, Las Vegas, grew from 8,422 to 24,624. Las Vegas posed special problems for the senator. The McCarran organization was weakest there, and the county had no equivalent of a Pete Petersen to tie things together. Outside the two largest counties, the population of the state was virtually stationary. The fifteen "cow counties," although they controlled the state legislature in those days before the Warren Court's decree of "one-man-one-vote," increased by only about 200 people during the decade.[2]

In addition, the basis of the state's economy was shifting. Mining and agriculture, Nevada's traditional major industries to which McCarran had been devoted, were in relative decline. This was particularly true of mining, where the number of employees fell from 6,262 in 1940 to only 3,315 in 1950.[3] In their place, by the late 1940s, gambling and related tourism were rapidly becoming the state's chief industries. This change apparently caught McCarran by surprise, even though he had intimate ties with the state's industrial and financial leaders.

Nevada gambling encountered dangerous shoals in the early 1950s. Because of his powerful position in state and national government, McCarran became intimately involved with the industry's problems; but his association with the gambling interests was eventually to tarnish his own reputation.

As noted, legal gambling is peculiarly vulnerable to federal intervention. On January 5, 1950, Senator Estes Kefauver of Tennessee called upon the Judiciary Committee to investigate the connection of "interstate gambling and racketeering activities" to organized crime. Initially the measure was referred to the Judiciary Committee, where McCarran succeeded in expanding the investigation's scope so it would not focus so narrowly on gambling. In time the resolution was amended to take the investigation out of the Judiciary Committee and create instead a special Senate committee, partly because of fears that McCarran might dominate a purely Judiciary Committee inquiry. The amended resolution passed the Senate on May 3, 1950, on a tie vote broken by the Vice-President. McCarran, having been outmaneuvered, was noticeable by his absence. Had he been present to vote against the special committee, it would have been defeated.[4]

This Special Committee to Investigate Organized Crime in Interstate Commerce (more usually referred to as the Kefauver Committee) was to make a huge splash in newspaper headlines as it conducted its sensational, televised hearings. Nevada and its peculiar institution became one of its prime targets. On November 15, 1950, the committee met in Las Vegas, and for the next five months it investigated organized crime in California and Nevada.

The Kefauver Committee's findings strongly condemned Nevada gambling, and provided generally unfavorable publicity for the state. Summarizing the committee's case, the final report declared, "As a case history of legalized gambling, Nevada speaks eloquently in the negative." Considerable, apparently damning evidence was provided to back up the statement.[5]

For one thing, the committee documented a chummy alliance between certain state officials and the gambling interests. Lieutenant Governor Cliff Jones, for example, was a partner in the Thunderbird Hotel and held stock in the Pioneer Club in Las Vegas. William J. Moore, a member of the Nevada Tax Commission which oversaw gambling, was himself part owner of a Las Vegas casino. This, in the eyes of the committee, was an obvious conflict of interest.[6]

According to the Kefauver Committee, Nevada also had done virtually nothing to keep undesirables out of its gambling. It charged that "the two major crime syndicates," one operating out of Chicago and the other New York, were present in Las Vegas. It named a number of Las Vegas and Reno gamblers who had previous arrest

and conviction records in other states, including, among many,
"Bugsy" Siegel (who was murdered in 1947, and who, according to
the Kefauver Committee, had been the gambling boss of Las Vegas),
Benny Binion, "one-time king of the rackets in Dallas," Moe Dalitz,
"an old-time bootlegger and gambler," and William Graham and
James McKay, ex-felons who owned the Bank Club in Reno.[7]

Nevada Tax Commission member William J. Moore was honest
enough about the state's policy of allowing ex-felons to conduct
gambling establishments. Committee Counsel Rudolph Halley asked
the key Questions:

Mr. HALLEY. You have a number of licensees here who have criminal
   records, do you not?
Mr. MOORE. That is right.
Senator TOBEY. . . . Shouldn't it be a condition precedent to giving him a
   license that the man is clean and has no criminal record?
Mr. MOORE. Frankly, no. That is my opinion. . . .
Mr. HALLEY. It makes no difference to you whether he gambles in a State
   where it is not legal?
Mr. MOORE. No. How is he going to learn the business.
Mr. HALLEY. In other words, you take the position that, because gam-
   bling is legal in the State of Nevada, that anybody who has been convicted
   for gambling in other States is not to be considered in any way disquali-
   fied; is that right?
Mr. MOORE. That is right.[8]

But according to the Kefauver Committee, Nevada also harbored
fugitives presently wanted in other states. Lieutenant George Butler
of the Dallas Police Department, read a statement by the city's
district attorney, alleging that Benny Binion, prominent in Las
Vegas, was the principal figure in an illegal Dallas policy game.
Binion's Dallas business supposedly grossed in excess of a million
dollars a year. Butler said:

   We have tried to extradite Binion from Nevada, but his extradition
   was denied by the Nevada Courts. We have reason to believe that he
   is continuing his interest in organized gambling in Texas under the
   protection accorded him by the Nevada courts against extradition. It
   is my belief he was guilty of income tax evasion for which he is cur-
   rently under investigation by various departments, including the Department of Justice and the Internal Revenue Department.[9]

Furthermore, although not directly related to gambling, the Kefauver Committee publicized an extortion racket already exposed by Ed Montgomery of the *San Francisco Examiner,* in which Nevada's Field Director of the Bureau of Internal Revenue, Pat Mooney (a McCarran appointee), sold worthless mining stock in a company of which he was an officer in return for providing tax favors. Those who refused to cooperate were hounded by Internal Revenue. The Internal Revenue Director for Nevada, Bob Douglass, a close McCarran ally, had already resigned in disgrace over the episode and subsequently committed suicide.[10] None of this, however, touched the senator himself.

McCarran did what he could to impede the investigation. When Kefauver requested that the president of the Senate issue warrants of arrest and have the sergeant-at-arms deputize federal officials to apprehend eleven missing witnesses, the Judiciary Committee issued a negative report under McCarran's guidance. But Kefauver, popular among the public if not the Senate leadership, carried his case to the Senate floor. There the request was upheld, 59 to 12, McCarran voting in the negative.[11]

McCarran was not alone among Nevadans in believing the Kefauver investigation was deliberately sensationalized and biased. Experienced hands wondered how there could be a successful gambling industry in any state unless it were run by professional gamblers. Simply put, the operator of a casino needs to know how to gamble. Otherwise the gambling business becomes too highly vulnerable to outside cheaters. The great majority of professional gamblers with the requisite skills had, by necessity, picked up their experience in violation of state and local laws elsewhere. Many Nevadans were therefore not particularly troubled that a good number of Las Vegas and Reno gamblers had run afoul of the police elsewhere, so long as they conducted their businesses honestly in Nevada. The typical attitude was well expressed by Robbins Cahill, longtime member of the State Gaming Commision: "Who owns a gaming place in Nevada is not nearly as important as to how it's run."[12]

Obviously, however, controls were needed, and the Kefauver investigations had exposed the inadequacy of Nevada licensing and policing procedures prior to 1951. If tighter controls were not imposed, the federal government was likely to move in and destroy the institution.

Leadership for these reforms would have to come from Governor Russell and the legislature. Even though McCarran was easily the state's most important political figure, and by 1950 could count on the loyalty of numerous state and federal officeholders, he did not lift a finger to clean up Nevada gambling. His response to the problem was to express his unswerving enmity toward Senator Kefauver.

The idea of a destructive federal tax on all gambling transactions had many important adherents in Congress. In 1951, a bill was introduced in the House of Representatives to institute a 10 percent tax on the gross receipts of all gambling transactions, which would have effectively ended legalized Nevada gambling. McCarran was in the forefront of the fight to save his state's chief industry. He urgently called Norm Biltz, Johnny Mueller, Marion Hicks and others to Washington, D.C., to organize the needed lobbying efforts. The gambling group which provided the greatest aid was the horse-racing lobby.[13]

Taking the lead among his colleagues in the Nevada delegation, McCarran made a strongly documented and effective plea to the Senate Finance Committee, where he stated the "cumulative result would spell tragedy for the State of Nevada."[14] In a long letter to Joseph McDonald, one of the most revealing he ever wrote, McCarran spelled out the need to defeat the bill. Gambling, in his view, had to be protected because it was now quite vital to the state's economy:

> The Committee on Ways and Means of the House of Representatives announced to the open session of the House of Representatives that they would bring in a bill with a 10 percent tax on the gross receipts of gambling. That was inserted in the Congressional Record and it was no idle threat. Ten percent of the gross receipts of gambling in the State of Nevada would close every gambling house, regardless of where it is located or how it is conducted. Virginia Street[15] would be in mourning and the gleaming gulch of Las Vegas would be a glowing symbol of funereal distress. . . . In the last few years the State of Nevada has woven gambling in its various forms into the warp and woof of the State's economic structure.
>
> Housing projects all over the State have been financed by the banks of the State. Millions of dollars have been hazarded by the banks in promoting these housing units. If these housing units are left empty or half occupied, the banks of Nevada would be squealing and I mean squealing. I remember when one set of 14 great strong banks had lent too much money on livestock and when the crash came and livestock went down, the banks closed their doors, never to open again.[16] I don't want that to be recurring, but it can be recurring under the existing economic structure of the State of Nevada. Gambling is now taxed in

Nevada aside from its being regulated and licensed. The State of Nevada has taken gambling into its financial structure. Never did I realize this so much as after I went into a study of the subject when the Committee on Ways and Means of the House made the announcement of a 10 percent tax on the gross business of gambling. I went into the subject earnestly than and I found one of the most difficult conditions of my whole public career.

McCarran wanted to spell out emphatically the seriousness of the threat; this was not to be considered just another amendment to a tax bill, which could be easily quashed. McCarran knew that his reputation in Nevada would be on the line. Although he realized his position might be used against him nationally, in the final analysis he had no choice; only he among the Nevada delegation had the necessary clout to defeat the amendment. His discussion on tactics was illuminating:

It isn't a very laudable position for one to have to defend gambling. One doesn't feel very lofty when his feet are resting on the argument that gambling must prevail in the State that he represents. The rest of the world looks upon him with disdain even though every other State in the Union is harboring gambling in one form or another, illegally, of course, and even though the State that he defends and represents, has legalized gambling, it doesn't take from the actuality in defending the thing in an open forum, where men of all walks of life and all particular phase and religious bents are listening and laughing, condemning or ridiculing. We have everything in the Congress of the United States from Orthodox Puritanical preachers to pill rollers. So, when the economic structure of one's state is so involved in the gambling business, or to put it another way, when the gambling business is involved in the economic structure of one's State, one must lay aside pride and put on the hide of a rhinoceros and go to it.

When one has to defend something that humanity generally looks down upon, he naturally must call upon every source of assistance that may be available. And in this gambling battle there are other gambling agencies that want help and one defending his State in its gambling policy must rub shoulders with those who need help. And so, your Senior Senator, standing alone in this battle, and while this battle was in the House of Representatives, at that, a body in which your Senior Senator is not a member, he was compelled to call upon every source of assistance, good, bad, and indifferent, and among those with the greatest influence in the House, with the strongest lobby in the Capitol of the Nation, and with a willingness to help us in the hour of our

greatest fight, was an outfit that had to do with the making of taxing
books and the publication of racing forms, etc. They came to our help
and they did valiant work, and the battle was won in the House because
I could call upon these people, and others like them, and because I had
individual friends in the Senate who in turn called their respective
Congressmen to help me defeat the movement in the Ways and Means
Committee, which movement would have meant the destruction of the
financial setup of my State.

   . . . The Special Committee Investigating Crime, headed by Senator
Kefauver of Tennessee, has introduced a number of bills, all aimed at
gambling in its various forms, and all aimed at Nevada because there
is the haven of legalized gambling. Senator Kefauver, the former Chairman of that Committee, has announced publicly that the tax bill as it
came from the House must be amended so as to tax all forms of
gambling—so the fight will be on again in the Senate. And Joe, I don't
care how much you love my colleague,[17] I don't care how much fraternal brotherhood there may be between you, I don't hesitate to say to
you that from a standpoint of rendering help, the answer is spelled out
in three letters—nil.

   Curiously, in this letter McCarran not only seemed somewhat
surprised at the ascendency gambling had gained in Nevada, but also
perturbed. He had battled long for the agricultural and mining interests of his state. His deep commitment to economic progress in the
west inclined him toward manufacturing—to belching smoke stacks
rather than tourism. And here was something else, unforeseen, that
one had to live with and protect. There is evidence, in fact, that
McCarran disliked gambling and gamblers, but believed that as a
representative of his state, he had to support the institution because
it had become so economically essential:[18]

   The State has builded its economy on gambling. Indeed so much so,
that I'm afraid we have blinked our eyes at that which to my mind is
the stronger form of economy, namely, payrolls on legitimate business
and payrolls coming from industry at its lowest ebb. Our agricultural
industry has been hard hit by the fact that the livestock population of
the State has dwindled. Our tax agencies have looked to the more lush
source from whence to derive additional taxes to maintain the State's
machinery. One scarcely thinks of these things, Joe, until he is brought
face to face with them as I was for two weeks while I conducted the
fight in the House of Representatives. . . .
   . . . What are you going to do with your tax structure when you have
woven gambling into it so that every thread in its warp and woof is

blended with a gambling phase of some kind. . . . I hope the time will come when the financial structure of the State of Nevada will not rest upon gambling. I hope the time will come when we point with pride to industries of all kinds in the State of Nevada, with payrolls that will sustain the economy of Nevada. But that isn't today, Joe, and it won't be tomorrow.

And it's going to take more than the building of housing projects for rental, financed by the banks of the state, to accomplish that result. The City of Reno has grown immensely in the past 20 years. The City of Las Vegas has come from a wide spot in the road to a community of 40,000 or more. That growth in neither instance was accomplished by industries with payrolls. It was acomplished by making the State of Nevada a playground to which the world was invited, and that playground has as its base gambling in all forms, and those who have been responsible for this growth upon this foundation cannot with propriety and good conscience take on a longhaired attitude overnight.[19]

This fight marks McCarran's acquiescence, despite his misgivings, to the aims of the gambling industry. Nowhere in this letter, nor anywhere else for that matter, did he indicate that the industry needed reforming. The tax bill was defeated in committee, due in part to McCarran's efforts.

For this reason, the gambling industry was more than ever indebted to him, a fact which it fully recognized. Some commentators suggested that McCarran deliberately sensationalized the seriousness of the threat from Washington, D.C., to make the gamblers more dependent on him. It was the familiar "Pat to the rescue" syndrome.[20] The end result, of course, was a heightening of McCarran's already considerable power in the state. Subsequently the Greenspun affair would show how effectively he was willing to use that power over the gamblers.

Although at the height of his political domination of Nevada in 1951, and seemingly unassailable, McCarran's prestige was soon to be put on the line. By the time of his death in 1954, his formidable organization was everywhere in retreat and McCarran's standing in Nevada had been damaged by several adverse circumstances.

Perhaps the most sensational item to batter McCarran's good reputation in and out of Nevada was the Greenspun affair. It not only tarnished his prestige, but is also an important incident in the history of the freedom of the press. Herman (Hank) Greenspun had had a varied background before becoming embroiled with the senator. Jewish, and very proud of it, he was born in 1909, and grew up in Brooklyn, New York and New Haven, Connecticut. He was admitted to the New York bar in 1937, speculated prosperously in various lucrative business ventures, served in World War II, and, in 1946, hit the Las Vegas scene—in the words of one reporter "a breezy, grinning fellow about the size of a light heavyweight, with deep-set, rather cold blue eyes in a craggy face—a typical hustler and as industrious a hand-pumper as any man in town." Since he had had a little publishing experience, quite a bit of business experience, and a strong penchant for self-advertisement, he became a public relations man for "Bugsy" Siegel, a leading gambler and a developer of the Las Vegas strip. After Siegel's gangland-style murder in 1947, he worked for Wilbur Clark of the Desert Inn. By associating with these men he gained entree among Nevada's gambling entrepreneurs.[21]

Greenspun was indicted by a grand jury and tried in 1949 for smuggling planes into Israel. Later he cheerfully admitted everything, believing it was his patriotic responsibility as a Jew to help the beleaguered state of Israel, then fighting for its independence. Although acquitted on the charge, he was indicted once again, in 1950, for violating the Neutrality Act, this time for smuggling "arms and ammunition" into Israel. He was found guilty, but instead of receiving a jail sentence, was fined $10,000. Greenspun was stripped of his civil rights, but was later pardoned by President John F. Kennedy in 1961. Those who hated Hank Greenspun (and their numbers were many) attempted to use this information to destroy his reputation, but he so disarmingly admitted to everything that the effort was considerably blunted.[22]

Until 1950, the dominant paper in Las Vegas was the *Review-Journal,* run by Al Cahlan, an important and conservative power in Democratic circles and one of McCarran's staunchest supporters. Its earlier competitors, the *Las Vegas Age,* and the *Morning Tribune,* died of economic malnutrition. Consequently, by 1950, Las Vegas was a rapidly expanding town with only one paper. The *Review-Journal* was entrenched and stodgy, a "home" newspaper, usually delivering the McCarran viewpoint.

Then Hank Greenspun entered the scene. In 1950, a triweekly paper, the *Free Press,* had been established by the International Typographical Union after the *Review-Journal* refused to negotiate with the union and locked out its printers. The *Free Press* venture appeared to be heading for predictable failure, when someone suggested that perhaps Greenspun would like to take over the sheet. The asking price for the *Free Press* was $104,000; and, after paying $1,000 down, Greenspun took over on June 21, 1950. In his first issue he promised what Nevada was to get: "I pledge that I will always fight for progress and reform: never tolerate injustice or corruption; never lack sympathy with the underpriviledged; always remain devoted to the public welfare; never be satisfied with merely printing news; always be drastically independent." As a journalistic guide for action, it was intriguing.[23]

The paper, renamed the *Sun* on July 1, 1950, caught on fast; whatever his faults, Greenspun was, and is, a talented newspaperman. The now daily *Sun,* published in the morning, was loud, brassy, opportunistic, flamboyant, occasionally irresponsible, and usually entertaining. With his daily column prominently featured on the front page, Greenspun imprinted his own personality and style onto the paper. In its first six months, the *Sun* made a $156 profit. By 1952, the newspaper had a circulation of 8,531 and appeared established against the *Review-Journal,* which by comparison had 12,535 circulation.[24]

Even though Greenspun had close ties with gamblers, his newspaper was the only one in Nevada which thoroughly covered the Kefauver hearings on Nevada gambling in 1950 and 1951. He soon became a vehement and vitriolic critic of Senator McCarran and his closest associates. Not only did the *Sun* bitterly and personally attack the senator, it went after Norm Biltz, Eva Adams, and all the rest, right down to the Senator's office staff. According to Greenspun, "I saw in McCarran what my old mentor, Fiorello La Guardia, had seen in Tammany Hall; a political machine bent on throttling all opposition, destroying policy, and thriving on the proceedings." The diatribes kept up day after day. McCarran became "the old buzzard."[25] The senator, who was sensitive to press criticism, had never known such relentless newspaper opposition in Nevada; other anti-McCarran journals such as the *Reno Evening Gazette* had always operated within far more gentlemanly and traditional bounds.

Also to be noted is that, in 1951, pro-McCarran Las Vegas Mayor Ernest Cragin had been defeated in his race for reelection by C. D. Baker, an up-and-coming politician who was completely independent of the senator.[26] This, combined with the rapid influx of newcomers into Clark County, demonstrated a weakening of the McCarran organization's influence, at least in southern Nevada.

At first it did not seem that way. Greenspun claims in his autobiography that on March 20, 1952, he was warned by Gus Greenbaum and Benny Binion, important Las Vegas gamblers, to stop criticizing McCarran. Greenbaum's words were "Hank, you've got to lay off. The Old Man has the power of life and death over us." Binion, according to Greenspun's account, cut in, "You know he pulls the strings behind the State Tax Commission. Those guys can ruin us! Look, on my bended knee I'm begging you!" Greenbaum added, "Look, Hank, I like your paper. I want to support it. But I'm afraid that you're going too far this time. I'm just warning you: they're driving us crazy from Washington!" Binion and Greenbaum refused to identify who "they" were, but there was only one "they" strong enough to suit the description—Senator McCarran himself.[27]

Four days later, the implied threat became a reality. The phone began constantly ringing for Norman White, the *Sun's* advertising manager. Soon White went over to Greenspun's desk and told the publisher, "We're in trouble." According to Greenspun, he asked White, "What kind of trouble?"

"Bad. During the past half hour, I've had ad cancellations from the Thunderbird, Hotel El Rancho, and the Last Frontier."

That was not the last of the calls. In one morning every big hotel and casino in Las Vegas, twelve in number, canceled their ads in the *Sun.* This represented thirty percent of the newspaper's advertising revenue. In the previous year this casino advertising revenue had varied from $7,000 per month to $9,000 per month.[28] According to Greenspun he whipped out of his office and drove down to the Desert Inn, where he confronted Moe Dalitz. Still according to Greenspun, he asked Dalitz "What's behind all these ad cancellations?"

Dalitz shrugged, "You should know. Why did you have to attack the Old Man?"

Greenspun, trying to speak quietly, asked, "What business is it of the Desert Inn, or any other hotel, what I print in my paper?"

"You've put us in a terrible position. You know as well as I that we have to do what he tells us. You *know* he got us our licenses. If we don't go along, you know what will happen to us."[29]

Mayor Baker called upon several of the principals in the case to meet in his office. Present were two prominent gambling operators, Fred Soly and J. Kell Houssels, Lieutenant Governor Cliff Jones, and Greenspun himself. At first the gambling operators told Baker that the boycott was "for economy reasons," because the *Sun* had increased its rates. That appeared to be the official line of the casino operators, as it was to be later in court.

But under Baker's interrogation, and it must be remembered this is still Greenspun's account, the story began changing:

> Jones started to repeat his statement, but Soly interrupted, "It was on account of pressure from Washington." Jones' face turned red.
> "From McCarran?" the mayor asked.
> "Sure it was McCarran!" Soly cried. Then Houssels confirmed it, saying, "Mr. Mayor, when my partners returned from a meeting of casino operators and told me what had taken place, I said 'we mustn't do it.'"
> "You mean, boycott the *Sun?*" I prodded.
> Houssels stood his ground. "I told them—my partners, I mean— look, we've always taken care of the Old Man with campaign contributions; we've given him suites at the El Cortez Hotel for free. And now he's putting us into the god-damndest jackpot we've ever been in, between himself and a newspaper!"
> Mayor Baker leaned forward. "Was it a call from Washington that triggered the boycott?"
> "Yes," Soly answered before Houssels could reply.[30]

This alleged telephone call from Washington provided Greenspun the opportunity to pin the blame on McCarran. Day after day the *Sun* ferociously concentrated its fire on the senator:

> People will stand for almost any kind of skullduggery on the part of some politicians, but one thing they will never tolerate is a threat to the freedom of the press. It took too much toil and effort to establish this newspaper to allow a phone call from Senator McCarran in Washington to Marion Hicks in Las Vegas, Nev. to completely undo the work of the Sun in the past two years.

Baker was more discreet and did not specifically or publicly name McCarran: "I am not arguing with their [the gamblers'] right to hold a meeting, but I am saying that outsiders have no right to dictate to the gambling industry or any other industry in the city of Las Vegas."[31]

Hank Greenspun's former legal training now was put to good use. Other journalists, such as Denver Dickerson, watched their papers go down the drain after having advertisements mysteriously pulled out, without realizing they might have recourse to the courts. But Greenspun went to federal court; he filed a $1,000,000 suit against a large group of Las Vegas casino operators, Senator McCarran, and his administrative assistant, Eva Adams, charging a boycott conspiracy to drive the *Sun* out of business. If the allegation were proven, it would constitute a violation of the federal antitrust laws. The *Sun,* for one, had no doubts as to who was primary instigator; it lashed out at the senator "in complete, undisputed control of Nevada [who] rules with as firm an iron fist as the most autocratic of all czars, dictators, or despots." McCarran's immediate public reaction was to assert that the suit was just an attempt to "advertise the fact that there is such a thing as the *Las Vegas Sun.* " "I don't have anything to advertise, so I haven't any advertising to withhold," he blandly added. "I don't control the people of Las Vegas. As far as I know, nothing had been done to withhold advertising from anyone. The whole thing is ridiculous."[32]

Greenspun obtained some high-powered talent for legal counsel. His Las Vegas attorney was George Marshall, the Republican candidate McCarran had defeated in 1950. Columnist Drew Pearson, who expressed a strong interest in the case, recommended his own Washington lawyer, William A. Roberts, to lend legal heft to the attack.[33]

District Federal Judge Roger R. Foley presided over the pretrial hearing, to decide if there was sufficient evidence for the matter to go to trial. Since McCarran had been responsible for Foley's appointment in 1945, there was considerable interest in Nevada as to just how impartial the jurist would be. Foley belied the skeptics by his absolute fairness during the proceedings.[34]

By now the Greenspun case was attracting some well-deserved national attention. The gamblers who testified before Foley steadfastly maintained there was no conspiracy. The boycott had been economically motivated and the idea of the casino owners themselves; there had been no telephone call from Washington pressuring them. Marion Hicks of the Thunderbird was among those who flatly denied all of Greenspun's allegations. Although Hicks admitted making a number of calls to the senator during March, 1952, and having received several, he said he was merely asking McCarran's advice on a proposed expansion of his hotel. Moe Dalitz also swore that McCarran had not pressured the casino owners. Instead he put the finger on Greenspun who, in his words, had threatened to "expose every stockholder in the strip hotels with information from his files" if the ads were not reinstated.[35]

It was Mayor C. D. Baker of Las Vegas who saved Greenspun's case at the pretrial hearing. Baker stated that his meeting with Soly, Houssels, Jones, and Greenspun had "established to his own satisfaction" that "outside pressure" had played a part in the situation. He testified that the gamblers had told him "a phone call" was responsible for the cancellation. Although this did not directly implicate Senator McCarran, many wondered who else had the clout to do this, if indeed there had been such a phone call. Baker's testimony was "hearsay evidence" and not admissable in an actual trial, but the implication of the mayor's account was that either he or the other witnesses had perjured themselves.

Baker's testimony probably was an important factor in determining Judge Foley's ruling that the hotels and casinos must resume their advertising in the *Sun.* The Judge further decided that there was a sufficient case to bring to trial. Although not mentioning the senator, it is significant that Foley did not remove McCarran or Adams from the suit. Foley adjudged accurately that the circumstances of the boycott itself indicated sufficient grounds for action. Otherwise, he observed, the "injunction would fall of its own weight." He also announced, rather sensationally, that in his opinion perjury had been committed in the court room.[36]

Part of Greenspun's charges were clearly true; the casino owners obviously had "conspired" to take their advertising out of the *Sun.* The fact that it was all done on the same day pointed up the stupidity of the action. Greenspun had a perfectly good legal case against the casino owners. If the advertising had been gradually withdrawn over a span of months, the casinos might have made the boycott work. As it was, their collusion was obvious.

But who was the primary instigator? Was it indeed McCarran, as Greenspun was convinced? It is difficult to believe that the casino operators were acting alone. Their claim that the *Sun's* rates caused them economic hardships is implausible. The *Sun's* advertising rates had indeed been raised, but so had its circulation; and the rates were still lower than those of the rival *Review-Journal.* The Kefauver committee had already established that casino profits were not modest. Las Vegas was a booming, prosperous town, and there was plenty of advertising money around. It should also be remembered that before the boycott, Greenspun had enjoyed agreeable relations with the casino operators, in fact he had worked among them for several years. His editorials were not directed at them. All the boycott could do would be to create political turmoil, presumably the last thing that any casino owner desired. Traditionally, gambling interests in Nevada have avoided such political controversy because it is to their best interests to play both sides.

Pete Petersen, Norm Biltz, and Eva Adams, the three closest intimates of the Senator, all later denied that McCarran was the prime mover of the boycott, yet they were all singularly unclear as to just who was. Biltz's words, reported in his memoirs for the University of Nevada Oral History Project, are especially ambiguous: "So it was decided, not entirely by McCarran, that they'd just pull the advertising away from Greenspun." Biltz appears, by his own testimony, to have been in on the decision, which seems to have been sort of cooperative determination. Both Biltz and Eva Adams knew that McCarran bitterly resented Greenspun's diatribes, and the personal attacks on both the senator and his staff.[37]

Although this type of evidence could obviously not be admitted in a court of law, virtually every politician and journalist in the state who was asked about the matter was convinced that McCarran was the primary instigator of the boycott. Comments ranged from, "Of course he was responsible" to "I cannot believe anything else." Although his information was second hand, at least one gambling operator has testified to McCarran's culpability. Twenty-five years after the event he told an interviewer, "They called me out on the Strip, and told me they was mad at him. And Gus Greenbaum said, 'We gonna bust him.'"[38]

It is impossible to avoid the conclusion that McCarran was ultimately the instigator of the boycott. Either he directly gave the word, or someone acting in his name did so. Although the decision to withhold advertising may have been a joint one, in the final analysis it was the senator's. The evidence is circumstantial, but such an analysis is the only one to make sense logically. Only he, or someone acting in his name, had the clout to persuade the casino operators to act in concert; a Norman Biltz, for example, acting alone, lacked the necessary power base in Las Vegas to persuade the casino owners. The operators were certainly heavily indebted to McCarran for his services in saving the industry from federal taxation in 1951, a favor for which the senator took entire credit. Contrarily, if someone had acted in McCarran's name without authorization—an unlikely possibility—the senator had the power and prestige to stop the boycott if he wished to. He did not, but left it instead to the courts. This conclusion is also supported by McCarran's well-documented and growing authoritarianism in state politics. It is entirely consistent with his record.

The trial did not take place until 1953. In the meantime, much detrimental publicity was heaped upon Greenspun; whether orchestrated by McCarran or not is unclear. Greenspun certainly had a record vulnerable to attack. Westbrook Pegler, the most vitriolic of columnists and now working for the Hearst newspapers, wrote darkly of the "Siegel-Greenspun clique." The FBI, he penned, "has the criminal record of Herman Greenspun of Brooklyn, who recently muscled into Nevada politics under the strange patronage of Drew Pearson, in an attempt of mysterious eastern forces to cut down Sen. Pat McCarran." He added an old, but true story that Greenspun had studied law in Vito Marcantonio's law office—Marcantonio being "the nearest thing to an avowed Communist ever to sit in our Congress." For his part, McCarran had the FBI make a rundown of Greenspun's activities, which he distributed to interested parties in Nevada. Apparently convinced that Greenspun was either a communist, or a communist fronter, the Senator asked Harvey Matusow, an ex-Communist witness before his committees, to dig up incriminating evidence on the publisher and his staff.[39] Greenspun was, by the way, a nominal Republican who was to run for the Republican gubernatorial nomination in 1962.

Senator Joseph McCarthy also visited Las Vegas, providing his own inimitable contribution to the furor. In a speech given in October, 1952, the Wisconsin Senator accused Greenspun of being an admitted "ex-communist," and called the *Sun* the "Local Daily Worker." Possibly he meant to call Greenspun an "ex-convict," but the words came out "ex-communist" instead. Greenspun, who was in the audience, rose in a fury and challenged McCarthy to debate the issue, whereupon McCarthy cut his speech short and hastily exited the auditorium. It must have been an interesting meeting. Greenspun, who could indulge in mean tactics himself, blazoned on his paper's front page the charge that McCarthy was a homosexual, "the most immoral, indecent and unprincipled scoundrel ever to sit in the United States senate."[40]

McCarran himself was depressed. The late 1952 election period was a hard time for him, and he eventually disavowed his party's nominees for president, Adlai Stevenson, and U.S. Senator from

Nevada, Tom Mechling. In a letter to his wife in the fall of 1952, he referred to "this red paper down here," meaning the *Sun*. His eldest daughter, Sister Margaret, fiercely loyal to her father, noticed that the affair was seriously affecting his mood. After seeing her father she commented:

> He keeps busy in a well-measured way so as not to be too preoccupied about the chicanery of Las Vegas. I did not press him to talk about that too much because he gets too unhappy about the traitors, the cowards, and the doubters. He remarked that the Savior's life was a model of the common man's. He finds it necessary to practice careful mental hygiene.[41]

In December, 1952, upon his return from a Latin American trip, Senator McCarran was required to submit a deposition, to support a motion by his attorneys that he be dismissed as a defendant.[42] In many ways this deposition was damaging to McCarran's reputation —at least the way it was reported in the press. In it, McCarran stoutly denied his involvement in the boycott. On the contrary, he declared that he originally had sympathetic feelings toward Greenspun and that he used his influence to keep Greenspun out of prison when he was convicted of running arms to Israel. In 1950, McCarran asserted, a Las Vegas politician, Guernsey Frazier, had told him that "Greenspun has a paper here and he is a pretty good scout. If you can keep him out of the penitentiary it would be worth while." It was then that McCarran intervened with the Department of Justice. The senator also claimed that he did not even know many of the gambling casino defendants in the case. He denied that he had ever met the famous "Bugsy" Siegel, much less intervened in his behalf.

But McCarran did admit, after intense questioning, that he often visited many of the leading Las Vegas and Reno hotels and casinos, and had stayed at most of the hotels. What especially interested the eastern press was McCarran's concession that he had received many services from the hotels and casinos absolutely free. Specifically, in 1944 and 1950, McCarran stated he had his headquarters in Las Vegas at the El Cortez Hotel, and his "recollection" was that "space was not charged for in which I had headquarters." He added, "As a rule, when I would go into any one of these hotels in the dining room, when I would ask for the check, any one of those hotels would say there is no check." It might be added that it was, at is, standard Nevada casino and hotel procedure that politicians are "comped," that is, given complimentary meals, rooms, and liquor. McCarran told the attorneys that he had indeed acted on a request by the Flamingo Hotel to modify its tax status, and had seen Charles Oliphrant, former counsel for the Bureau of Internal Revenue, on the matter.

On his relationship with the press, McCarran made some revealing statements, as quoted in the *Washington Post:*

> That in 1947, William Green, the late head of the AFL, wrote to AFL officials in Nevada threatening to withdraw support of the Nevada State Labor News unless it ceased criticizing McCarran, "one of the staunchest friends of the AFL." . . .
>
> That last summer, upon the recommendation of McCarran, Denver Dickerson, editor of the Nevada State News, which had sometimes criticized McCarran, was made a State Department press attaché and shipped to Rangoon, Burma. McCarran said yesterday: "I think it's a good thing for him [Dickerson] to get the experience."
>
> That McCarran once protested that Moritz Zenoff, editor of the Boulder City News, also was printing a newspaper at the Air Force Base at Las Vegas which contained political criticism. McCarran said he protested to the Air Force. Zenoff ultimately lost the contract. McCarran said Zenoff later told him "he was sorry about the attitude he had taken about me."[43]

Actually there was nothing specific in the deposition that was vitally damaging. Yet the cumulative effect in the eastern press was to portray McCarran as a rather sinister influence, a man who accepted favors from gambling sources, and who did favors for them.

Even though Eva Adams, among others, believed the senator would be taken out of the case, Judge Foley decided otherwise. Although he ruled that Greenspun could claim only damages treble the actual amount of alleged financial loss (which reduced the suit from $1,000,000 to $225,000) he refused to delete McCarran's name from the list, ruling instead that "there was sufficient evidence to make McCarran a defendant in the case.[44]

The trial finally began on February 4, 1953, but a behind-the-scenes settlement came almost immediately. The Greenspun forces located the telephone operator who could identify the calls from Washington to Marion Hicks during the crucial week in March, 1952. This took the telephone-call issue from the category of hearsay evidence and made it admissible in court. The settlement, which was supposedly secret, ordered the defendants to pay Greenspun $80,-

500, which was paid by the casino operators, and to give a "gen-tleman's understanding" that casinos and hotels would continue with their *Sun* ads. McCarran admitted nothing but neither was he exonerated. It was generally admitted that Greenspun had won a genuine victory. The story is told that the flamboyant Greenspun, after insisting on being paid off in cash, got into his flashy, red convertible and drove up and down the Strip, waving the money as he went past the respective casinos.[45]

McCarran publicly broke the silence on the supposedly secret agreement in a statement:

> The settlement was between the plaintiff and certain defendants other than myself. I was here in Washington when the case was settled. I took no part in the trial or in the settlement. I did not participate in negotiations for settlement, nor did any attorney representing me. I gave no consideration for the settlement. I have not given or agreed to give any money or any promise or any other thing of value for the settlement, or as damages to the plaintiff. I consented to dismissal of the action against me only on the condition that it be dismissed with prejudice. I consider the fact that this action had been dismissed as an open admission by the plaintiff that the charges which he brought against me during the recent political campaign were entirely un-founded.[46]

This statement was, to say the least, misleading, as McCarran well knew. The fact that McCarran was in Washington while the case was settled in Las Vegas fooled no one. McCarran's lawyers actively participated in the settlement. McCarran did not have to pay dam-ages because the casinos picked up the tab for him. At no time was his name or Eva Adams's removed from the list of defendants. The statement that Greenspun could not resue McCarran only indicated that the settlement was a final one.

Privately McCarran was depressed and discouraged, belying his public stance. He tended to blame the sad state of affairs on the twelve lawyers he had on the case. Two days before the trial, he despairingly wrote his wife, "They never seem to get together. There is no established policy in this case. Some want to settle some don't some don't care. Just so they get a fee—it's a hell of a thing."[47]

The settlement saddened him despite his outward confidence. He was old now and lacked his previous resilience. The "mental hy-giene" of which Sister Margaret had written was not working, per-haps a casualty of Greenspun's continuous sniping. The increasingly protective Eva Adams wrote Sister Margaret about the Senator's deteriorating mood:

> This whole thing, Sister Margaret, has been a heartbreak all the way through. I just don't know what to do. We have been quietly working trying to find a way to silence Greenspun. I am enclosing a photostat of his latest blast. The facts are wrong but the viciousness is there and I am told that it will get worse. . . .
>
> The thing that breaks my heart most in this matter is that the Senator has lost so much faith in so many people. He feels most unhappy at the way the thing was handled. . . . no Nevada attorney has ever had any experience in anti-trust law. . . . Mr. Leahy is very able and in several instances did a magnificent job of presenting the Senator's case. However, the Senator doesn't feel that they really fought for him and I can appreciate why he has that reaction.
>
> Looking backward doesn't help. We have to look toward the coming months now. The Senator feels that all the people in Las Vegas have sold him down the river. That makes him feel very unhappy as it is only a comparatively small group actually fighting him. The majority of people are just so occupied with their own affairs that they pay no attention unless they want something. . . . However, even the Senator realizes keeping this fire burning only makes the scars deeper for him. I just can't believe other than that time will turn the tables and God will somehow allay this great sorrow which has come to him, and put some kindness in Greenspun's horrible heart.[48]

Greenspun was not "silenced," his "horrible heart" did not become noticeably kinder toward the senator, and McCarran, by now an old, bitter man, could not do much about it.

Other enemies needed attention and retribution, however. In 1952, the Senate Internal Security Subcommittee, headed by Senator McCarran, investigated the International Union of Mine, Mill, and Smelter Workers. This union, a descendant of the old Western Federation of Miners, was strong in the Ely area. In 1950, it had been expelled from the CIO along with ten others for its communist domination.[49] Although this was not as important nationally as some of the subcommittee investigations, McCarran made it into a personal vendetta, with implications for Nevada.

The investigation seemed a natural one. But why did the subcommittee focus on this particular union when there were certainly many other and more important unions to be investigated? The ostensible reason given by the subcommittee was that the International Union of Mine, Mill, and Smelter Workers had disrupted national copper production by calling strikes twice since the beginning of the Korean War. McCarran declared that he had been told the communists in the union were planning further strikes in the crucial copper industry under the guise of demands for higher wages.[50]

Yet these official reasons do not quite satisfy. Of all the allegedly communist-dominated unions, the Mine, Mill, and Smelter Workers was the only one with any strength in Nevada. It had vehemently fought McCarran in 1944 and 1950, and McCarran was not one readily to forgive such bitter opposition. As recently as August, 1952, Graham Dolan, an official for the union, described McCarran in its newspaper as "a vindictive old man," "one of the Senate's most expendable," and "the senatorial voice of the Kennecott Copper Corporation."[51] The investigation was thus also an attempt to settle old scores, to crush an enemy, and, timed as it was only a month before an important election, to weaken its political influence.

Along with several other members of the subcommittee, McCarran brought the hearings to Salt Lake City, on October 6 through 9, 1952. The union, for its part, placed a full page ad in the *Salt Lake Tribune* castigating McCarran for his "witch-hunts and concentration camps." McCarran's reaction was that the ad "carries out exactly the Communist line. For years now we have become acquainted with it, reviling, abusing, and vilifying the members of the committee."[52]

Certainly the committee had all the information it needed to demonstrate the communist leanings of the union leadership. And since the union leaders all took the fifth amendment, the "investigation" became simply an exercise in public relations. It afforded a splendid opportunity for McCarran to bully and snarl at the union officials, an opportunity he did not let pass.[53]

One problem with investigating a labor union, even a communist-dominated one, was that McCarran had always boasted an impeccable labor record. In these hearings, he put himself in the light of persecuting the labor movement, so the senator went to great pains to defend his prolabor credentials:

> The chairman of the Judiciary Committee of the United States Senate, the chairman of this committee, came from the loins of labor. He was born and reared in a labor home. Everything that surrounded him

in his boyhood days was labor. He played on the streets of Virginia City
and Gold Hill where the first miners' union was organized, the first
miners' union in all America.

After reviewing his prounion record, McCarran stated the problem
was communism, not the labor movement:

> There is no slavery in the world like the slavery of communism.
> There is no enemy in the world of labor like communism. And if labor
> permits itself to be dominated by communism either in this union or
> in any other union, then labor will lose the fine things that we have
> worked out for labor by legislation during the past quarter of a century.
> ... In God's name and in the name of the country to which you
> belong, to which you give your loyalty as a citizen, ... in God's name
> as American citizens awaken to the situation that you may cleanse
> yourself of this situation and not wait for law to deal with these individ-
> uals.[54]

From a publicity standpoint, the hearings went well, although
nothing was discovered that either the investigators or the government did not already know. McCarran was so pleased by the testimony provided by Harvey Matusow in particular (who later
confessed that it was fraudulent), that he set up a private interview
with the informer to see if Matusow might be useful in another
Nevada connection. During the course of their conversation he asked
Matusow if he would investigate Hank Greenspun. According to
Matusow, "He asked me if I knew Hank Greenspun.... McCarran
said he thought Greenspun was Communist, or a Communist
fronter. He wanted to know if I, through my connections, could
establish this fact." Matusow was glad to comply; as a first course
of action he asked the senator to furnish him with a list of all the
Sun's employees: "My plan was to try to pin the 'Communist label'
on his staff."[55]

Nothing came of this, of course, as Greenspun and the *Sun,* had
impeccable anticommunist credentials. The fate of the International
Union of Mine, Mill, and Smelter Workers was less happy, although
it is not clear whether the Senate Internal Security Subcommittee
contributed to that fate. It was on the run throughout the 1950s,
losing its collective bargaining status in Ely among other things, and
passed out of existence in 1967, by merger with the United Steel
Workers.

Contemporary with these events was the campaign of 1952, which also clearly demonstrated the growing ineffectiveness of the McCarran organization, particularly in Clark County, and the senator's increasing political impotency and despondency. Seemingly, 1952 was Alan Bible's year to go to the U.S. Senate. When the popular Bible, formerly state attorney general, and universally and correctly considered McCarran's protégé, announced for the office, virtually every political observer believed him a shoo-in, at least for the Democratic nomination. Most commentators foresaw an eventual victory over Republican Senator Malone as well. Everyone liked Bible; he was, and is, a friendly, personable man. The only major criticism of him was his supposed subservience to McCarran; and there were rumors that Bible was attempting to counteract this by avoiding any visible link to McCarran.[56]

The Democratic primary campaign for senator took a strange twist, however, with the challenge of Tom Mechling, a 31-year-old Washington, D.C., newspaperman. Mechling had married a Nevada woman, the daughter of a wholesale liquor dealer in the Wells area, which was just about as close as he had ever come to Nevada. Mrs. Mechling had worked in McCarran's office, and doubtless had given her husband an earful of office gossip. Mechling was frankly ambitious, and believed that the quickest way to political advancement was to win a U.S. senatorship from the nation's smallest state. Mechling was totally unknown in Nevada when he announced; the astute Pete Petersen had never even heard of him.[57]

Mechling turned out to be an extraordinarily talented campaigner. Soon many were attracted to the young man with the engaging manner. Mechling was prepared to spend his total savings of $12,000 on the effort. He systematically mapped out the state and its population and shopping areas, and coolly determined to shake hands with every registered voter in Nevada. So the young candidate hitched his trailer to a car, and drove out on every possible road and byway. By April, 1952, he estimated that he had already rung 25,000 doorbells, visited 5,000 stores and offices, and made 123 speeches; and the campaign was only half over.[58] Hank Greenspun, who really did not think Mechling could make it, applauded the youth's perseverence. He was not alone in his praise:

> I don't know whether to admire young Tom Mechling, candidate for the Democratic nomination for the U.S. Senate, for his exceptional courage or to dismiss him as a presumptuous upstart. How any man

can expect to capture the nomination using his tactics is beyond me.

The fellow is working 18 hours a day—up every morning at 5 A.M. to meet the early rising workers such as railway men, service trades, and miners—then punches doorbells to talk to housewives until noon; luncheon speaking engagements and back to doorbells until supper with veteran's and other meetings occupying his time until almost midnight.

A schedule which he expects to maintain for the next eight months and which will carry him into every crossroad hamlet in the state. Before the election in the fall, young Tom and his pretty wife should meet every registered voter in the state—some of them more than once.[59]

To the more romantic, Mechling seemed a shining young knight. He rallied around himself many of the Democrats who opposed McCarran's conservative voting record, by advocating a Fair Employment Practices Commission (FEPC), public power, Truman's foreign policy, and public disclosure of campaign donations. He opposed the Taft-Hartley Act. By comparison, Bible appeared to speak only in generalities, and conservative ones at that. Mechling impressed everyone with his clean-cut youthful good looks and his determination: "Win or lose, at least I think I will have done something toward better government. What I saw up close of self-serving politicians in Washington made me mad—mad enough to jump down out of the press gallery and into politics with both feet." More pointedly, he made the McCarran domination of Nevada politics and the senior senator's dictatorial tactics one of his chief issues.[60]

But the McCarran forces probably felt little cause for worry during the summer of 1952. The organization appeared to be operating smoothly enough, controlling the various county conventions and the state convention in Wells. On a national level, Senator McCarran espoused the presidential aspirations of Senator Richard Russell of Georgia. Russell was a man who had no popular support in Nevada, but McCarran got his way. As one Democrat responded, "Why, I guess we'll do whatever Pat tells us to do."[61]

The old domination appeared unchallenged. Russell was not really popular in the Nevada delegation and the senior senator employed some high-handed methods to gain his way. Representative Walter Baring independently declared to McCarran that he could not bring himself to vote for Russell, and that Adlai Stevenson was a more appealing candidate. In front of several bystanders, including reporters, McCarran bluntly told the congressman, "You will vote for

Russell, or I will personally see to it that you're beaten in this fall's election." Baring had the courage to vote for Stevenson and was indeed defeated in the fall. But the Nevada delegation as a whole gave 8 of its 10 votes to Russell.[62]

By the time of the national convention, everyone agreed that Mechling's chances were improving but Bible would win anyway—probably by a 60 percent margin. The confident Bible was not campaigning very hard, and emphasized the fact that Mechling was a new arrival to the state. Just to make sure things did not go awry, McCarran came out with a ringing endorsement of Bible "He is no carpetbagger," the senior senator announced.[63]

Unfortunately, all this effort boomeranged. Hank Greenspun asserted on his paper's front page, "If I ever had any doubts about being on the right candidate, it has been dispelled by events of the past few days. McCarran's unqualified endorsement of the Bible candidacy . . . makes Mechling's independence shine like a beacon." Although Bible and McCarran did not realize it, the candidate was in major trouble in Clark County. Len Carpenter warned McCarran from the marshal's office that Bible had to campaign a lot harder in Clark County: "That place is growing to be more of a hotbed every day. I know that personally I have never seen so many radicals in one small area in my experience ever before."[64]

The election result was a humiliating surprise for McCarran. Mechling narrowly defeated Bible by 15,914 votes to 15,439, although he carried only three counties. But he swamped McCarran's protégé in Clark County, by an overwhelming 7,080 ballots to 4,223. Newspapers generally blamed Bible's defeat on McCarran, which might have been unfair since Mechling had waged an unusually effective campaign. The *Fallon Eagle* proclaimed "Alan Bible was defeated by Senator Pat McCarran." The *Elko Free Press,* usually not unfriendly to the senior senator, opined that "it was the revolt of the Democrats against Sen. Pat McCarran and his ruthless control over political affairs in this state." The *Reno Evening Gazette* even believed that if McCarran had been running he would have been defeated. Certainly the election demonstrated that the McCarran forces were in appalling disarray in Clark County, by now the state's most populous. Elsewhere though they appeared reasonably solid.[65]

After his victory, Mechling continued his denunciations of McCarran. By now he was generally favored over Malone. In retrospect, it would better have served Mechling's interest to cool his attacks on the senior senator, and focus instead on healing the divisions within the Democratic party. Malone, whom McCarran disliked as he did all his junior colleagues, was, after all, a vulnerable candidate. But Mechling was riding high from his victory, and he began demonstrating an overly dramatic, opportunistic, and even reckless streak which would eventually work against him. In the final analysis Mechling defeated himself.

On October 17, 1952, Mechling made several sensational and unnecessary charges, accusing Republican candidate Malone of accepting McCarran's undercover support. According to the Democratic aspirant, "two of Senator McCarran's acknowledged spokesmen" had approached Mechling on September 6, four days after his primary victory. He stated that they offered McCarran's support in return for two things: allowing the senior senator to okay all appointments and patronage that Mechling "would normally make," and accepting McCarran's guidance in all matters, particularly those pertaining to Nevada politics. Ads were placed in Nevada newspapers asserting Mechling's indignant refusal of the proposal and McCarran's subsequent support for Malone.[66] After his eventual defeat, Mechling was to repeat the charges to a larger, national audience:

> For several days McCarran refused to talk. He hinted that he would not support me and would even cross party lines to beat me. But a few days later his representatives approached me. They brought with them his price, the price I was expected to pay for a unified party. . . .
>
> But the price was ridiculous for anyone who prized his independence. McCarran wanted me to clear every political decision with him, just as if I were one of his errand boys. In short, I was to help him rebuild the machine we had wrecked in the primary. With McCarran it was either rule or ruin.
>
> With all this activity going on against me in my own party, I felt it was high time to publicize the deal that had been offered me in return for McCarran's support. I decided to make it an issue in the campaign.[67]

It was Mechling's charge that made McCarran's public opposition inevitable. Obviously Mechling welcomed the opposition; but, in retrospect, nothing was gained by it. From the beginning, many Nevada observers suspected the charges were made up, at least in part. It was certainly characteristic of McCarran that he would attempt to dominate any junior senator from Nevada, but there was something strange in the accusation that McCarran tried immediately to make compromise overtures to a man he obviously despised. It would have been more typical of the senior senator to refuse any contacts with such a person, and then quietly try to crush him.

The inevitable happened—forced in this instance by Mechling. On October 23, 1952, McCarran went on statewide radio, to broadcast his opposition to the Democratic candidate for Senator. By all testimony he was by this time an embittered man who found supporting Malone a completely distasteful task.[68] McCarran termed Mechling's statement an "unmitigated lie. I sent no spokesmen to either candidate for the Senate, or to any other candidate. So far as I know, the whole incident which Mr. Mechling purported to describe was either a figment of his imagination, or a deliberate misrepresentation."

McCarran demanded that Mechling name the so-called spokesmen. He stated that he realized Mechling's defeat might cause him to lose the chairmanship of the Judiciary Committee, if the Republicans should organize the Senate. But it was not to the state's interests to elect such an unreliable man:

> I have come to the conclusion that Thomas B. Mechling is untrustworthy, untruthful, and unfit to represent the people of Nevada in the United States Senate. Having come to this conclusion, I felt it was my duty to communicate with the people of Nevada. The decision was reached reluctantly; but I have no reluctance in disclosing it to you. I will not be a hypocrite. I will not campaign in this election for any candidate; but my own vote will be cast against Mr. Mechling and I shall ask my friends throughout the state to cast their votes that way.[69]

Interestingly enough, McCarran avoided mentioning Malone's name, so the broadcast was hardly a resounding endorsement of his Republican colleague. It was an anti-Mechling protest, not a pro-Malone one.

McCarran's active role in the campaign was over; now it remained for several of his friends to secure Mechling's defeat. They received no little help from Mechling himself. Statewide controversy forced Mechling to name the two men he said had approached him on September 6. On October 24, a day after McCarran's radio speech, Mechling released a carefully worded statement that seemed to answer all the questions. Upon closer reading it answered none. Many Nevadans began to suspect that there might be some foundation for

McCarran's accusations that Mechling was untruthful. Mechling's statement was hotheaded and desperate:

> It is now apparent to all Nevada voters where Sen. McCarran stands. He has found Republican Sen. George Malone easier to do business with. Mr. Malone has accepted the deal which I rejected seven weeks ago and has paid the price of servitude for the senior senator's endorsement.
>
> Fortunately that deal made in secret several weeks ago, has now been forced out into the open—for all Nevadans to see and consider and to decide whether they want to elect an independent senator or one who has crawled into Mr. McCarran's pocket.
>
> This is a wonderfully free country, so any man can support anyone he chooses. And any man can bow his neck to another if he chooses. . . .
>
> I have been asked to name names—as if they were more important than the principle involved—so the spokesmen of Mr. McCarran can add their denials to Mr. McCarran's, even though the results of the deal they so vigorously deny is plain to everyone.
>
> Do you think men like Norm Biltz and Johnny Mueller would hesitate to do anything to protect their benefactor—Sen. McCarran?
>
> . . . McCarran has chosen to make it his word against mine. You are asked to believe a man who says he is a Democrat, who stood on the same Democratic platform with Vail Pittman . . . pledging his support and then throwing that support to Republican candidate Charles Russell in a last-minute double cross.
>
> The plain fact is: Mr. McCarran will not support any man he can't control, regardless of the party, regardless of the office. I will have no part of "two-faced" politics.
>
> So now, Mr. McCarran, start your smear campaign and order your henchmen to lie for you.[70]

The statement appeared to name Biltz and Mueller as the men who had approached Mechling on September 6, but actually it did not. The statement also appeared to indicate an attempted deal on McCarran's behalf, but a closer reading does not establish even that. It was obvious that Mechling was in serious trouble. The day following his statement, both Mueller and Biltz vociferously denied Mechling's imputation, Mueller calling it a "filthy lie" and Biltz a "deliberate lie."[71]

On October 26, in a radio broadcast, Mechling specifically identified Biltz and Mueller as the two men who had tried to arranged the September 6 deal. Mechling said he had been asked again who the "spokesmen" were. He replied, "How many times do I have to say

Mueller and Biltz. Biltz and Mueller." Then he spelled out the two names: "B-i-l-t-z and M-u-e-l-l-e-r."[72]

Two facts, however, discredited Mechling's statement. For one thing, Biltz and Mueller both had alibis for September 6. Mechling's activities on that date were well documented. He had driven from Wells to Tonopah in the morning and then attended the meeting of the Democratic state central committee in Tonopah. But Biltz, according to a number of witnesses, had spent the day at his Lake Tahoe home, entertaining a fairly large party of friends well into the night. And Mueller was registered at the Mark Hopkins hotel in San Francisco. No one had seen either of them in Tonopah, which is not, after all, a large town.[73]

More damning for Mechling's veracity, Biltz, on October 28, released taped extracts of a conversation which had in fact taken place among Mechling, Biltz, and Mueller. Biltz taped the conversation without Mechling's knowledge. By the evidence of the extracts, the meeting had not taken place on September 6, as Mechling had alleged, but on September 27, in Biltz's office in Reno. If taken at face value, the tapes demonstrated that it was Mechling who set up the meeting, not Biltz or Mueller. The tapes also indicated, although this was not quite clear, that the initial overtures had come from Mechling, who apparently was seeking McCarran's support. The tapes contained nothing particularly incriminating for Mechling, except that his previous statements were shown to be lies. Biltz had kept the tapes secret for a month, and released them only when Mechling's accusations were causing him considerable heat, and after McCarran's statement that he would not vote for Mechling.[74]

Mechling replied in the only way left to him, charging that the tapes had been doctored. In his seemingly open manner, Mechling came back with a strong attack. In an October 29 radio speech he stated:

> You remember that when I exposed these double-dealing politicians a few weeks ago—and was called a liar for it—I asked if you citizens of Nevada thought that men like Norman Biltz and John Mueller would hesitate to do anything to protect their benefactor, Senator McCarran.
> I said that the smear campaign would start soon, and that Mr. McCarran would order his henchmen to lie for him.
> They are now doing a good job of following his orders. . . .
> Let's open the book on that tape-recording. Let's let the people of Nevada hear it in its entirety . . . not just carefully edited excepts, dubbed in or cut out.

Let's let the people of Nevada hear all of it—all of our long conversation. I will buy the necessary radio time, and pay for it personally. I challenge them to let the people of Nevada hear the whole truth in their own words.

I challenge them as a man who stands openly on the street to express his views, instead of resorting to Gestapo tactics of hidden tape recordings.

I challenge Mr. Biltz and Mr. Mueller to replay the conversation in its entirety—uncut, uncensored, unedited. And you, the people of Nevada, will then hear in their own words.

. . . how they offered the McCarran deal in exchange for control of my Senate seat.

. . . how they offered to make me, how they threatened to break me.

. . . how they bragged about the housing deal of Henderson, Nevada, "The Great Henderson Steal."

. . . how they bragged they had knifed Vail Pittman for their stooge, Charlie Russell, in the 1950 governor election.

. . . how they assured me that they spoke for McCarran.[75]

This was a shrewdly conceived statement on Mechling's part since he knew that Biltz's profanity was so rampant that no radio station could possibly have played the tapes. But Biltz retaliated by inviting two dozen newspaper and radio men to his office to hear the hour-long tape. The reporters heard dialogue that convinced most of them that Mechling had previously misled them and that, indeed, it had been Mechling who had made the overtures for reconciliation. The September 27 date was corroborated by references to Mueller's birthday the previous day, and it was stated on the tapes that this was the first meeting of the three. The reporters also heard plenty of Biltz braggadocio—how he had elected Russell for example—not all of it creditable for Biltz; but that only seemed to heighten the tape's authenticity. They heard Mechling make statements such as, "I would tell him [McCarran] face to face I need somebody to show me around, and I hope to hell it's my own senators. I don't want to go out and have somebody else like Paul Douglas or another of my friends show me around. I mean it would be better if we worked together." Later Mechling declared, "We want to win this election. Ah, we don't want to keep this party split up."[76]

Most of the reporters, although skeptical men, were convinced. It is important to note that although most of the publishers in the state were supporting Malone, with the exception only of the *Las Vegas Sun* and the *Wells Progress,* the reporters were generally for Mechling. Yet the dialogue sounded just like Mueller and Biltz to them.

Further evidence that Mechling had made misleading statements in the campaign, and that he had indeed sought McCarran's support while purporting the reverse, comes from Pete Petersen. In his oral autobiography, Petersen declares that Mechling had called him at home immediately after the primary and insisted that he make an appointment with the senator, so McCarran and Mechling could straighten things out. Mechling said, in Petersen's words, "I demand it." Biltz, in his oral autobiography, alleges that Mechling "said that if we would back him we could have anything we wanted. We could have fifty percent of him. That was his expression."[77]

The effect of Biltz's tapes immediately before the election was devastating. It was the tapes, not McCarran, that beat Mechling. If newspaper comments are to be believed, McCarran's support of Malone helped Mechling, if anything. By now it was entirely believable for the senior senator to be supporting men in the opposite party. But the tapes hurt badly. They tore Mechling's previous stories to shreds. The young man was attracting an enormous amount of controversy, of a type which made him appear erratic at the very least. That kind of reputation could only injure his campaign. In the end, he beat himself, McCarran had little to do with it.

Mechling came close though, especially if one considers that he was running against an Eisenhower landslide. Malone edged him by only 41,906 to 39,184 votes, a margin of 2,722, while Eisenhower was winning the state by 18,814. Although Mechling took Clark County by a margin of 5,775 ballots, Malone did well enough in Washoe and the rest of the state to make up the loss.[78] Mechling ran for governor of Nevada in 1954, and lost rather badly in the Democratic primary. Subsequently he left the state.

Many observers who supported him in 1952, later came to distrust him. Despite his surface openness, Mechling seemed devious, and self-serving. After the 1952 election, Ed Olsen, then head of the Associated Press in Reno, went to dinner with reporter Frank McCulloch and Mechling, and their wives. When they were all in the car afterwards, Mechling suddenly asked, "How about the money now?" Olsen replied, "What money?" Mechling said, "You guys promised to give me the money to buy a radio station." The reporters, needless to say, had never made such an offer, and anyway were earning only $40 and $50 a week.[79]

The 1952 election was a bad period for McCarran. His former resiliency had disappeared and his private letters were despondent. Mechling's primary victory over Bible, the continuing nastiness from the *Las Vegas Sun,* and what he considered the disastrous policies of the majority wing of the Democratic party had cut deep. He publicly announced his refusal to vote for Adlai Stevenson, whom he considered a friend of the British Socialist party: "That party is the child of the Fabians of England and the head of the Fabians at the present time is Comrade Joe Stalin. Stalin and all he stands for is anathema to me. I wonder if Mr. Stevenson can say the same."[80] His alienation from his own party was all but official.

McCarran poured out his despair in letters to his wife. Occasionally his bitterness reached beyond coherence.* He wrote at various times during the fall of 1952:

> I don't know whether Malone can win or not, he's awful weak and so many people speak disparagingly of him and her.[81] She is out front all the time and the biggest part of her is her mouth. Meckling is a "Commy" plant in Nevada but people dont seem to get on. Clark County is the worst mess I ever saw.[82]

> This place [Las Vegas] is a political mess—the worst I ever saw. . . . There is no enthusiasm for either one of the candidates for president nor for either candidate for Senator. It's the same all over the state. This fellow Stevenson is a liar along with everything else. He answered my wire saying he was not an A.D.A. yet the A.D.A. paper of February carries an article on his membership. He says he didn't seek the Presidency yet in his explanation of his spending the slush fund he had he shows the largest sum was spent for a publicity man for the purpose of boosting him for President. Some man he, Stevenson, is. Well Isenhower would at least clean out the rats from the White House. But hes saying nothing only shaking hands with my friends and being seen. This red paper down here now wants to withdraw its suit. [83] I'm saying nothing to that either.[84]

> This election campagne is surely getting dirty. Truman will go down in history as the dirtiest as well as the most ignorant of all presidents. This pissant in human form is a disgrace to his country. . . . [85]

> It seems both Stevenson and Isenhour are dumb as to law. They both show gross ignorance as to my bill. They dont even read the bill. The Jews are misleading both of them. This fellow who has the democratic nomination here—Mechling is going wild with his lies about me, and

---

*McCarran's private comments, written in longhand, here and at footnote 120 in this chapter, retain the original punctuation and spelling.

I'm going to answer him on the radio. He too is being led by eastern Jews, and "Commies."

Its a stormy time for me but these storms make us strong when we know we are right. And I'm right these Commy rats cant cower me with their threats; this land is worth fighting for, and should not be turned over to the criminal and the insane of the weak decrepit old world of graft and slavery—So we fight on.[86]

I see on my return that Stevenson has taken a rap at me. I gave my answer last night. Its in the Journal this morning and on the wires as well. The damn fool why does he want to alienate democrats. He belongs to the A.D.A. He lied to me by his letter when he said he was not a member of the A.D.A. He belongs to that red outfit.

This is the dirtiest of dirty campagnes. The worst is yet to come.[87]

Today is the day and only God knows what it will bring.

The way this Meckling man has conducted his campagne you would think I was a candidate against him. He has lied and lied from the first day he came to the state and he has been caught in all of his lies. There is a great movement of new people into the state. There are four thousand people living in trailors in Clark County alone and as many more here [Reno]. They are on wheels, so to speak and really don't belong here.

I think Malone will win but not certainly. I think Isenhour will carry this state. I hope he carries the nation. There's no hope for democracy with Stevenson in.[88]

The election did little to satisfy these sad ravings. Eisenhower won and so did Malone, a man McCarran disliked but infinitely preferred to Mechling. But Hank Greenspun in effect won his suit, and the McCarran organization was obviously in trouble in Clark County, by now the state's most populous. He did not understand the new-comers who "really don't belong here" and they obviously did not understand the old paternalism. McCarran remained in this bitter mood until his death.

By now Norman Biltz was one of McCarran's most intimate associates, and the senator's Nevada dealings became closely intertwined with those of Biltz. Biltz had a colorful and varied background, straight out of Horatio Alger. Born in Bridgeport, Connecticut, in 1902, he had been an entrepreneur almost from the beginning. Even at the age of ten he had a shoe shine operation and a sausage route, at least by his later account. Biltz never completed high school, he was expelled from a military academy. He went west and arrived in Los Angeles with $14 in his pocket. There he worked for a while on the docks and ships. In 1927, Biltz began his speculations in real estate at Lake Tahoe. These dealings at Tahoe and nearby Donner Lake later extended to land developments around Reno. In time, Biltz ventured into mining and ranching operations, but, interestingly enough, not into gambling. By the early 1950s he had amassed a personal fortune estimated at eight to ten million dollars.[89]

Along with this money, Biltz also accumulated considerable power, enough for him to be called, by 1954, "the Duke of Nevada." His fortune was not the sole basis of this power; Biltz also had a forceful, but charming personality. He was trusted and generally considered honest. His word was universally regarded as good. One Nevadan declared, "If Norm is a dragon, he is a friendly dragon." Another described Biltz as "an extremely likeable son of a bitch," and a third responded that Biltz "could charm anyone right out of the trees." Everyone attested to his salesmanship and his personality. He lacked academic training, in fact he never felt at ease reading. Yet he had an intuitive understanding of other human personalities. He listened to them. He knew their frailties and their worth.[90]

His power stemmed in great measure from his personal contacts. Biltz had persuaded many wealthy men to make their permanent homes in Nevada in order to avoid heavy taxes elsewhere. He had been the person mainly responsible for an amendment to the Nevada constitution forbidding assessment of estate taxes by the state, the only such law among the forty-eight states. After passage of the amendment, Biltz made up a list of millionaires in the nation worth $20,000,000 or more and systematically went down the list, attempting to persuade them to move to Nevada. He helped to entice millionaires like automobile and aviation magnate E. L. Cord and gin-and-yeast king Max Fleischmann to the state; and they, in turn, aided in maintaining Biltz's power.[91]

Biltz was closely connected with the political powers of the state as well. He was a good friend of George Wingfield in and after his heyday. By 1944, Biltz was devoting considerable attention to the increasingly important Senator McCarran, and he raised money for the senator's tight race with Vail Pittman. Biltz also had political and financial contacts outside the state. Some of this came through his marriage, in 1929, to his third wife, originally Esther Auchincloss. She was an aunt to John and Jacqueline Kennedy, and that, of course, brought additional influence.

Although Biltz was a Republican, by the 1950s this was no liability in his relationship with McCarran. In fact it was a distinct asset to the senator, for Biltz could tap Republican campaign sources in Washoe County and elsewhere which might otherwise have been closed to the Democratic McCarran. But party affiliation did not mean much in Nevada anyway; in McCarran's estimation, politics was more good guys versus bad guys.[92] And Biltz was distinctly a good guy.

Biltz's ideal of a viable party system, shared by now by McCarran, was distinctly bipartisan. Biltz declared, "What most of us are interested in is getting the right kind of people, and we don't give a damn whether they are Democrats or Republicans." Good government has nothing to do with party politics, what was needed was stability and men one could trust. "I have a philosophy," said Biltz, "that the hardest thing in the world to do is to protect yourself against a liar or a thief, and if you've got a liar or a thief governing your present and future ambitions or life, you're in trouble. I mean you're in deep trouble." Essentially Biltz wanted a government that ran smoothly, one he could deal with smoothly. To his way of thinking, Ed Flynn of the Bronx, who had a Nevada ranch, represented the finest in American government. Flynn's word was good and he represented "clean government."[93]

In the political sphere, Biltz and McCarran were close to John Mueller, with whom Biltz also had some business associations. Mueller had never held high office in Nevada but had long been one of the true kingpins of the state. A former state engineer, from the mid-1930s until his death in 1962, he was the leading lobbyist in the Nevada state senate. Biltz later described the foundation of Mueller's power:

> He had much of the same regard for politics as McCarran had for the law. He just abhorred any semblance of dishonesty or unfairness. And he was called the eighteenth senator.[94] Which is very true. . . . I don't believe there was one Senator that disliked John Mueller or distrusted John Mueller. He was working twenty-four hours a day, thirty days a month, and year after year, giving assistance to these men, whether they were in financial trouble, or mental trouble, or whatever their problems were. Johnny was always the father confessor and Johnny was the boy that went to work.[95]

But Republican Mueller's immense power stemmed from more than hard work and personal character. It also derived from the peculiar structure of Nevada's governmental system, in particular from the way the state senate was elected. Each of Nevada's 17 counties had equal representation in the state senate, in flat contradiction to a section of the Nevada constitution (Article 1, section 13) which stated, "Representation shall be apportioned according to population." Thus there was the anomaly of tiny Esmeralda County (614 people in 1950), Storey County (671 people), and Eureka County (896 people) together being able to outvote Washoe County (50,205) and Clark County (48,289) in the state senate. The disparity in population between the largest and smallest counties in Nevada was almost 100 to 1 (it was 200 to 1 after the 1960 census); yet they were entitled to the same representation. This system was upset in the early 1960s by the landmark *Baker* v. *Carr* and *Reynolds* v. *Sims* decisions of the United States Supreme Court. But in 1950, Washoe and Clark counties together had well over half the state's population and elected only two senators out of seventeen.

Since most small counties in Nevada were Republican, the Republicans controlled the state senate for 25 years, even in a state which usually voted Democratic. The situation meant consistent one-party domination of the legislature's upper house. Mueller had the prestige and knowledge to dominate this vital segment of Nevada government without himself ever being a member of the state senate.

McCarran cooperated with Biltz and Mueller; they, like him, were practical men who got things done, and they did not look too closely at a man's political affiliation. As indicated, Biltz and Mueller provided Republican financing for him; in turn, McCarran could provide business favors for them in Washington, D.C. Biltz, in particular, helped McCarran with his private finances, which were often in a chaotic state. His assistance extended to sending expensive new suits as gifts to the Senator,[96] and making sure McCarran's expenses for room and food were taken care of in hotels and casinos. More than that, Biltz provided friendship and emotional companionship more than did most members of McCarran's own often turbulent family. In one letter, McCarran indicated his trust and friendship for Biltz, who knew how to reach out to the essentially lonely senator:

> I want you to know, Norman, that I have never had many close friends in my life. I don't know whether this is good or bad, but I do

know that in these last years I have had a great joy and rare privilege in feeling close to you. I have a confidence in you which is rare and I know would never be misplaced. You never ask anything for yourself and I wonder if you know that the greatest happiness I could have would be to do something for you, my friend.[97]

In a letter to Biltz written after McCarran's death, Eva Adams told the Nevada entrepreneur that she remembered the senator saying to Adams that Biltz "is like my own son to me."[98] This was no exaggeration of the sincerely strong bonds that had developed between the two men.

The McCarran-Biltz-Mueller combine soon ran afoul of newly elected Governor Charles Russell. From the moment of his accession, Russell was in a difficult position, partly because of the peculiarities of his election. Although Russell was ostensibly the head of the minority party in the state, everyone realized that he had been elected because of the McCarran organization. The governor was to discover, as had E. P. Carville in 1939, that McCarran did not work for anyone's election without exacting something in return. The senator was not without ideas as to who should be appointed to various state offices. And his good friend, Norman Biltz, was even more insistent about having a voice in the governor's administration.[99]

Russell's dilemma was that complete acquiescence to McCarran's suggestions could ruin him within his own party. Therefore the governor attempted to be bipartisan in his appointments, and ended, not surprisingly, by fully satisfying nobody.

Although not following all of McCarran's suggestions, Russell made it a policy to avoid any appointments that might be anathema to the senior senator.[100] Two of his most important appointments did, in fact, originate with McCarran. Horace (Chet) Smith, a member of McCarran's staff in Washington, D.C., was named the state's budget director at McCarran's suggestion, although Smith was also a close friend to Russell, and Russell had served as best man at his wedding.[101] Russell also fired J. G. Allard as chairman of the Public Service Commission, replacing him with Robert Allen, who in previous years had been an important part of McCarran's organization. This change was also made at McCarran's suggestion. Interestingly, the chairman of the Public Service Commission also sat in on meetings of the Nevada Tax Commission, which oversaw gambling licenses, a matter in which McCarran frequently interested himself.[102]

Because of these appointments, newspapers in the state generally criticized the new governor. The *Elko Independent* was representative in its comments:

> Certainly it couldn't be that Charlie Russell in the few short months that he has been in office, could have found so many democratic office holders inefficient and unfit for further service. Nor, being a Republican, could it have been possible for him to have found affront in the particular democratic office holders he has seen fit to dispense with so quickly any more than any other democrats. And even were those dismissed on Russell's black list for some reason or another, isn't it a strong coincidence that they all happened to be personally obnoxious to Senator Pat McCarran, too?
>
> And isn't it even stranger that many of the democrats being dismissed are being replaced with democrats, instead of Republicans? And isn't it also mighty strange that Democrat Bob Allen, newly rewarded for his efforts against Vail Pittman, should be appointing republicans to jobs created by his ousting of Pittman men?
>
> Strange. It's the worst political fiasco Nevada has seen since the Wingfield-Thatcher bi-partisan machine ran the state of Nevada.[103]

Some of the fired officeholders lost no time in blaming Russell—and McCarran. J. G. Allard lambasted both men in a statement reproduced universally in the Nevada press. "I have always done the best job possible without bowing to the demands of political overlords," the fired Public Service Commission chairman righteously declared. "Apparently my greatest sin has been my refusal for many years to bow at the throne of Senator McCarran and the present purge is being directed by the Senator." The bitter Allard added, "It is obvious that Senator McCarran's domination of the state political setup in Nevada is complete with the governor merely carrying out the orders as they emanate from Washington."[104]

What probably hurt Russell more, however, was that he was accused by his own party's state chairman, Harold N. Stocker, of being "a tool of Senator Pat McCarran," and of "selling his soul for a handout." Pointing out Russell's "anxiety to do McCarran's bidding," Stocker maintained that the Nevada chief executive had "abandoned bona-fide members of his party since he took office."[105]

However, Governor Russell was to prove an effective and honest administrator for the state of Nevada. He also was to demonstrate a surprising and growing amount of policital courage. It did not take Russell long to discover he could not serve two masters, and in the end he became loyal to the Republican party. Although the relationship between the governor and McCarran certainly cooled, there was no irreparable break. The real break was with Norman Biltz, who all along had desired control of the Russell administration for himself.

Upon assuming office, Russell found considerable potential scandal. For one thing, purchasing of materials was based on political pull rather than open bidding, a practice that cost the state thousands of dollars annually. The office of state purchasing agent was one that McCarran had strongly desired to fill with one of his own men.[106] One of Russell's first actions as governor was to propose the establishment of a state purchasing department, which would place on bid the major items to be used by the state. The legislature agreed to the suggestion. But by so acting, Russell alienated some of his financial backers, particularly Biltz:

> Rather interesting was that when I went into office, I was frankly told that if the state of Nevada would purchase some of their heavy equipment—tractors and so on—from a specific company that in turn, it had been a custom for years that approximately two per cent of the purchase price would be put into a governor's fund. It would be used by the governor and made available to him when he ran for office again. I stated that this would not be done, and this same group in the legislature fought the purchasing department. Under the purchasing act it could not be done, and consequently then, I lost some of my closest supporters of my first election, who were against me then when I ran for office in the second election.[107]

Russell also discovered that Norm Biltz was gaining secret information from the governor's office, obtaining, for example, minutes of the confidential meetings of the tax commission concerning the granting of gambling licenses. When the governor voted against some of Biltz's and McCarran's wishes on gambling licenses, the news was in Biltz's hands almost immediately. Eventually the governor was able to trace the leak and fire the assistant who was reporting the information.[108]

However, disagreement over disposal of the Basic Magnesium complex at Henderson was the chief reason for the Russell-Biltz breakup. In March, 1951, the legislature approved the principle that the state's BMI holdings should be sold to private interests. In September, 1951, Biltz publicly announced that he would put in a bid for the property.[109] Later Biltz declared that the bid, financed through the New York Life Insurance Company, was for $39,000,-000, and would have assured the state of Nevada a handsome profit. There is, however, a real question as to the validity of Biltz's figure, because it is more than twice as large as the bid eventually accepted by the governor. Since Biltz knew of the other bid, it is unlikely he would have doubled it; rather it appears that he was attempting to make Russell appear foolish by giving an inflated figure. Whatever the actual bid, Biltz and his group were planning to resell the components of BMI at a considerable profit to themselves. Beneficence toward the state of Nevada was thus hardly the chief determinant of their bidding.[110]

To Blitz's surprise, the governor was not enthusiastic about his offer. When Biltz reported to Russell that he wished to bid on BMI (and there is no dispute that he and his group would have been the highest bidder) the governor coolly replied, "Well, Norm, I'm afraid it would be embarrassing to me if you happen to buy it." Biltz answered, "How can it be embarrassing to you if I'm the high bidder? I'm not asking any favors. I'm not asking to see the bids. I'm not asking anything. I just want it to go on bid." It was also made clear to Russell that if he went Biltz's way, money would be put in a safety deposit box for his use. Biltz apparently did not realize that this approach was inappropriate for the governor, who was a man of great personal rectitude.[111]

Many rumors about the Biltz offer floated around the state, surmising that it would be "the greatest steal in the history of the state." There were even rumors that McCarran would be in for a cut of the profits, that there was some sort of syndicate. But Charles Russell later emphatically denied that McCarran had pressured him in any way to accept the offer, and there is no direct evidence of McCarran's involvement with the scheme. Biltz broke with Russell over this matter, and McCarran did not. It thus seems clear that Biltz, not McCarran, stood to gain.[112]

Unfortunately for Biltz and his cohorts, the lessees at BMI also put in a bid for the plant. They offered to pay off the remainder of what the state owed the federal government—$19,000,000. By statute the lessees had to be given preference in any sale of BMI, and an acceptable offer of purchase would eliminate the need for public bidding.

Russell deemed the offer acceptable; and in May, 1952, a final contract was completed, selling most of the facilities of the Henderson townsite and the BMI plant to the lessees.[113]

It is probable that the state of Nevada lost considerable money from Russell's decision, but so did Biltz and his group. Biltz never forgave the governor, stating afterward that Russell had sold directly to the lessees because of his overly cautious regard for public opinion, his fear of embarrassment, and the feeling that people would criticize him if Biltz, his greatest campaign supporter in 1950, had won the bid:

> Charlie's a very honorable man, very honest, and rather timid, very
> nervous about criticism. And you can't be, in this job. You know you
> have to lay your back open to the whip. Like Truman said, "If you can't
> take the heat, stay out of the kitchen."[114]

Many of Biltz's friends argued that Russell lacked basic intelligence, was just not bright enough to know where the main chance was. However, the failure of insight was on Biltz's part, not Russell's. Biltz simply could not understand Russell's unbending honesty and conscience. What was principle to Russell became deficient intelligence for Biltz and his associates. Biltz failed to realize that it was Russell who was the more skilled politician, that perhaps the governor had used Biltz and McCarran to win a victory in 1950 that would not otherwise have been possible. Certainly Russell had enough political skill to be reelected in 1954, even though Biltz tried determinedly to bring about his defeat.

By 1954, McCarran's position in the Nevada Democratic party was obviously declining, as demonstrated by the circumstances of the 1954 gubernatorial race. The senior senator had no protégé seeking the Democratic nomination for governor, and public support for the Republican Russell was precluded by Biltz's break with the governor. Certainly the list of possible, and announced, Democratic candidates aroused little enthusiasm on McCarran's part. The possibilities, in descending order of merit from McCarran's viewpoint, were Archie Grant of Las Vegas, who had not been unfriendly to McCarran but was independent of him, Vail Pittman, and Thomas Mechling. Another possibility, who eventually decided not to announce, perhaps so he could challenge McCarran in 1956, was

Mayor C. D. Baker of Las Vegas, who had given vital support to Greenspun's suit against the senator.[115]

But McCarran and his organization, although frayed, still retained enough clout to dominate the state party machinery, mainly because of the senator's uncontested control of the cow counties. The January, 1954 Clark County convention was a complete disaster for the McCarran forces, with at least 60 percent of the delegates to the state convention favorable to the gubernatorial aspirations of the unspeakable Baker, and the rest split between Grant and Pittman. Even in the Washoe County convention, the McCarran delegates endured the ignominy of being forced to combine with previously anti-McCarran Democrats to win the day against a strong Mechling challenge. After winning, the victors instituted a unit rule for the Washoe delegation at the state convention. This provided an opportunity for convention delegate Reverend Jules Bagneris, minister of the Bethel African Methodist Church in Reno, to ask whether the unit rule worked the same in Nevada as it did in Georgia. When the chairman explained to him how the rule worked in Nevada, the Reverend Bagneris replied, "that's the way it works in Georgia," and sat down.[116]

At the state convention in Boulder City, February 5 and 6, 1954, there was a hot battle for state chairman between Las Vegas attorney Joe Foley, backed by the Clark County delegates, and Keith Lee of Reno. Foley made McCarran the issue, stating he was unalterably opposed to "jumping parties" and charging that in the past the senior senator had thrown official party support to Republican candidates —a situation that Foley found "intolerable." The "paramount issue," as Foley defined it, was Senator McCarran's past domination of the state chairmanship. The Clark County attorney's determined anti-McCarran stand earned him over 40 percent of the votes at the state convention. Lee defeated him by only 231 to 167.[117]

The proud old man's resentments boiled over at a banquet held for President Celal Bayar of Turkey, February 11, 1954. The seat of honor at the banquet was given to Mayer C. D. Baker of Las Vegas, at that time a widely mentioned candidate for governor. "Since when," the senator thundered at the State Department personnel who had worked out the seating, "does the Mayor of a city come before a United States Senator?" The officials tried to mollify McCarran by pointing out that the mayor was the official host, but that he —the senior senator—was to introduce the president to the audience. "I will not," the senator announced in a voice that carried through the audience. "I'll walk out first. Since when," he repeated, "does the Mayor of a city come before a U.S. Senator?" The situation eased only when Mayor Baker was asked to move over one seat, and the senator was installed in the seat of honor. As one newspaper put it, "Although McCarran and Baker sat side-by-side for the rest of the evening, a chilling silence separated them."[118]

The gubernatorial primary turned into a three-man contest between Grant, Pittman, never forgiven for his 1944 transgression and the unmentionable Mechling. At first McCarran supported Grant, who, although never in the senator's camp, was certainly the least obnoxious of the three. But McCarran's sentiment for Grant cooled noticeably after a Tonopah meeting between the two. There is no record of what transpired there, but Grant probably would not pay McCarran's price for support. In the end, McCarran officially supported no one.[119] He seemed left out of the campaign and, as was increasingly the case, bitter:

> I never saw the political game so slow and uninteresting. I don't know who has the best of it. Grant is so slow and dead and the rest of them the same. This Guy Mechling is making the best campaigne but that would be awful if he should win. Then there is a fellow named Ryan running for Lieutenant Governor, who is a second Harry Bridges, a Communist and he looks dangerous and that would be awful.[120]

On June 1, 1954, Vail Pittman won the Democratic primary rather handily, with 14,427 votes compared to Archie Grant's 9,660 and Thomas Mechling's 9,270. Although McCarran privately continued to dislike and mistrust Pittman, much to the surprise of many observers, he publicly indicated on June 3, 1954, that he would campaign for the entire Democratic state ticket. The reasons for this announcement are not really difficult to understand. It seems unlikely, as McCarran's daughter asserts, that the senator desired to elect a Democratic United States Senate so he could regain his chairmanship of the Judiciary Committee. The election of a Democratic governor in Nevada would have made no difference in the composition of the United States Senate, and no seat was at stake in Nevada.[121]

Instead, the reason undoubtely lies in McCarran's weakening position within the Nevada Democratic party. He probably desired a fifth term if his health held up, and perhaps even if it did not. Threats on his own political future hand hitherto made little difference to him, and he had supported Republican candidates in 1946, 1950, and 1952, when he was riding high. But now he was more vulnerable. Walter Baring, who was running for congressman at the time, has stated that it was labor, specifically the AFL, which pressured McCarran to support Pittman and Baring, with the explicit threat that otherwise he would never again receive crucial labor support. Others have argued that strong party pressure was put on McCarran, forcing him to go out on the hustings and campaign.[122]

McCarran surely would have preferred Pittman's defeat. He privately told Governor Russell that he was going to have to make a series of speeches on Pittman's behalf, but promised that he would leave the state when the campaign got hot. In a letter to Pete Petersen, the senior senator wishfully anticipated Pittman's early demise: "They say that Pittman will be elected, but his age and infirmities look toward his expiring in his term of service." Pittman, incidentally, was seven years younger than McCarran and outlived him by nine years. McCarran died two months after sending the letter.[123]

McCarran's public support for Pittman strengthens the contention that he was planning to run for a fifth term in 1956, a view almost unanimously held by Nevada commentators at the time of his death. He certainly sought to keep his options open. Otherwise, there was no need to campaign for a man he had so consistently opposed on previous occasions. As noted, the McCarran office, staff, and operations had become a full-time, self-perpetuating industry. It is not easy to stop such an operation; even if the senator himself had wished to retire, he surely recognized the dependence of many others upon him. Over the years he had convinced himself that he was indispensable in Washington, D.C., in the battle against communism. Furthermore, politics was McCarran's whole life; he was a man of few hobbies and interests outside of his work. Running for office had become a habit; he had run in 1902, 1904, 1906, 1908, 1912, 1916, 1918, 1926, 1932, 1938, 1944, and 1950—twelve times. Retirement at the age of 80 would have meant the end of the power that McCarran so thoroughly enjoyed. The bitterness and frustration increasingly evident in his last letters do not indicate a desire for retirement; that would mean the takeover of the state party by his many enemies. The evidence is that Pat McCarran was still spoiling for a fight.

Although his daughter believed that McCarran intended to retire, such a decision would have been entirely uncharacteristic. Eva Adams thought he would have run if his health had permitted, and

Pete Petersen declared that he was campaigning in 1954 for Pittman "to get a little harmony in the Democratic party" so he could make the run in 1956.[124]

But by 1956, McCarran would have been highly vulnerable in a reelection effort. He had caused bitter divisions within the state party and had broken relations with the national Democrats. Thus he might very well have suffered defeat by an aggressive challenger like C. D. Baker. A Republican contender such as Cliff Young, the popular young congressman, running on Eisenhower's coattails, could have been a formidable opponent even if McCarran had survived the primary. Defeat would have been the greatest humiliation for McCarran, but by 1954 it was a distinct possibility.

The question is academic. On September 19, 1954, at a rally attended by Vail Pittman, Walter Baring, and other leading Democrats, McCarran died of a heart attack.

CHAPTER 10

EPILOGUE

ALTHOUGH he retained most of his old vitality, Senator McCarran had suffered declining health for almost a decade. In December, 1946, he had endured an apparent heart attack while traveling east by train, necessitating a ten-day stay at St. Mary's hospital in Reno.[1]

In August 1947, he suffered a more severe heart attack in Tonopah, just before he was to deliver an address to the local chamber of commerce. Initially taken to the naval hospital at Hawthorne, he was then sped by ambulance to St. Mary's. Press notices quoted his personal physician as being "fairly confident" the senator would recover. But McCarran initially required three blood transfusions and early reports indicated he would need "three or four more" to remedy an anemic condition brought on by a series of hemorrhages of the intestinal tract.[2] The following year the senator had prostate surgery at the Mayo clinic, where he remained for two months.[3]

On November 1, 1951, Senator McCarran was admitted to St. Mary's hospital in Reno after complaining of not feeling well. Three days later hospital spokesmen announced that the senator had sustained still another heart attack and his condition was "serious." Although his office continued issuing the usual press releases as if nothing had occurred, speculation abounded in Nevada that the "old man" might not make it this time. He did eventually recover, but was forced to remain in the hospital for two months.[4]

Interspersed with these major attacks were various hospital "rests." For example in February, 1954, the senator checked into St. Mary's hospital for two weeks, suffering from bronchitis. He stayed at Bethesda Naval Hospital with regularity. For the most part he was able to see visitors, take telephone calls, and transact business during these hospital rests. But he had been told by his doctors that he was living on borrowed time.[5]

Despite all these attacks, the senator not only survived, he retained much of his vigor. Only three months after his 1951 attack he could write that "I feel like a million, for which I thank God every day." Although some observers were expecting McCarran's death at any time, most, perhaps fooled by his vigor, took him quite for granted. When one young man observed that McCarran could not go on forever, a companion responded, "You're talking silly, man. When I'm 85 McCarran will be 125."[6]

In 1953; McCarran celebrated both his fiftieth wedding anniversary and the fiftieth anniversary of his entry into active political life. These anniversaries occasioned many celebrations of his career throughout Nevada, as if it was now the appropriate time for valedictories. In August, 1953, the senator, his wife, and all five children went to Bermuda to celebrate his fiftieth wedding anniversary. When asked by reporters to outline his recipe for a happy marriage, McCarran answered, "My recommendation to a young married man are these—Let the wife run the home, you take care of things on the outside and you'll get along all right."[7]

The following month, on September 19, 1953, the Washoe County Fair celebrated Pat McCarran Day. Serialized articles on McCarran's life, written in the senator's office, ran in many Nevada newspapers. Republicans and Democrats alike joined in the ceremony, as if to testify that the senator had risen above partisanship. The truth is that he had devoured both political parties in Nevada. Governor Charles Russell presented a Nevada map, made of copper, jointly contributed by the Anaconda and Kennecott copper companies. Eulogies by prominent members of congress and other government officials were delivered personally and by tape recording Harolds Club provided the fireworks, and the Masons placed a green fez on the Catholic senator's head. The *Nevada State Journal* commented that this represented "the general wholesome atmosphere that prevails in Nevada when all join hands in paying tribute where tribute is due, regardless of creed, color, or political affiliation." The senator himself testified to the ecumenical spirit, "When a Masonic order bestows this honor on a Catholic, I say this indeed is America."[8]

Barely a year remained to McCarran. Strangely, the high honors and acclaim did nothing to raise the senator's spirits. Instead he became increasingly bitter and alienated, as is clearly demonstrated by his private correspondence. Mechling was a "commie plant" in

Nevada, the *Las Vegas Sun* was a "red paper," Truman was a "pissant in human form," Jews were "misleading" prominent Americans, Stevenson was a "damn fool." McCarran was profoundly depressed by the serious threat from atheistic communism and predicted inevitable war. On a more local level, enemies were appearing everywhere. The 1954 accommodation with Vail Pittman revealed only McCarran's growing political impotence, not any increasing tolerance. There was still much the senator felt he should do, but now so little time left.

Most of those closely associated with him testified to his continued strength and mental sharpness, but his letters and certain incidents demonstrate that the McCarran of 1954 was not mentally the McCarran of 1935—more because of a changed outlook on life than of declining mental acuity. McCarran had lost his earlier mental resiliency. Many on his staff later asserted that Eva Adams was assuming an ever heavier burden of office duties, and her own letters testify to her concern over the senator's health. The last session of Congress he attended left him profoundly tired; he felt buffeted by the young, energetic minority leader, Lyndon Johnson.

Some observers even believed they detected paranoia. In early 1953, a young Reno reporter, Ed Olsen, was astonished to see McCarran under strange circumstances. Some years later, he told the story to an interviewer:

> But after the Mechling episode, well, McCarran just sort of disappeared after the election. He disappeared from Washington, he disappeared from here; nobody knew where he's been for six or eight weeks. And one night I was in the Riverside with Melvin Belli, the lawyer who subsequently defended Jack Ruby. . . . I was in the Riverside with Belli at the bar, and he nudges me and he says, "Isn't that your senator over there?" And sure enough, by God, here, off eating dinner at a table was Pat McCarran with dark glasses on. So instead of perhaps being a little more polite and waiting until the man had finished dinner, I decided I'd better take the opportunity, since he was there right now, to go talk to him and find out what he'd been doing and where he'd been. So I went over—I'd met him, oh, dozens of times, but introduced myself again and my association with the AP.
>
> He very nastily said something to the effect of, "Well, what do you want?"
>
> And I said, "Well, I just wanted a story of what you've been doing the last six or eight weeks. Have you been on vacation or what? Everybody's been speculating about where you've been."

He says, "How do I know that you're who you say you are?"

I said, "Well, I don't know. You know me, but I'll produce some identification if you want." I didn't really have anything except a driver's license and a gasoline credit card or something like that; we never did have press cards. So I took those out and put them on the table in front of him, and he studied them and shoved them back across the table at me and bellowed out, "You're nothing but a Goddam Communist that's been following me across the country, that's what you are!"

And with that, he picked up the table with all its dishes and food and steak and cups and everything and threw it at me! He tipped the whole thing over in the middle of the dining room and got up and stomped out. . . . He apparently was in a tremendously emotionally overwrought state. It was certainly a shocking experience.[9]

Undoubtedly a sense of his imminent death and deepening loneliness fostered the senator's desire that his two oldest daughters, both sisters in the Roman Catholic church, live near him. Sister Mary Mercy's later book, *Once There Was a Nun,* reveals the levers he often pulled to gain special favors for the two girls. When Sister Mary Mercy went to Europe in 1953 and 1954, he made sure she was under both FBI ("a nice gesture from my good friend, the Director") and State Department escort and protection. McCarran was quite anxious that she return to the United States as soon as possible. He also wished Sister Margaret to be closer than Oakland, California, and in 1954, he made a determined, but unsuccessful effort to have her hired by Catholic University's history department.[10]

When Sister Mary Mercy returned from her European trip on July 19, 1954, she was met by her father and other family members at the dock in New York. Her initial impression was that her father had "failed." At that time the congressional session still had approximately a month to run. As she observed her father go about his senatorial labors, she noticed he "looked so exhausted some days, that I really marvelled at his constant patience, his ever ready smile, his attention to detail and his enormous capability." She was not alone in her anxiety. The ever solicitous Eva Adams wrote Sister Margaret almost at the session's end that the days were "long and tiring" for the senator, although she was impressed by his recuperative powers.[11]

When the session finally adjourned on August 20, McCarran went to Florida for three days on internal security business. Upon his return to Washington he checked into Walter Reed Hospital "and did exactly as the doctor ordered":

> He had no phone in his room. He went very quietly and almost incognito so no visitors would come; he ate only what was given— because the doctor wanted him to lose ten pounds. He read only light literature and he had a radio. Mother and I went to see him each day. We found him so sweet always; but he seemed so lonely to me.[12]

After two weeks of rest the "terrible fatigue seemed to have passed." He took a train west by way of Mayo Clinic, where Mrs. McCarran received a checkup. On September 22, 1954, he addressed a mining convention in San Francisco, and also saw Sister Margaret. But he was in a hurry to get home to Reno, where he finally arrived September 23.

On the morning of September 28, the senator told Mrs. McCarran he was going to Hawthorne, 130 miles southeast of Reno, to give a political talk. He planned to stay overnight and return about noon the next day, in order to celebrate his son Sam's birthday. Chester Smith of his office staff drove him to Hawthorne. On the way, he stopped at the family ranch, now rented, to inspect a new mowing machine. As the two drove on, "he slept a little and . . . once or twice he took a pill" (nitroglycerin).

Arriving in Hawthorne he received a shave and went to dinner with the commandant at the naval base there. After dining, the senator rode in an open car with the 1954 state Democratic candidates, including Vail Pittman and Walter Baring. McCarran's brief political message included an endorsement of all the Democratic candidates. "Every man on the ticket is my candidate," he said. "It is imperative that a Democratic Congress be elected in order that your Senior Senator may resume his position as head of the Judicial Committee of the Senate and continue his fight against Communism." Thus did McCarran call for unity for the Democratic state ticket and for the party, a party which he had divided more than any other individual. His conclusion touched a by now typically somber theme. "At no day in history," he declared, "has the U.S. been in such jeopardy as it is today. It is beset with enemies from within and from abroad in greater numbers than ever before."

Finishing his remarks, McCarran resumed his seat, and the meeting adjourned. As he stepped from the platform, some of the audience went forward to greet him. After talking to a woman who had a simple request, he started to turn away. Suddenly his knees buckled, and he fell backward to the floor before anyone could break his fall. There were no words at all. He died instantly and had no chance to use the nitroglycerin which was in his hand when he collapsed.[13]

Eulogies and comments poured in from politicians, newspapers, friends and enemies. The newspapers of Nevada all mentioned his great contributions to the state and his sincere interest in his constituents. All declared that a giant had died. The *Nevada State Journal,* which had always championed him, commented, "Senator McCarran's career . . . was marked by many political fights, some of them unnecessary and by a devotion to Nevada interests never exceeded by any member of Congress from this state." The *Reno Evening Gazette* was more critical in its assessment:

> Senator McCarran commanded either unquestioned loyalty or black hatred in Nevada. There was no neutral ground. And he likewise bestowed his complete friendship or loosed implacable fury. There was no middle ground for him, either.
> ✳ Over the years of his senate service, he brought great benefits to the state of Nevada, and his importance on the national scene brought reflected prestige to this state✳But his dominance of state political affairs and his demands for complete subservience from those who received his favors were scarcely beneficial.

One Reno newspaperman was the most unforgiving of all: "McCarran was a son of a bitch alive and he's a son of a bitch dead." But Hank Greenspun, who could have been expected to print a vitriolic assessment, did not. One suspects he was going to miss the senior senator. He penned the following:

> McCarran died as he lived—fighting. He could fight in fierce anger, courageously, with the power of a lion or he could do battle shrewdly, vindictively, with the cunning of a fox. And it mattered not whether the cause be just or popular. If he had taken a stand to defend it, he fought. And who today can say what his motives were, because though we may examine a man while he lives, it is beyond our power to judge him after death.
> There are men who pass through life barely producing a ripple, neither strongly liked or disliked, while others can barely stay afloat in

the mountainous waves created by the passionate loves and violent
hatreds which mark their stormy existence.

McCarran was a man of action[14]

McCarran's death aroused much national comment as well. The
Washington Post, which had consistently fought him, declared, "He
often used his power shortsightedly and for narrow ends. But no one,
even while disagreeing with him, could challenge his sincerity of
purpose."[15] On the other side, J. Edgar Hoover, in a telegram to the
widow, expressed a feeling common among the senator's supporters:
"His work will remain a living inspiration to those dedicated to
preserving the American way of life."

On November 8, eulogies for Patrick McCarran were presented in
the United States Senate. Significantly, of the senators who spoke, 18
were Republicans and only 11 were fellow Democrats, and most of
those were Southerners. Typically, Senator Joseph McCarthy, facing
imminent censure, turned part of his eulogy into a nasty diatribe
against the *Communist Daily Worker.* Minority Leader Lyndon
Johnson asserted, rather blandly, "There were many people for Pat
McCarran and against him. But nobody was indifferent. He loomed
too large on the national scene to be ignored." It was Senator Richard Russell of Georgia, however, one of the most powerful of all
senators, who pinpointed McCarran's achievement as a senator:
"Needless to say, he was an able and effective legislator. I doubt
whether any man who ever served in this body sponsored the passage
of more legislation, in wider and more varied fields, than did this
great Senator from the state of Nevada." The senator from Georgia
continued, voicing a universal sentiment: "No greater tribute can be
paid any Member of the Senate than to say that he stood for something. Senator McCarran stood for the things in which he believed,
and stood there fearlessly."[16]

McCarran's body was brought back to Reno. Eva Adams flew in
from Washington, D.C., to take charge of the funeral arrangements.
The family decided to have a church service first and then a state
service. On Friday night, October 1, a rosary was said for Patrick
McCarran in the St. Thomas Aquinas Church in downtown Reno.
The bishop officiated. The Fourth Degree Knights of Columbus, in
full regalia, kept guard over the body as the casket was opened, and
the public filed mournfully by for much of the night.

On Saturday morning, Solemn High Mass was held at St. Thomas
Aquinas. Pallbearers included those men closest to McCarran: Pete

Petersen, Alan Bible, Norman Biltz, Jay Sourwine, Chester Smith, Joseph F. McDonald, Jr., and Joe T. McDonnell, among others. United States Senators attending were majority leader William Knowland of California, Barry Goldwater of Arizona, Herman Welker of Idaho, George Malone of Nevada, Styles Bridges of New Hampshire, and Dennis Chavez of New Mexico. All, except for Chavez, were Republicans.

After the mass the cortege moved to the State Building. Preceding the hearse were the Knights of Columbus in their uniforms. They proceeded slowly up Arlington Street, crossed the Truckee River, passed the McCarran home, then turned left on Court Street past the Wingfield home, to the State Building, where the public funeral was to take place. There, Senator Bridges, perhaps the closest of all McCarran's colleagues, gave the principal address.

After the ceremony, the cortege proceeded to Mountain View Cemetery, three miles west of downtown Reno. The stores of the senator's native city were closed, and office and public buildings shut down in respect. Senator McCarran was laid to rest in the cemetery Mausoleum until a proper sarcophagus could be made. Mary Mercy's last view in leaving the cemetery was of the floral pieces, "One was a shamrock, one a cross, one was the American flag!" Pat McCarran was to be buried next to his mother and father, in the Nevada soil he so loved.[17]

On balance, the senator's contributions to Nevada politics were mixed. He gained much in the way of material rewards for his state, but politically, because of his temperament, his influence was divisive. Because his only criterion for patronage was personal loyalty, he contributed little to the improvement of state government. One important politician, who wished to remain anonymous, later alleged that "McCarran wrecked the Democratic party in this state." This accusation seems true enough if one evaluates the cohesiveness of the party and its unity of purpose.

One problem was that McCarran stayed on too long. Personality characteristics that were attractive in his youth—a take-charge, helpful spirit and great energy—intensified with age into an insatiable desire to dominate. The vindictive side of his nature was amply demonstrated in his later years. He was a man who knew his enemies and did not forgive them their sins. Yet his great power did not satisfy him personally. He could not relax, but became disappointed, melancholic, and bitter. He was a giant of a man, but something went wrong as he grew older.

Since McCarran's organization had only one goal—his own political aggrandizement—it did not outlast his death. The benefits of his extraordinary career for Nevada were far less than they should have been.

NOTES

Chapter 1

1 Patrick A. McCarran, "Autobiography," (Undated, unpublished typeset MS., personal possession of author), p. 1; Sister Margaret P. McCarran, "Patrick Anthony McCarran, 1876–1954," *Nevada Historical Society Quarterly,* XI(Fall-Winter, 1968), 10; *Appendix to Journals of Senate and Assembly of the Eighth Session of the Legislature of the State of Nevada,* III (Carson City: John J. Hill, 1877), 629; Richard H. Orton, *Records of California Men in the War of the Rebellion, 1861–1867* (Sacramento: J. D. Young, 1890), p. 290; *Territorial Enterprise,* April 26, May 29, 1889; Storey County Criminal Court Records, 1889; Interview with Sister Margaret P. McCarran, Oct. 16, 1974.

2. McCarran, "Autobiography," pp. 2–3; Sister Margaret P. McCarran, "McCarran," *op. cit.,* 10.

3. McCarran, "Autobiography," p. 2.

4. Patrick A. McCarran to Sister Margaret P. McCarran, April 5, 1939, McCarran Collection, Nevada Historical Society.

5. McCarran, "Autobiography," p. 3.

6. McCarran, "Autobiography," p. 3.

7. P. A. McCarran to Libbie Booth, Sept. 15, 1915, McCarran Collection.

8. McCarran, "Autobiograpy," p. 3; Commencement Invitaion, June 24, 1897, McCarran Collection. Mary Doten was the wife of Comstock figure and publisher Alf Doten. See Walter Van Tilburg Clark, ed., *The Journals of Alfred Doten, 1849–1903,* 3 vols. (Reno: University of Nevada Press, 1973) for an unusually rich view of Nevada society in the late nineteenth century.

9. Grades, 1897–1901, Registrar's Office, University of Nevada-Reno; McCarran, "Autobiography," p. 4; P. A. McCarran to T. L. Withers (Reno), Feb. 10, 1915, McCarran Collection.

10. McCarran, "Autobiography," p. 4.

11 *Nevada State Journal,* Oct. 15, 1901; McCarran, "Autobiography," p. 5.

12. McCarran, "Autobiography," p. 5; quoted in Howard Rushmore, "The Gentleman from Nevada," *American Mercury,* LXXVIII (June, 1954), 131.

13. *Nevada State Journal,* Aug. 30, 1902, Sept. 24, 1902; *Reno Evening Gazette,* Sept. 16, 1902.

14. Sister Margaret Patricia McCarran, "McCarran," *op. cit.,* 15; *Nevada State Journal,* Nov. 1. 1902, Nov. 6, 1902.

15. *Reno Evening Gazette,* Feb. 11, 1903.

16. Sister Margaret Patricia McCarran, "McCarran," *op. cit.,* 15–16; Interview with Sister Margaret Patricia McCarran, Oct. 16, 1974. Martha Harriet was born in 1882 and died in 1963, nine years after her husband.

17. *Reno Evening Gazette,* July 25, 1904.

18. Sister Margaret has written *Fabianism in the Political Life of Britain, 1919–1931* (Chicago: The Heritage Foundation, 1954) and *The Fabian Transmission* (Unpublished manuscript, Hoover Library, Palo Alto, Calif.). The publishing of this latter work was forbidden by the Order of the Holy Names. Sister Margaret is a woman of strongly conservative opinions who adulates the memory of her father. She vigorously endorsed and encouraged his investigations into internal communism in the early 1950s, and often discussed with him her views. Her two articles on her father may be found in *Nevada Historical Society Quarterly,* XI (Fall-Winter, 1968), 5–66, and XII (Spring, 1969), 5–75.

19. Mary wrote a revealing autobiography in collaboration with Ruth Montgomery, *Once there was a Nun, Mary McCarran's years as Sister Mary Mercy* (New York: G. P. Putnam's Sons, 1962). The rather gushy style in this book is more typical of Montgomery's writing than of Mary, who probably would have done better without a collaborator. Mary left the order after her father's death, to take care of her mother and sister Norine. She died in 1966, beloved by all who knew her. Norine died in 1980.

20. McCarran, "Autobiography," p. 7; *Nevada State Journal, Nov. 11, 1904.*

Chapter 2

1. Patrick A. McCarran to Sister Mary Mercy, Aug. 27, 1937, McCarran Collection.

2. The only extensive study of George Wingfield is Barbara Thornton, "George Wingfield in Nevada from 1896 to 1932" (Unpublished M. A. thesis, University of Nevada, Reno, 1967). This information was taken from pp. 1–3. See also Francis Wilfred Barsalou, "An Economic Analysis of Commercial Banking in Nevada" (Unpublished Ph. D. dissertation, University of Southern California, 1953), pp. 116–24).

3. May Wingfield, plaintiff vs. George Wingfield, defendant, Aug. 15, 1906, McCarran Collection.

4. Russell R. Elliott, *History of Nevada* (Lincoln: University of Nebraska Press, 1974), p. 222.

5. U.S. Congress, House, *Papers Relative to the Labor Troubles at Goldfield, Nevada, Message from the President of the U.S. transmitting Report of Special Commission on Labor Troubles at Goldfield, Nevada, and Paper Relating Thereto,* 60th Cong., 1st Sess., House Ex. Doc. 607 (1908).

6. Elliott, *History of Nevada,* p. 222.

7. Murray, Neill, Smith, to the President, Dec. 20, 1907, Jan. 4, 1908, *Papers Relative to the Labor Troubles at Goldfield,* pp. 8–9.

8. *Ibid.,* pp. 15–16.

9. *Bullfrog Miner,* Jan. 18, 1908.

10. Key Pittman to Frank P. Mannix, Aug. 15, 1908, Box 2, Pittman Papers, Library of Congress, reproduced in McCarran Collection.

11. Key Pittman to G. G. Rice, Aug. 15, 1908, Box 2, Pittman Papers, Library of Congress, reproduced in McCarran Collection.

12. Key Pittman to Sam Davis, Aug. 15, 1908, Box 2, Pittman Papers, Library of Congress, reproduced in McCarran Collection.

13. *Tonopah Weekly Bonanza,* Sept. 6, 1908.

14. *Nevada State Journal,* Jan. 2, 1911.

15. Quoted in Ronald Lee Watson, "The Personality and Politics of Patrick Anthony McCarran," (Student paper for Political Science 497, Aug., 1968, University of Nevada–

Reno), p. 18. The men quoted are George Smilanich and Frankie Davie. In personal possession of Jerome Edwards.

16. A number of people tell this story. My source is John Sanford, "Printer's Ink in My Blood" (Oral autobiography, University of Nevada–Reno Library, 1971), pp. 248–49; Interview with John Sanford, March 13, 1975.

17. A discussion of this case is Jerome Edwards, "Mary Pickford's Divorce," *Nevada Historical Society Quarterly*, XIX (Fall, 1976), 185–91.

18. Files, 1909–12, McCarran Collection.

19. *In Re Bailey*, 40 Nev. 142–43 (1916).

20. P. A. McCarran to Key Pittman, Sept. 29, 1911, Box 4, Pittman Papers, Library of Congress, reproduced in McCarran Collection. *Reno Evening Gazette*, Aug. 31, 1912.

21. *Nevada State Journal*, Sept. 1, 1912.

22. Both the *Reno Evening Gazette*, Oct 21, 1912, and the *Nevada State Journal*, Nov. 4, 1912, supported Bartlett, citing McCarran's lack of background in civil as opposed to criminal law.

23. Patrick McCarran to Pete Petersen, April 9, 1947, Petersen Papers, University of Nevada Library, Reno.

24. *State* v. *Scott*, 37 Nev. 432–33 (1914).

25. *State* v. *MacKinnon*, 41 Nev. 191 (1917).

26. Most of the material on pp. 16–26 concernng McCarran's tenure on the Nevada Supreme Court has appeared, in similar form, in Jerome Edwards, "Patrick A. McCarran: His Years on the Nevada Supreme Court, 1913–1918," *Nevada Historical Society Quarterly*, VIII (Winter, 1975), 185–205, particularly pp. 186–93. This article also analyzes his most important court decisions.

27. Nevada Constitution, Article VI, Section 11.

28. The most generally available book on Newlands is Arthur B. Darling, ed., *The Public Papers of Francis G. Newlands*, 2 vols. (Washington, D.C.: W. F. Roberts, 1937). A more biographic work is William Lilley, "The Early Career of Francis G. Newlands, 1848–1897" (Unpublished Ph.D. dissertation, Yale University, 1966). William D. Rowley of the University of Nevada–Reno history faculty is presently working on a political biography of Newlands.

29. The only available biography of Pittman is Fred L. Israel, *Nevada's Key Pittman* (Lincoln: University of Nebraska Press, 1963).

30. P. A. McCarran to John Redden, June 12, 1913; P. A. McCarran to Key Pittman, June 13, 1913, McCarran Collection.

31. P. A. McCarran to Richard Galligan, Aug. 28, 1913, McCarran Collection.

32. Sam P. Davis to Key Pittman, March 26, 1914, Pittman Papers, Library of Congress, reproduced in McCarran Collection.

33. J. M. McNamara to P. A. McCarran, Jan. 9, 1913, McCarran Collection.

34. P. A. McCarran to James D. Finch, Jan. 6, 1914, McCarran Collection; A. B. Gray to Key Pittman, Jan. 7, 1914, Box 28, Pittman Papers.

35. Sam P. Davis, *The History of Nevada* (Reno, Los Angeles: The Elms Publishing Co., 1913), pp. 11, 1172.

36. P. A. McCarran to J. M. McNamara, Jan. 12, 1914; P. A. McCarran to P. W. Feeley, Feb. 24, 1914, McCarran Collection.

37. See e.g., *Reno Evening Gazette*, Feb. 26, 1914, March 10, 1914.

38. J. M. McNamara to P. A. McCarran, Jan. 19, 1914; James D. Finch to P. A. McCarran, Jan. 29, 1914, McCarran Collection.

39. P. A. McCarran to Richard Galligan, July 30, 1914, McCarran Collection.

40. A. B. Gray to Key Pittman, Feb. 4, 1914, Box 28, Pittman Papers.

41. P. A. McCarran to C. M. McGovern, Oct. 10, 1914, McCarran Collection.

42. *Nevada State Journal*, Oct. 31, 1914.

43. P. A. McCarran to Joe Kelly, Sept. 23, 1915, McCarran Collection; Key Pittman to J. T. Goodin, Dec. 6, 1914, Box 6, Pittman Papers.

44. See Israel, *Nevada's Key Pittman,* pp. 32–33, 35–36; an official letter of the International Association of Machinists to its Nevada membership, July 26, 1916, endorsed Pittman, Box 12, Pittman Papers.

45. P. A. McCarran to Mrs. Jane Gourney Yoakum (Louisville, Ky.) Sept. 1, 1915, McCarran Collection. George B. Thatcher was attorney general of Nevada 1912–18; Denver S. Dickerson had been governor of the state, 1908–10.

46. William Woodburn to Key Pittman, Aug. 17, 1915, Pittman Papers, reproduced in McCarran Collection. Woodburn had been Washoe County district attorney, 1908–14, when he was appointed U.S. Attorney for Nevada. He was the son of William Woodburn, Sr., who had been Congressman from Nevada, 1875–76, and 1885–88.

47. P. A. McCarran to Sam M. Pickett, May 24, 1916, McCarran Collection.

48. P. A. McCarran to Miss M. Ethel Berlin, June 19, 1916, McCarran Collection.

49. *Reno Evening Gazette,* July 23, 1915.

50. Mrs. Denver Dickerson to Key Pittman, April 18, 1916, Pittman Papers, reproduced in McCarran Collection.

51. *Reno Evening Gazette,* Oct. 7, 1915, March 2, 1916, Oct. 29, 1916; Pat A. McCarran to A. W. Hendricks, March 9, 1915, McCarran Collection.

52. Key Pittman to William Woodburn, July 21, 1916, Box 10, Pittman Papers, reproduced in McCarran Collection; *Reno Evening Gazette,* Nov. 30, 1915.

53. P. A. McCarran to Pittman, Aug. 10, 1916, Box 8, Pittman Papers.

54. A. B. Gray to Key Pittman, June 23, 1916, Box 7, Pittman Papers, reproduced in McCarran Collection.

55. Key Pittman to William Woodburn, April 11, 1916, Box 10, Pittman Papers.

56. Interview with Sister Margaret Patricia McCarran, Oct. 16, 1974.

57. P. A. McCarran to Francis G. Newlands, March 1, 1917, P. A. McCarran to Key Pittman, March 1, 1917, McCarran Collection.

58. P. A. McCarran to Judge J. P. O'Brien, Dec. 8, 1917, P. A. McCarran to Key Pittman, Dec. 8, 1917, P. A. McCarran to Francis G. Newlands, Dec. 8, 1917, McCarran Collection.

59. Woodrow Wilson to Key Pittman, undated [December, 1917], McCarran Collection.

60. P. A. McCarran to Thomas E. Kepner (Reno), Dec. 26, 1917, McCarran Collection.

61. A. B. Gray to Key Pittman, Jan. 10, 1918, Box 7, Pittman Papers, reproduced in McCarran Collection.

62. A. B. Gray to Key Pittman, Feb. 24, 1918, Box 7, Pittman Papers, reproduced in McCarran Collection.

63. William Woodburn to Key Pittman, March 25, 1918, Box 10, Pittman Papers, reproduced in McCarran Collection.

64. A. B. Gray to Key Pittman, Nov. 11, 1918, Pittman Papers, reproduced in McCarran Collection.

65. P. A. McCarran to J. H. Causten, April 18, 1918, McCarran Collection.

66. P. A. McCarran to Joe M. McNamara, May 13, 1918, McCarran Collection.

67. P. A. McCarran to A. G. Stebbenne, Dec. 9, 1918, McCarran Collection.

68. P. A. McCarran to J. G. Thompson, Nov. 19, 1918, McCarran Collection.

Chapter 3

1. F. W. Barsalou, "The Concentration of Banking Power in Nevada: An Historical Analysis," *Business History Review,* XXXIX (Dec., 1955), 355–56, 359; Barsalou, "An Economic Analysis of Commercial Banking in Nevada," p. 217.

2. Thornton, "George Wingfield in Nevada from 1896 to 1932," p. 23.

3. Thornton, "George Wingfield in Nevada from 1896 to 1932," p. 56, quoted from *Nevada State Journal,* July 2, 1912.

4. George Wingfield to George A. Bartlett, May 18, 1910, Box 4, Bartlett Papers, University of Nevada–Reno Library.

5. Thornton, "George Wingfield in Nevada from 1896 to 1932," p. 32, gives many of these names, quoting *Reno Evening Gazette,* May 7, 1927.

6. Sanford, "Printer's Ink in My Blood."

7. Thomas Miller to Tasker Oddie, Aug. 21, 1920, quoted in Loren B. Chan, *Sagebrush Statesman: Tasker L. Oddie of Nevada* (Nevada Studies in History and Political Science No. 12, Reno: University of Nevada Press, 1974), p. 96

8. Sanford, "Printer's Ink in My Blood," p. 46.

9. Thomas W. Miller, "Memoirs of Thomas Woodnutt Miller, a Public Spirited Citizen of Delaware and Nevada" (Oral autobiography, University of Nevada–Reno Library, 1965), pp. 219–20. See also Sally Springmeyer Zanjani, *The Unspiked Rail, Memoir of a Nevada Rebel* (Reno: University of Nevada Press, 1981), pp. 303–25.

10. Harry Atkinson, "Tonopah and Reno, Memoirs of a Nevada Attorney" (Oral autobiography, University of Nevada-Reno Library, 1970), pp. 65–66, 69.

11. Joseph F. McDonald, "The Life of a Newsboy in Nevada" (Oral autobiography, University of Nevada–Reno Library, 1970), pp. 152–53.

12. The information on Baker came from the obituary notices in the *Nevada State Journal* and the *Reno Evening Gazette,* April 29, 1935. See also Chan, *Sagebrush Statesman,* p. 115.

13. Campaign Brochure, "Pat McCarran for United States Senator, 1926," McCarran Collection.

14. *Ibid.*

15. *Nevada State Journal,* Sept. 5, 1926.

16. *Nevada State Journal,* Aug. 22, 1926.

17. *Reno Evening Gazette,* Sept. 8, 1926; William McKnight to Key Pittman, July 12, 1926, Box 13, Pittman Papers, Library of Congress, reproduced in McCarran Collection; William Woodburn to Key Pittman, July 19, 1926, Box 16, Pittman Papers, Library of Congress.

18. William D. Swackhammer, *Political History of Nevada, 1973* (Carson City, 1974), p. 209.

19. Thornton, "George Wingfield in Nevada from 1896–1932," pp. 32–33.

20. Sanford, "Printer's Ink in My Blood," p. 48.

21. *Reno Evening Gazette,* Sept. 7, 1927.

22. Many suggestions for this discussion of the Cole-Malley trial were gained from the insightful paper by Erin B. Engelmann, "Nevada, As Seen Through Her Newspapers October 1, 1926–April 30, 1928" (Paper for History 914, University of Nevada–Reno, Dec. 16, 1974. Personal Possession of Russell R. Elliott). Also see Thornton, "George Wingfield in Nevada from 1896–1932," p. 33.

23. *Ibid.,* pp. 34–35.

24. *Ibid.,* p. 35; Agreement of May 27, 1927, McCarran Collection.

25. Thornton, "George Wingfield in Nevada from 1896–1932," pp. 35–36.

26. Quoted in *Nevada State Journal,* May 8, 1927; *Reno Evening Gazette,* May 7, 1927.

27. *Reno Evening Gazette,* May 7, 1927, May 10, 1927, May 13, 1927.

28. *Nevada State Journal,* June 5, 1927; Engelmann, "Nevada, As Seen Through Her Newspapers," p. 21.

29. *Reno Evening Gazette,* May 13, Aug. 22, 1927.

30. *Reno Evening Gazette,* Sept. 2, 1927; Engelmann, "Nevada As Seen Through Her Newspapers," p. 15.

31. *Reno Evening Gazette,* Sept. 12, 1927.

32. Thornton, "George Wingfield in Nevada from 1896–1932," p, 37.

33. Engelmann, "Nevada As Seen Through Her Newspapers," p. 21.

34. *Nevada State Journal,* May 8, 1927.

35. *Statutes of Nevada,* 1911, p. 295; Engelmann, "Nevada As Seen Through Her Newspapers," p. 21.

36. *Nevada State Journal,* Sept. 2, 1927.

37. P. A. McCarran to Ed Mulcahy, July 11, 1944, McCarran Collection.
38. *Reno Evening Gazette,* Aug. 25, 1927.
39. Interview with John Sanford, March 13, 1975.
40. See Sanford, "Printer's Ink in My Blood," pp. 51–53.
41. Elliott, *History of Nevada,* p. 272; Thornton, "George Wingfield in Nevada from 1896 to 1932," p. 44; *Reno Evening Gazette,* Feb. 3, 1928.
42. W. A. Kelly to Key Pittman, Nov. 15, 1931, Box 13, Pittman Papers, Library of Congress.
43. Chan, *Sagebrush Statesman,* p. 149.
44. *Las Vegas Review-Journal,* March 25, 1932.
45. *Nevada State Journal,* March 20, 1932.
46. *Reno Evening Gazette,* March 18, 1932.
47. Pete Petersen, "Reminiscences of My Work in Nevada Labor, Politics, Post Office and Gaming Control" (Oral autobiography, University of Nevada–Reno Library, 1970), p. 26.
48. *Nevada State Journal,* May 22, 1932.
49. *Nevada State Journal,* June 29, 1932; Interview with Tom Craven, Jan. 9, 1975.
50. P. A. McCarran to Sister Margaret P. McCarran, Feb. 12, 1933, McCarran Collection.
51. *Nevada State Journal,* June 28, 1932.
52. *Nevada State Journal,* July 1, 1932.
53. *Ibid.*
54. *Reno Evening Gazette,* Oct. 1, 1932
55. *Nevada State Journal,* June 30, 1932.
56. P. A. McCarran to Sister Margaret P. McCarran, Feb. 12, 1933, McCarran Collection.
57. J. T. Crawford to Tasker Oddie, October 15, 1932, quoted in Chan, *Sagebrush Statesman,* p. 152.
58. *Reno Evening Gazette,* Oct. 22, 1932.
59. *Nevada State Journal,* Oct. 18, 1932.
60. Pete Petersen, "Reminiscences of My Work in Nevada Labor, Politics, Post Office and Gaming Control," p. 27.
61. *Nevada State Journal,* Oct. 29, 1932.
62. *Reno Evening Gazette,* Oct. 31, 1932.
63. Tasker Oddie to H. N. Lawrie, Aug. 26, 1932, quoted in Chan, *Sagebrush Statesman,* p. 151.
64. These official returns are from John Koontz, *Political History of Nevada,* 5th edition (Carson City, 1965), p. 195
65. "Cow counties" is not used as a term of opprobrium, but as a convenient, popular phrase to denote the counties of Nevada exclusive of Washoe and Clark. It must be remembered that the economies of several of these counties, e.g., Ormsby, Storey, and White Pine, depend little on "cows."
66. *Reno Evening Gazette,* Nov. 12, 1932; Loren Chan, *Sagebrush Statesman,* p. 155.
67. *Reno Evening Gazette,* Nov. 9, 1932.
68. P. A. McCarran to Sister Margaret P. McCarran, Feb. 12, 1933, McCarran Collection.
69. Norman Biltz, "Memoirs of the Duke of Nevada" (Oral autobiography, University of Nevada–Reno Library, 1967), pp. 131–32.
70. Quoted in Clel Georgetta, *Golden Fleece in Nevada* (Reno: Ventura Publishing Company, 1972), p. 410.
71. *Reno Evening Gazette,* Nov. 18, 1932; *Las Vegas Age,* Nov. 19, 1932; "Report of the Joint Committee on Investigation of Closed Banks," pp. 8–9, in *Appendix to Journal of Senate and Assembly, Nevada, 37th Session, 1935,* Vol. 2 (Carson City: State Printing Office, 1935); James S. Olson, "Rehearsal for Disaster: Hoover, the R.F.C., and the Banking Crisis in Nevada, 1932–1933," *Western Historical Quarterly,* VI (April, 1975), 153 gives a total of $5,170,000 for RFC aid to the Wingfield organization. Mr. Olson contends that by its stringent repayment requirements, the RFC loans added pressures to the financially straitened institutions and hastened their failure (p. 155).

72. Georgetta, *Golden Fleece in Nevada,* p. 405; Chan, *Sagebrush Statesman,* p. 154; Jesse H. Jones, *Fifty Billion Dollars; My Thirteen Years with the R.F.C., 1932–45* (New York: Macmillan, 1951), pp. 42–43.

73. Georgetta, *Golden Fleece in Nevada,* p. 405.

74. P. A. McCarran to Sister Margaret P. McCarran, Feb. 12, 1933, McCarran Collection.

Chapter 4

1. See Fred Israel, *Nevada's Key Pittman* and Gilman M. Ostrander, *Nevada, The Great Rotten Borough, 1859–1964* (New York: Alfred A. Knopf, 1966), pp. v–viii.

2. Interview with Eva Adams, May 10, 1975.

3. See Chapter VI for a fuller development of this theme.

4. Pat McCarran to Joe McDonald, June 25, 1933, McDonald Papers, University of Nevada–Reno Library.

5. P. A. McCarran to Sister Margaret P. McCarran, Aug. 4, 1946, McCarran Collection.

6. The previous statistics are from U.S. Bureau of Census, *Fifteenth Census of the United States, 1930, Population,* I (Washington, G.P.O., 1931), 695–97, III, pt. 2 (Washington: G.P.O., 1932), 129–49; U.S. Dept. of Commerce, *Statistical Abstract of the United States,* 1934, 576ff, 655ff.

7. George Creel, "Under the Underdog," *Collier's,* April 6, 1935, McCarran Collection; *Time Magazine,* March 5, 1934, p. 8, scrapbook 1, McCarran Collection.

8. *Washington Daily News,* April 25, 1935, scrapbook 3, *Life Magazine,* Nov. 29, 1937, scrapbook 5, *New York Times,* Sept. 8, 1938, scrapbook 6, McCarran Collection.

9. Pat McCarran to Joseph McDonald, Aug. 19, 1933, McDonald Papers. Senator Pittman strongly concurred that too many Republicans were appointed to lower-echelon positions in the Roosevelt administration. He complained that men such as Ickes and Wallace "absolutely ignore any plea on the grounds of Democracy." Key Pittman to William McKnight, Aug. 17, 1933, Box 13, Pittman Papers, Library of Congress.

10. Pat McCarran to Joe McDonald, June 25, 1933, McDonald Papers.

11. Key Pittman to Pat McCarran, March 8, 1934, Box 13, Pittman Papers, Library of Congress; Many of the key documents of the 1934 McKnight controversy are reprinted in U.S. Senate, Committee on the Judiciary, *Hearings before a Subcommittee . . . on the Nomination of William S. Boyle to be United States Attorney for the District of Nevada, April 19, 27, and May 3, 1939,* 76th Congress, 1st session, pp. 81–87.

12. *Reno Evening Gazette,* Dec. 30, 1933, scrapbook 1, McCarran Collection. J. B. Clinedinst to Key Pittman, Nov. 6, 1934, Box 11, Pittman Papers, Library of Congress.

13. Interview with Tom Craven, Jan. 9, 1975.

14. Key Pittman to Pat McCarran, April 28, 1934, Pat McCarran to Key Pittman, May 1, 1934, Pittman Papers, Library of Congress.

15. Telegram from William McKnight to Key Pittman, May 4, 1934, Pittman Papers, Library of Congress.

16. *Reno Evening Gazette,* May 15, 1934, scrapbook 2, McCarran Collection.

17. U.S. Senate, Committee on the Judiciary, *Hearings . . . on the Nomination of William S. Boyle,* p. 43.

18. *Reno Evening Gazette,* May 19, 1934, scrapbook 2, McCarran Collection.

19. *Humboldt Star,* Sept. 26, 1934, *Elko Free Press,* Sept. 29, 1934, scrapbook 2, McCarran Collection.

20. Pat McCarran to William Woodburn, June 29, 1933, Box 16, Pittman Papers, Library of Congress; George B. Thatcher to Key Pittman, July 1, 1933, Pittman Papers, Library of Congress, reproduced in McCarran Collection.

21. William Neblett to Senator Harry Ashurst, Dec. 28, 1933, McCarran Collection; *Reno Evening Gazette,* Jan. 9, 1934, *Las Vegas Review-Journal,* Feb. 6, 1934, scrapbook 1, McCarran Collection.

22. The rumor of the $80,000 fee is from *Reno Evening Gazette,* May 12, 1934, scrapbook 2, McCarran Collection. On the Owl Drug bankruptcy see John Sanford, "Printer's Ink in My Blood," pp. 85–87, and most especially U.S. Senate, 73rd Cong., 2nd Session, Committee on the Judiciary, *Nomination of Frank H. Norcross, Hearings before a Subcommittee of the Judiciary . . . and before William H. Neblett* (Washington, D.C.: Government Printing Office, 1934).

23. Quoted in *ibid.,* p. 441.

24. William Neblett to Harry Ashurst, Dec. 28, 1933, McCarran Collection; *Humboldt Star,* Feb. 24, 1934, scrapbook 1, McCarran Collection.

25. U.S. Senate, Committee on the Judiciary, *Nomination of Frank H. Norcross* pp. 427, 429.

26. *Reno Evening Gazette,* June 13, 1934, June 15, 1934, scrapbook 2, McCarran Collection.

27. *Reno Evening Gazette,* Jan. 3, 1935, scrapbook 2, McCarran Collection.

28. Key Pittman to Frank Middleton, June 11, 1937, Box 16, Pittman Papers, Library of Congress; Joseph F. McDonald, "The Life of a Newsboy in Nevada," p. 160; Pat McCarran to Joseph McDonald, June 25, 1933, Pat McCarran to Joe McDonald, Aug. 19, 1933, McDonald Papers.

29. Key Pittman to William Woodburn, Oct. 4, 1933, Box 16, Key Pittman to Frank Middleton, June 11, 1937, Box 16, Pittman Papers, Library of Congress.

30. Harvey Dickerson to Pat McCarran, Feb. 15, 1935, McCarran Collection; Frank Middleton to Key Pittman, June 17, 1937, Box 16, Pittman Papers, Library of Congress.

31. Pat McCarran telegram to Richard Kirman, Jan. 11, 1935, S/A/K2/2/2, Kirman Papers, Nevada State Archives, Carson City; *Reno Evening Gazette,* Dec. 22, 1934, scrapbook 2, McCarran Collection.

32. *Reno Evening Gazette,* Dec. 30, 1936, scrapbook 3, McCarran Collection.

33. Les Kofoed, "Kofoed's Meanderings in Lovelock Business, Nevada Government, the U.S. Marshal's Office, and the Gaming Industry" (Oral autobiography, University of Nevada–Reno Library, 1971), pp. 119–20.

34. Raymond Moley, *The First New Deal* (New York: Harcourt, Brace and World, 1966), pp. 368–70.

35. Harold T. Smith, "New Deal Relief Programs in Nevada, 1933 to 1935" (Unpublished Ph.D. dissertation, University of Nevada, 1972), pp. 69–70, 74, 225; *Reno Evening Gazette,* June 27, 1934, Dec. 22, 1934, scrapbook 2, McCarran Collection. Key Pittman to John F. Kuns, Box 13, Pittman Papers, Library of Congress.

36. *Washington Star,* Feb. 9, 1934, scrapbook 1, *Washington Post* Feb. 9, 1934, scrapbook 1, *Reno Evening Gazette,* Dec. 22, 1934, scrapbook 2, *Reno Evening Gazette,* March 23, 1935, scrapbook 3, *Las Vegas Review-Journal,* April 3, 1935, story by Al Cahlan, scrapbook 3, McCarran Collection.

37. Key Pittman to Vail Pittman, April 28, 1934, Box 14, Pittman Papers, Library of Congress.

38. Key Pittman to Franklin D. Roosevelt, Aug. 10, 1934, Box 23, Pittman Papers, Library of Congress, reproduced in McCarran Collection.

39. Pat Mooney to Key Pittman, Aug. 8, 1934, Box 21, Pittman Papers, Library of Congress, reproduced in McCarran Collection; Pat McCarran to Joseph McDonald, June 15, 1934, McDonald Papers.

40. Fred L. Israel, *Nevada's Key Pittman,* p. 111.

41. Key Pittman to Pat McCarran, Jan. 3, 1935, Box 13, Pittman Papers, Library of Congress.

42. Robbins Cahill, "Recollections of Work in State Politics, Government Taxation, Gaming Control, Clark County Administration, and the Nevada Resort Association" (Oral auto-

biography, University of Nevada–Reno Library,) I, 107–10; Sally Springmeyer Zanjani, *The Unspiked Rail,* pp. 241–42.

43. Sister Margaret P. McCarran, "McCarran," XI, 31.

44. W. J. Harris to Pat McCarran, March 28, 1933, April 26, 1933, Sept. 30, 1933, Jan. 11, 1934, McCarran Collection.

45. See p. 183.

46. *Reno Evening Gazette,* March 9, 1936, scrapbook 2, McCarran Collection.

47. *Ely Record,* June 19, 1936, scrapbook 3, undated and unattributed newspaper article, scrapbook 3, *Washington Times,* Aug. 21, 1936, scrapbook 3, McCarran Collection.

48. Joseph Alsop and Turner Catledge, *The 168 Days* (Garden City, N.Y.: Doubleday, Doran & Co. 1938), p. 259.

49. Mrs. Harriet McCarran to "Margie and Mercy," Aug. 22, 1937, Pat McCarran to Mary Mercy, Aug. 27, 1937, Pat McCarran to Sister Margaret, Sept. 10, 1937, Mrs. Harriet McCarran to Sister Margaret, Dec. 19, 1937, McCarran Collection

Chapter 5

1. Harry S. Truman, *Memoirs,* Vol. I. *Year of Decisions* (Garden City, N.Y.: Doubleday & Company, 1955), p. 156; Alfred Steinberg, *The Man from Missouri, The Life and Times of Harry S. Truman* (New York: G. P. Putnam's Sons, 1962), pp. 145–46; Margaret Truman, *Harry S. Truman* (New York: William Morrow & Company, 1972), pp. 103–4.

2. *Caliente Herald,* Feb. 18, 1937, scrapbook 4, *The Literary Digest,* Feb. 13, 1937, p. 7, P. A. McCarran to *New York Times,* Feb. 8, 1937, McCarran Collection.

3. Lester D. Summerfield to P. A. McCarran, March 4, 1937, McCarran Collection.

4. Sister Margaret P. McCarran, "McCarran," XI, 45.

5. Patrick A. McCarran to Sister Mary Mercy, May 24, 1937, McCarran Collection.

6. *Elko Free Press,* April 29, 1937, *Reno Evening Gazette,* April 29, 1937, *Las Vegas Review-Journal,* May 4, 1937, scrapbook 4, McCarran Collection.

7. James Farley, *Jim Farley's Story, The Roosevelt Years* (New York: McGraw-Hill, 1948), pp. 74, 88; Joseph Alsop and Turner Catledge, *The 168 Days* (Garden City, N.Y.: Doubleday, Doran & Co., 1938), pp. 190–92; Leonard Baker, *Back to Back; The Duel between FDR and the Supreme Court* (New York: Macmillan, 1967), pp. 210–15; Burton K. Wheeler with Paul F. Healy, *Yankee from the West* (Garden City, N.Y.: Doubleday & Company, 1962), pp. 342–47.

8. Farley, *Jim Farley's Story,* p. 88.

9. *Washington Daily News,* July 19, 1937, *New York Times,* July 11, 1937, scrapbook 4, McCarran Collection; Alsop and Catledge, *The 168 Days,* p. 259.

10. July 10, 1937, *Congressional Record,* LXXXI, Pt. 6, p. 7022.

11. This statement poses a problem: who does McCarran mean by "Mr. Farley's candidate"? He is probably referring to William Boyle, who made no bones about his political ambitions and his close association with Farley. There is a possibility he is alluding to Senator Key Pittman.

12. *Ibid.,* p. 7020.

13. *Ibid.,* p. 7024.

14. *New York Times,* July 11, 1937, *Washington Post,* July 12, 1937, scrapbook 4, McCarran Collection.

15. *Nevada State Journal,* July 11, 1937, quoted in Fred E. Whited, *The Rhetoric of Senator Patrick Anthony McCarran* (Unpublished Ph.D. dissertation, University of Oregon, 1973), p. 211. *Elko Free Press,* July 12, 1937, scrapbook 4, McCarran Collection.

16. Pete Petersen to Patrick A. McCarran, July 12, 1937, Al Cahlan to Patrick A. McCarran, July 10, 1937, E. M. Steninger to Patrick A. McCarran, July 15, 1937, Julian Thruston to Patrick A. McCarran, July 20, 1937, McCarran Collection.

17. *Nevada State Journal,* Aug. 2, 1937, *Reno Evening Gazette* Aug. 14, 1937, scrapbook 5, McCarran Collection; Interview with Walter Baring, May 14, 1975.

18. Farley, *Jim Farley's Story,* pp. 120–22, 124, 133.

19. Key Pittman to Jack Robbins, April 19, 1937, Key Pittman to Richard Kirman, June 11, 1937, Box 16, Pittman Papers, Library of Congress.

20. *Carson City Chronicle,* Aug. 5, 1938, "Salmagundi," scrapbook 5, McCarran Collection. The "Salmagundi" column was written by Denver Dickerson, for many years one of the most astute reporters of the Nevada political scene. *Washington Herald,* July 24, 1938, *Las Vegas Review-Journal,* July 23, 1938, scrapbook 5, McCarran Collection.

21. *Reno Evening Gazette,* May 7, 1938, scrapbook 5, McCarran Collection; Albert Hilliard to Joseph McDonald, May 5, 1938, McDonald Papers.

22. *Elko Free Press,* June 17, 1938, scrapbook 5, McCarran Collection.

23. Full page advertisement, *Gardnerville Record Courier,* Nov. 4, 1938, 1938 campaign brochure, "The Record of Pat McCarran on Mining Nevada, A Friend of Silver," McCarran Collection.

24. Key Pittman to R. L. Douglass, May 27, 1938, Box 11, Pittman Papers, Library of Congress.

25. These accounts are taken from *New York Times,* July 14, 1938 and *Reno Evening Gazette,* July 13, 1938.

26. R. L. Douglass to Key Pittman, July 20, 1938, Box 12, Pittman Papers, Library of Congress.

27. *New York Times,* July 14, 1938, *Reno Evening Gazette,* July 14, 1938.

28. Franklin D. Roosevelt to James Roosevelt, July 15, 1938, Elliott Roosevelt, ed., *F.D.R., His Personal Letters, 1928–1945,* II (New York: Duell, Sloan and Pearce, 1950), p. 798.

29. U.S.Senate, Committee on the Judiciary, *Hearings before a Subcommittee on the Nomination of William S. Boyle to be United States Attorney for the District of Nevada, April 19, 27, and May 3, 1939,* 76th congress, 1st session, pp. 49–51; *Las Vegas Review-Journal,* April 21, 1936, column by Al Cahlan, *Elko Free Press,* June 15, 1938, *Carson Chronicle,* July 8, 1938, "Salmagundi," scrapbook 5, McCarran Collection.

30. U.S. Senate, Committee on the Judiciary, *Hearings . . . on the Nomination of William S. Boyle,* pp. 44, 62; *Ely Times,* July 11, 1938, scrapbook 5, McCarran Collection.

31. Key Pittman to William S. Boyle, Feb. 5, 1937, Box 11, Pittman Papers, Library of Congress.

32. William S. Boyle to Key Pittman, July 25, 1938, Box 11, Pittman Papers, Library of Congress.

33. Advertisement in the *Reno Evening Gazette,* Aug. 16, 1938, scrapbook 6, McCarran Collection.

34. *Chicago Daily News,* Sept. 7, 1938, scrapbook 6, McCarran Collection.

35. *Elko Daily Free Press,* Oct. 1, 1938, comments by E. M. Steninger, scrapbook 6, McCarran Collection.

36. Chan, *Sagebrush Statesman,* pp. 165–66; *Las Vegas Review-Journal,* Oct. 18, 1938, Nov. 5, 1938, scrapbook 6, McCarran Collection.

37. Key Pittman to John E. Robbins, Nov. 30, 1938, Box 15, Pittman Papers, Library of Congress.

38. Pete Petersen to Patrick A. McCarran, Jan. 30, 1939, Petersen Papers.

39. Pete Petersen to Patrick A. McCarran, Feb. 1, 1939. Peterson Papers.

40. U.S. Senate, Committee on the Judiciary, *Hearings . . . on the Nomination of William S. Boyle,* pp. 2–4; Pete Petersen, "Reminiscences of My Work in Nevada Labor, Politics, Post Office and Gaming Control," pp. 45–46.

41. U.S. Senate, Committee on the Judiciary, *Hearings . . . on the Nomination of William S. Boyle,* p. 16.

42. *Ibid.,* pp. 26–29.

43. *Ibid.,* p. 42.

44. *Ibid.,* p. 99.

45. *Ibid.,* p. 100.

46. *Ibid.,* p. 102.

47. Patrick A. McCarran to Pete Petersen, May 8, 1939, Petersen Papers.

48. *Reno Evening Gazette,* May 6, 1939; *Nevada State Journal,* May 6, 1939; Patrick A. McCarran to Pete Petersen, June 2, 1939, Petersen Papers.

49. U.S. Senate, Committee on the Judiciary, *Hearings . . . on the Nomination of William S. Boyle,* pp. 101–6.

50. *Reno Evening Gazette,* May 29, 1939, scrapbook 7, McCarran Collection.

51. *New York Herald Tribune,* June 20, 1939, scrapbook 7, McCarran Collection.

52. *Reno Evening Gazette,* June 30, 1939, scrapbook 7, McCarran Collection; *Congressional Record,* LXXXIV, Pt. 8, pp. 8221–28.

Chapter 6

1. See Von Pittman, Jr., "Senator Patrick A. McCarran and the Politics of Containment" (Unpublished Ph.D. dissertation, University of Georgia, 1979), pp. 35–54. Petersen's comments are on p. 47.

2. See, e.g., *Congressional Record,* LXXXVIII, Part 7, Dec. 7, 1942, pp. 9355–64, Dec. 8, 1942, pp. 9370–91; *Reno Evening Gazette,* Dec. 8, 1942, Dec. 14, *Los Angeles Times,* undated [Dec. 1942], scrapbook 11, McCarran Collection.

3. See Pittman, "Senator Patrick A. McCarran," pp. 58–73.

4. Pete Petersen, "Reminiscences of My Work in Nevada Labor, Politics, Post Office and Gaming Control," p. 39; Pete Petersen to Pat McCarran, Dec. 30, 1938, Pete Petersen to Pat McCarran, Nov. 4, 1940, Petersen Papers.

5. Pete Petersen to Pat McCarran, Dec. 30, 1938, Petersen Papers.

6. Pat McCarran to Pete Petersen, Jan. 3, 1939, Petersen Papers.

7. Pete Petersen to Pat McCarran, Jan. 16, 1939, Petersen Papers.

8. Pete Petersen to Pat McCarran, June 14, 1939, Petersen Papers.

9. Pat McCarran to Pete Petersen, Jan. 3, 1939, Pete Petersen to Pat McCarran, Jan 23, 1939, Petersen Papers.

10. Pat McCarran to Edward Carville, Feb. 26, 1940.

11. Edward Carville to Pat McCarran, March 7, 1940, S/A/F1/4/3, Carville Papers.

12. Claude J. Mackey to Key Pittman, Dec. 4, 1939, Box 13, Pittman Papers, Library of Congress; *Carson City Chronicle,* Dec. 1, 1939, "Salmagundi," scrapbook 7, *Carson City Chronicle,* Feb. 2, 1940, "Salmagundi," scrapbook 8, McCarran Collection.

13. *Carson City Chronicle,* Jan. 12, 1940, "Salmagundi," scrapbook 8, McCarran Collection.

14. Key Pittman to Joe Cleary, May 18, 1940, Box 13, Pittman Papers, Library of Congress.

15. Pete Petersen to Pat McCarran, June 17, 1940, Petersen Papers.

16. Key Pittman to William S. Boyle, May 14, 1940, Box 13, Pittman Papers, Library of Congress.

17. Key Pittman to Vail Pittman, June 12, 1940, Box 14, Pittman Papers, Library of Congress.

18. Pete Petersen to Pat McCarran, Aug. 12, 1940, Pat McCarran to Pete Petersen, Aug. 31, 1940, Petersen Papers.

19. Pat McCarran to Pete Petersen, July 10, 1940, July 31, 1940, Nov. 6, 1940, Petersen Papers; Key Pittman to Ed Clark, July 10, 1940, Box 11, Pittman Papers, Library of Congress, *Elko Free Press,* July 7, 1950, scrapbook 8, McCarran Collection.

20. Pat McCarran to Pete Petersen, Aug. 14, 1940, Pete Petersen to Pat McCarran, Aug. 12, 1940, Petersen Papers.

21. Pete Petersen to Pat McCarran, Oct. 25, 1940, Petersen Papers.

22. Pete Petersen to Pat McCarran, Nov. 4, 1940, Petersen Papers.

23. Pat McCarran to Pete Petersen, Dec. 21, 1940, Petersen Papers.

24. Pete Petersen, "Reminiscences of My Work in Nevada Labor, Politics, Post Office and Gaming Control," p. 42; John Sanford, "Printer's Ink in My Blood," p. 238. Interview with Eva Adams, May 10, 1975.

25. Interview with Berkeley Bunker, Oct. 31, 1974; Pat McCarran to Pete Petersen, Dec. 21, 1940; Pete Petersen to Pat McCarran, Dec. 19, 1940, Petersen Papers.

26. Pete Petersen, "Reminiscences of my Work in Nevada Labor, Politics, Post Office and Gaming Control, pp. 43–44.

27. Interview with Berkeley Bunker, Oct. 31, 1974.

28. *Reno Evening Gazette,* March 15, 1941, "Politics," scrapbook 9, McCarran Collection.

29. Pete Petersen to Pat McCarran, April 1, 1941, Petersen Papers.

30. Pat McCarran to Pete Petersen, Nov. 8, 1941, McCarran Collection.

31. Pete Petersen to Pat McCarran, July 8, 1941, McCarran Collection; Pete Petersen to Pat McCarran, Aug. 5, 1941, Petersen Papers.

32. Pat McCarran to Pete Petersen, April 19, 1941, Petersen Papers.

33. *Reno Evening Gazette,* Jan. 27, 1941, scrapbook 9, McCarran Collection.

34. James Scrugham to Thomas Miller, Jan. 30, 1941, Thomas Miller Papers, University of Nevada–Reno Library.

35. Pete Petersen, "Reminiscences of My Work in Nevada Labor, Politics, Post Office and Gaming Control," p. 44.

36. Pete Petersen to Pat McCarran, May 12, 1942, Petersen Papers.

37. Interview with Berkeley Bunker, Oct. 31, 1974.

38. Pat McCarran to Pete Petersen, May 30, 1942, Petersen Papers.

39. Pat McCarran to Pete Petersen, Sept. 4, 1942, Petersen Papers.

40. Les Kofoed, "Kofoed's Meanderings in Lovelock Business, Nevada Government, the U.S. Marshal's Office, and the Gaming Industry," pp. 101–2.

41. Pat McCarran to E. P. Carville, Feb. 16, 1940, S/A/F1/4/3, Carville Papers.

42. Pat McCarran to Pete Petersen, May 29, 1939, Petersen Papers.

43. Pete Petersen to Pat McCarran, May 29, 1939, Petersen Papers.

44. Pete Petersen to Pat McCarran, May 3, 1939, June 6, 1949, Petersen Papers.

45. Pete Petersen to Pat McCarran, Nov. 3, 1941, McCarran Collection.

46. Pat McCarran to Pete Petersen, July 10, 1941, McCarran Collection.

47. James Whalen to Pat McCarran, May 7, 1941, Petersen Papers.

48. Pat McCarran to Pete Petersen, May 14, 1941, Petersen Papers.

49. Pat McCarran to Pete Petersen, July 15, 1941, Petersen Papers.

50. Pat McCarran to Pete Petersen, Aug. 1, 1941, McCarran Collection.

51. Pat McCarran to Pete Petersen, Oct. 31, 1941, McCarran Collection.

52. *Carson City Chronicle,* May 15, 1942, "Salmagundi," scrapbook 10c, McCarran Collection.

53. Pat McCarran to Pete Petersen, March 28, 1942, April 20, 1942, Petersen Papers.

54. *Carson City Chronicle,* March 27, 1942, "Salmagundi," scrapbook 10c, McCarran Collection.

55. Pat McCarran to Pete Petersen, March 28, 1942, Petersen Papers.

56. Pete Petersen to Pat McCarran, March 31, 1942, Petersen Papers.

57. Pat McCarran to Pete Petersen, Oct. 15, 1943, Petersen Papers.

58. See Wallace Turner, *Gambler's Money, The New Force in American Life* (Boston: Houghton Mifflin, 1965), pp. 274–75; Edward Montgomery of the *San Francisco Examiner* received the Pulitzer Prize in 1951 for these findings.

59. Pat McCarran to Pete Petersen, Oct. 15, 1943, Petersen Papers.

60. Pat McCarran to Pete Petersen, April 19, 1943, Petersen Papers.

61. *Carson Chronicle,* May 14, 1943, "Salmagundi," Sept. 3, 1943, "Salmagundi," scrapbook 11, McCarran Collection.

62. *Sparks Tribune,* June 8, 1943; *Carson Chronicle,* Aug. 20, 1943, scrapbook 11, McCarran Collection; Pete Petersen to Pat McCarran, June 29, 1943, Petersen Papers.

63. *Reno Evening Gazette,* Sept. 11, 1943, Nov. 5, 1943, Dec. 10, 1943, scrapbook 12, McCarran Collection; Pete Petersen, "Reminiscences of My Work in Nevada Labor, Politics, Post Office, and Gaming Control," pp. 53–54.

64. Pat McCarran to Pete Petersen, March 10, 1943, April 8, 1943, Petersen Papers; *Reno Evening Gazette,* Oct. 27, 1943, Oct. 30, 1943, "Politics", *Las Vegas Review-Journal,* April 6, 1944, scrapbook 12, McCarran.

65. Pat McCarran to E. C. Mulcahy, July 11, 1944, *Reno Evening Gazette,* Sept. 23, 1944, scrapbook 13, McCarran Collection; Pete Petersen to Pat McCarran, May 9, 1944, Petersen Papers. Thomas Miller, "Memoirs of Thomas Woodnut Miller, a Public Spirited Citizen of Delaware and Nevada"(Oral autobiography, University of Nevada-Reno Library, 1965), pp. 176–177.

66. Pete Petersen, "Reminiscences of My Work in Nevada Labor, Politics, Post Office and Gaming Control," pp. 46–47.

67. *Ibid.,* pp. 54–55.

68. Interview with Eva Adams, May 10, 1975, Joseph F. McDonald, Jr., March 26, 1975, Walter Baring, May 14, 1975, Charles H. Russell, "Reminiscences of a Nevada Congressman, Governor and Legislator" (Oral autobiography, University of Nevada-Reno Library, 1967), p. 94, used by permission of the author.

69. Postcard for McCarran, 1944 material, McCarran Collection.

70. *Las Vegas Morning Tribune,* June 14, 1944, *Elko Free Press,* June 21, 1944, scrapbook 12, McCarran Collection.

71. *Reno Evening Gazette,* June 26, 1944, July 8, 1944, "Politics," scrapbook 12, McCarran Collection.

72. Pat McCarran to Rex Nicholson, July 14, 1944, McCarran Collection.

73. *Labor,* March 4, 1944, scrapbook 10c, *Nevada State Journal* May 31, 1944, *Labor,* July 22, 1944, scrapbook 12, *Las Vegas Review-Journal,* July 29, 1944, scrapbook 13, McCarran Collection.

74. *Nevada Labor News,* July 28, 1944, *Reno Evening Gazette,* July 29, 1944, "Politics," scrapbook 13, McCarran Collection; Nevada State Federation of Labor, *Official Proceedings of the Second Annual Convention, 1944,* pp. 68–69, 80–81.

75. Eric, N. Moody, *Southern Gentleman of Nevada Politics: Vail M. Pittman* (Reno: University of Nevada Press, 1974), pp. 37, 38.

76. Quoted in *ibid.,* p. 37.

77. *Fallon Standard,* Aug. 16, 1944, scrapbook 13, McCarran Collection.

78. Ralph H. Rasmussen to Members of International Union of Mine, Mill and Smelter Workers, June 21, 1944, McCarran Collection.

79. Moody, *Southern Gentleman of Nevada Politics,* pp. 36–37.

80. *Salt Lake Tribune,* Aug. 27, 1944, scrapbook 13, McCarran Collection.

81. *Ely Daily Times,* July 29, 1944, *Chicago Tribune,* Sept. 7, 1944, scrapbook 13, McCarran Collection.

82. *Reno Evening Gazette,* Sept. 9, 1944.

83. Moody, *Southern Gentleman of Nevada Politics,* pp. 43–44 has an extensive discussion of this problem. *Las Vegas Review-Journal,* Sept. 9, 1944, scrapbook 13, McCarran Collection; Vail Pittman to Private Denver Dickerson, Oct. 20, 1944, Vail Pittman Papers, University of Nevada-Reno Library.

84. Moody, *Southern Gentleman of Nevada Politics,* p. 43.

85. Vail Pittman to Denver Dickerson, Oct. 20, 1944, Vail Pittman Papers.

86. Pat McCarran to Mike Dowd, Sept. 9, 1944, McCarran Collection; Moody, *Southern Gentleman of Nevada Politics,* p. 44.

87. *Ely Daily Times,* Nov. 9, 1944, scrapbook 13, McCarran Collection.

88. See any Hearst newspaper, Sept. 17, 1944, *Reno Evening Gazette,* Sept. 27, 1944, scrapbook 13, McCarran Collection.

89. *Labor,* Oct. 7, 1944, *Labor,* Oct. 14, Oct. 21, 1944, carried many of the same charges, scrapbook 13, McCarran Collection.

Chapter 7

1. *Nevada State Journal,* scrapbook 23, McCarran Collection.
2. McCarran radio talk, Dec. 6, 1948, typed copy, McCarran Collection; press release, March 4, 1953, McCarran Collection.
3. Norman Biltz, "Memoirs of the Duke of Nevada," pp. 216–217, Interview with Robert Laxalt, June, 1976.
4. McCarran Collection, correspondence.
5. *Nevada State Journal,* Dec. 27, 1941, scrapbook 10c, McCarran Collection; Navy Dept. to Mrs. J. F. McDonald, Dec, 24, 1941, McDonald Papers.
6. L. B. Combs, Navy Dept. Bureau of Yards and Docks, to Joseph McDonald, Feb. 26, 1942, McDonald Papers.
7. *Las Vegas Age,* June 26, 1942, scrapbook 10c, McCarran Collection.
8. Pat McCarran to Joe McDonald, June 16, 1942, McDonald Papers.
9. Eva Adams to Joe McDonald, March 4, 1942, Eva Adams to Joe McDonald, Sept. 26, 1942, Cordell Hull to Pat McCarran, June 4, 1943, Pat McCarran to Joe McDonald, Jr., April 29, 1943, Joe F. McDonald, Jr. to parents, April 14, 1944, McDonald Papers.
10. Pat McCarran to Joseph F. McDonald, June 21, 1943, McDonald Papers.
11. *Las Vegas Review-Journal,* April 18, 1941, "Salmagundi," scrapbook 9, McCarran Collection.
12. *Reno Evening Gazette,* May 9, 1942, "Politics," scrapbook 10c, McCarran Collection.
13. Interview with John Sanford, March 13, 1975; Joseph F. McDonald, "The Life of a Newsboy in Nevada," p. 179.
14. Interview with Denver Dickerson, May 1, 1975.
15. See, among many possible examples, Eva Adams to Joseph T. McDonald, Jan. 20, 1944, McDonald Papers.
16. Interview with Eva Adams, May 10, 1975.
17. *Carson City Chronicle,* Nov. 28, 1941, "Salmagundi," scrapbook 10c, McCarran Collection.
18. Pat McCarran to Paul K. Gardner, April 17, 1942, McCarran Collection.
19. Robert Allen and William V. Shannon, *The Truman Merry-Go-Round* (New York: The Vanguard Press, Inc., 1950), p. 225; Alfred Steinberg, "McCarran, Lone Wolf of the Senate," *Harper's Magazine,* CCI (Nov., 1950), 90; Interview with Joseph F. McDonald, Jr., March 26, 1975.
20. *Nevada State Journal,* Jan. 20, 1949, scrapbook 26; *New York Sun,* Sept. 28, 1948, scrapbook 26, McCarran Collection.
21. Norman Biltz, "Memoirs of the Duke of Nevada," p. 181.
22. *Ibid.;* Interview with Jay Sourwine, May 1, 1975; Interview with Eva Adams, May 10, 1975.
23. Interview with Jay Sourwine, May 1, 1975.
24. Interview with Joseph T. McDonnell, May 6, 1975; Interview with Eva Adams, May 10, 1975.
25. *Ibid.,* Interview with Jay Sourwine, May 1, 1975; Interview with Joseph T. McDonnell, May 6, 1975.
26. *Nevada State Journal,* Sept. 30, 1954; *Nevada State Journal,* Sept. 28, 1970; Interview with Jay Sourwine, Aug. 4, 1969; Interview with Howard Cannon, July 28, 1969; Interview with Charles Sobsey, July 24, 1969.
27. Interview with Grant Sawyer, Oct. 29, 1974; *Time Magazine,* LXIV (Oct. 11, 1954), 30.

Chapter 8

1. *Time Magazine,* LV (March 20, 1950), 18; Herbert Block, *The Herblock Book* (Boston: The Beacon Press, 1952), pp. 24–25.

2. *Washington Times-Herald,* Feb. 8, 1945; *Nevada State Journal,* Feb. 8, 1945, *Sacramento Bee,* Feb. 12, 1945, scrapbook 13, McCarran Collection.

3. *Carson Appeal,* March 1, 1945, *Reno Evening Gazette,* March 2, 1945, scrapbook 14, McCarran Collection; Pat McCarran to Norman Biltz, Feb. 21, 1945, Norman Biltz Papers, University of Nevada–Reno.

4. Pat McCarran to Pete Petersen, March 6, 1945, Petersen Papers.

5. Pat McCarran to Pete Petersen, Aug. 3, 1945, Petersen Papers.

6. Confidential source.

7. *Las Vegas Review-Journal,* Jan. 4, 1946, "Nevada Politics," scrapbook 16, *Reno Evening Gazette,* Aug. 17, 1946, "Politics," *Nevada State Journal,* Sept. 1, 1946, scrapbook 20, McCarran Collection.

8. Pat McCarran to Pete Petersen, Aug. 3, 1945, Petersen Papers; Pat McCarran to Thomas Miller, Oct. 1, 1945, Miller Papers, University of Nevada-Reno Library.

9. Pat McCarran to Pete Petersen, June 1, 1946, Petersen Papers.

10. Thomas W. Miller, "Memoirs of Thomas Woodnutt Miller, a Public Spirited Citizen of Delaware and Nevada," p. 180.

11. Interview with Charles Russell, Nov. 26, 1974; Pat McCarran to Mrs. Harriet McCarran, Sept. 9, 1946, McCarran Collection.

12. Thomas W. Miller, "Memoirs of Thomas Woodnutt Miller, a Public Spirited Citizen of Delaware and Nevada," p. 205.

13. Pete Petersen, "Reminiscences of My Work in Nevada Labor, Politics, Post Office and Gaming Control," p. 66

14. Moody, *Southern Gentleman of Nevada Politics,* p. 79.

15. Pat McCarran to Pete Petersen, June 21, 1947, Pete Petersen to Pat McCarran, Jan. 7, 1949, May 3, 1949, April 1, 1950, Petersen Papers.

16. Pat McCarran to Pete Petersen, March 16, 1948, McCarran Collection.

17. *Nevada State Journal,* Aug. 14, 1948, scrapbook 26, McCarran Collection.

18. Pat McCarran to Pete Petersen, Jan. 19, 1950, Petersen Papers.

19. Pete Petersen to Pat McCarran, April 13, 1950, McCarran Collection.

20. Leggett was angry and hurt that he had been forced by Petersen to act this way. In Petersen's words, "We had a little difficulty in the beginning with Les Leggett. That was not exactly due to him not being loyal to you, but primarily for the reason that he thought a county convention should be conducted in the same manner as a fraternal organization," *ibid.*

21. *Reno Evening Gazette,* April 11, 1950, scrapbook 32, McCarran Collection.

22. Pete Petersen to Pat McCarran, Jan. 6, 1950, Petersen Papers.

23. Pat McCarran to Pete Petersen, Jan. 19, 1950, Petersen Papers.

24. *New York Journal American,* May 25, 1950, scrapbook 32, *Reno Evening Gazette,* July 8, 1950, "Politics," *Nevada State Journal,* July 9, 1950, "Nevada Politics," scrapbook 33, McCarran Collection.

25. Quoted in Alonzo L. Hamby, *Beyond the New Deal: Harry S. Truman and American Liberalism* (New York and London: Columbia University Press, 1973), pp. 288–89.

26. *Nevada State Journal,* Sept. 24, 1950, "Nevada Politics," scrapbook 37, McCarran Collection.

27. *Reno Evening Gazette,* June 3, 1950, "Political Scene," scrapbook 33, McCarran Collection.

28. Pete Petersen to Eva Adams, July 18, 1950, Petersen Papers.

29. Report of Research Services, Inc., Denver, Colorado, in behalf of William Wright, McCarran Collection. A copy of this report was sent to McCarran by Pete Petersen, Aug. 6, 1950.

30. Pete Petersen to Pat McCarran, Feb. 14, 1950, June 1, 1950, Petersen Papers.

31. Interview with Charles Russell, Nov. 26, 1974.

32. *Ibid.*

33. *Ibid.*

34. "Charles" to Norm Biltz, May 10, 1950, Biltz Papers.

35. Pat McCarran to Pete Petersen, June 16, 1950, Petersen Papers; an identical letter addressed to Norm Biltz is in the Biltz Papers.

36. Pete Petersen to Pat McCarran, July 10, 1950, Petersen Papers.

37. Interview with Eva Adams, May 10, 1975.

38. Norm Biltz, "Memoirs of the Duke of Nevada," p. 149.

39. *Ibid.,* pp. 151–52, 165–66.

40. Pete Petersen to Pat McCarran, Aug. 16, 1950, Petersen Papers.

41. Pat McCarran to Pete Petersen, March 8, 1949, McCarran Collection.

42. *New York Times,* May 8, 1951. Edward S. Montgomery of the *San Francisco Examiner* won a Pulitzer Prize for this finding.

43. Interview with Charles Sobsey, July 24, 1969; *Las Vegas Sun,* April 19, 1952, "Where I stand," by Hank Greenspun.

44. Entry for Feb. 12, 1952, Drew Pearson, *Diaries, 1949–1959,* ed. by Tyler Abell (New York: Holt, Rinehart and Winston, 1974), pp. 201–2.

45. *Reno Evening Gazette,* Feb. 3, 1951, "Political Picture," scrapbook 38, *Nevada State Labor News,* June 1, 1951, "Salmagundi," scrapbook 39, McCarran Collection.

46. *Boulder City News,* June 22, 1951.

47. Pat McCarran to Leonard Carpenter, Aug. 7, 1950, McCarran Collection.

48. *Elko Free Press,* March 14, 1952, scrapbook 42, McCarran Collection.

49. *Congressional Record,* June 18, 1952, XCVIII, Part 6, pp. 7496–98.

Chapter 9

1. *Washington Post,* July 10, 1952, scrapbook 47, McCarran Collection.

2. U.S. Bureau of the Census, *Census of Population: 1950.* Vol. 1, *Number of Inhabitants* (Washington, D.C.: G.P.O., 1952), pp. 28–4 to 28–6.

3. U.S. Bureau of the Census, *Census of Population: 1950,* Vol. II, *Characteristics of Population,* Part 28, pp. 28–25 to 28–26.

4. William Howard Moore, *The Kefauver Committee and the Politics of Crime, 1950–1952* (Columbia: University of Missouri Press, 1974), pp. 49–66; Interview with Jay Sourwine, May 1, 1975; *Congressional Record,* May 3, 1950, XC, Part 5, pp. 6244–45; U.S. Senate, Special Committee to Investigate Organized Crime in Interstate Commerce, *Third Interim Report,* 82nd Congress, 1st Session, S. Report No. 307 (Washington, D.C.: G.P.O., 1951); Joseph Bruce Gorman, *Kefauver, a Political Biography* (New York: Oxford University Press, 1971), pp. 75–76.

5. U.S. Senate, Special Committee to Investigate Organized Crime, *Third Interim Report,* p. 94.

6. *Ibid.,* pp. 90–91; U.S. Senate, Special Committee to Investigate Organized Crime in Interstate Commerce, *Investigation of Organized Crime in Interstate Commerce, Hearings,* Part 10, *Nevada-California* (Washington, D.C.: G.P.O., 1951), pp. 2–34.

7. U.S. Senate, Special Committee to Investigate Organized Crime, *Third Interim Report,* pp. 90–94.

8. U.S. Senate, Special Committee to Investigate Organized Crime, *Investigation of Organized Crime in Interstate Commerce, Hearings,* Part 10, *Nevada-California,* pp. 10–11, 24.

9. *Ibid.,* p. 943.

10. References to this are sprinkled throughout the Kefauver hearings and report; a comprehensive discussion is found in U.S. Senate Special Committee to Investigate Organized Crime, *Third Interim Report,* pp. 99–100.

11. Moore, *The Kefauver Committee,* pp. 158–60.

12. Robbins Cahill, "Recollections of Work in State Politics, Government, Taxation, Gaming Control, Clark County Administration, and the Nevada Resort Association," (oral autobiography, University of Nevada–Reno Library, 1976), p. vi.

13. An interesting discussion of this is found in Norman Biltz, "Memoirs of the Duke of Nevada," pp. 228–31.

14. Statement by Pat McCarran before the Senate Finance Committee, Aug. 15, 1951, McCarran Collection.

15. The main gambling street in Reno.

16. This refers to the closure of the Wingfield banks in October, 1932.

17. Senator "Molly" Malone.

18. Robbins Cahill, "Recollections of Work in State Politics, Government, Taxation, Gaming Control, Clark County Administration, and the Nevada Resort Association," p. 1150.

19. Pat McCarran to Joseph F. McDonald, July 3, 1951, McCarran Collection. See also Pat McCarran to Pete Petersen, June 23, 1951, McCarran Collection.

20. *Las Vegas Sun,* Feb. 6, 1955.

21. Hank Greenspun with Alex Pelle, *Where I Stand, The Record of a Reckless Man* (New York: David McKay Company, 1966), pp. 1–74; Richard Donovan and Douglass Cater, "Of Gamblers, a Senator, and a Sun that Wouldn't Set," *The Reporter,* VIII (June 9, 1953), 26. Most of the material on pp. 155–167 concerning Senator McCarran and the *Las Vegas Sun* has appeared, in similar form, in Jerome Edwards, "The *Sun* and the Senator," *Nevada Historical Society Quarterly,* XXIV (Spring, 1981), 3–16.

22. Greenspun, *Where I Stand,* pp. 74–181, 188–92.

23. Greenspun, *Where I Stand,* pp. 181–86.

24. *Ibid.,* p. 184; N. W. Ayers & Sons, *Directory, Newspapers and Periodicals, 1952.* p. 1187.

25. Greenspun, *Where I Stand,* pp. 195–96.

26. *Nevada State Labor News,* May 11, 1951, "Salmagundi," scrapbook 39, McCarran Collection.

27. Greenspun, *Where I Stand,* pp. 199–200.

28. *Ibid.,* p. 200; *Las Vegas Sun,* March 28, 1952, Greenspun column; *Las Vegas Sun,* April 9, 1952; Donovan and Cater, "Of Gamblers, a Senator, and a Sun that Wouldn't Set," 196.

29. Greenspun, *Where I Stand,* pp. 200–1.

30. *Ibid.,* pp. 201–2.

31. *Las Vegas Sun,* March 27, 1951, Greenspun column; *Las Vegas Sun,* March 31, 1952.

32. Interview with Denver Dickerson, May 1, 1975; *Las Vegas Sun,* April 9, 1952, *Las Vegas Sun,* April 19, 1952, "Where I Stand" by Hank Greenspun; *New York Times,* April 10, 1952, scrapbook 44, *Nevada State Journal,* April 10, 1952, scrapbook 45, McCarran Collection.

33. Greenspun, *Where I Stand,* pp. 203–4.

34. *Ibid.,* p. 204.

35. *Ibid.,* pp. 204–5; *Las Vegas Sun,* May 23, 1952; *Reno Evening Gazette,* May 23, 1952, scrapbook 45, McCarran Collection.

36. Greenspun, *Where I Stand,* p. 205; *Las Vegas Sun,* June 7, 1952; *Reno Evening Gazette,* May 21, 1952, scrapbook 45; *Reno Evening Gazette,* May 22, 1952, scrapbook 45, *Reno Evening Gazette,* June 7, 1952, scrapbook 46, McCarran Collection.

37. Norman Biltz, "Memoirs of the Duke of Nevada," p. 174; Interview with Eva Adams, May 10, 1975.

38. Benny Binion, "Some Recollections of a Texas and Las Vegas Gaming Operator" (Unpublished oral autobiography, University of Nevada-Reno Library 1976), p. 85.

39. *New York Journal American,* Nov. 25, 1952, Westbrook Pegler column, McCarran Collection; John Sanford, "Printer's Ink in My Blood," p. 421; Interview with John Sanford, March 13, 1975; Harvey Matusow, *False Witness* (New York: Cameron & Kahn, 1955), pp. 160–61.

40. Greenspun, *Where I Stand,* pp. 209–22; *Elko Free Press,* Oct. 14, 1952, *Las Vegas Review-Journal,* Oct. 14, 1952, *Nevada State Journal,* Oct. 15, 1952, scrapbook 48, McCarran Collection; *Las Vegas Sun,* Oct. 14, 1952; Perry Bruce Kaufman, "The Best City of Them All: A History of Las Vegas, 1930–1960" (Unpublished Ph.D dissertation, University of California, Santa Barbara, 1974), pp. 504–6.

41. Patrick McCarran to Mrs. Patrick McCarran, Oct. 2, 1952, Sister Margaret Patricia McCarran to Mrs. Patrick McCarran, Sept. 18, 1952, McCarran Collection.

42. *Las Vegas Review-Journal,* Nov. 28, 1952; scrapbook 49, McCarran Collection.

43. *Washington Post,* Dec. 30, 1952, scrapbook 53, *Nevada State Journal,* Dec. 30, 1952, scrapbook 49, McCarran Collection.

44. Eva Adams to Jay Sourwine, Dec. 20, 1952, McCarran Collection, *Nevada State Journal,* Dec. 25, 1952, Jan 18, 1953, scrapbook 49, McCarran Collection.

45. Greenspun, *Where I Stand,* pp. 225–28; *Nevada State Journal,* Feb. 14, 1953, Feb. 15, 1953, scrapbook 49, McCarran Collection; Interview with Bryn Armstrong, Oct. 30, 1974.

46. Quoted in *Elko Independent,* Feb. 19, 1953, scrapbook 49, McCarran Collection.

47. Patrick McCarran to Mrs. Patrick McCarran, Feb. 2, 1953, McCarran Collection.

48. Eva Adams to Sister Margaret P. McCarran, March 25, 1953, McCarran Collection.

49. David M. Oshinsky, "Labor's Cold War: the CIO and the Communists," in Robert Griffith and Athan Theoharis, *The Specter; Original Essays on the Cold War and the Origins of McCarthyism* (New York: New Viewpoints, 1974), pp. 118–70.

50. McCarran Office press release, undated [Dec. 1952], Speech of McCarran to American Mining Congress, Sept. 23, 1952, McCarran Collection.

51. *The Union,* XI (Aug. 25, 1952), 3, Vail Pittman Papers, University of Nevada-Reno Library.

52. U.S. Senate, Committee on the Judiciary, Subcommittee to Investigate the Administration of the Internal Security Act and Other Internal Security Laws, *Communist Domination of Union Officials in Vital Defense Industry—International Union of Mine, Mill and Smelter Workers,* 82nd Congress, 2nd Session (Washington, D.C.: G.P.O., 1952), p. 2.

53. See *ibid.,* pp. 225, 250, 261 for examples.

54. *Ibid.,* pp. 158–59.

55. Matusow, *False Witness,* pp. 160ff.

56. *Reno Evening Gazette,* July 21, 1951, "Political Picture," scrapbook 39, *Nevada State News,* April 2, 1952, "Salmagundi," scrapbook 45, McCarran Collection.

57. Pete Petersen, "Reminiscences of My Work in Nevada Labor, Politics, Post Office and Gaming Control," p. 62.

58. *Washington Daily News,* April 14, 1952, Peter Edson column, scrapbook 44, *Nevada State News,* May 30, 1952, "Salmagundi," scrapbook 45, McCarran Collection; John Sanford, "Printer's Ink in My Blood," pp. 339–40.

59. *Las Vegas Sun,* Feb. 19, 1952, Greenspun column, scrapbook 42, McCarran Collection.

60. *Washington Evening Star,* Sept. 4, 1952, scrapbook 47, *Louisville Courier Journal,* Sept. 4, 1952, scrapbook 48, McCarran Collection.

61. *Reno Evening Gazette,* March 15, 1952, "Nevada Political Picture," scrapbook 42, McCarran Collection; C. C. Smith and Charles Kinsman, Jr., "Nevada," in Paul T. David, Malcolm Moos, Ralph Goldman, eds., *Presidential Nominating Politics in 1952,* V *The West* (Baltimore: The Johns Hopkins Press, 1954), pp. 112–13.

62. *Reno Evening Gazette,* July 25, 1952, July 26, 1952, "Nevada Political Picture," scrapbook 46, McCarran Collection; Interview with Walter Baring, May 14, 1975.

63. *Elko Free Press,* Aug. 29, 1952, scrapbook 48, McCarran Collection; Pete Petersen, "Reminiscences of My work in Nevada Labor, Politics, Post Office and Gaming Control," p. 62; Joseph F. McDonald, "The Life of a Newsboy in Nevada," p. 173; Interview with Alan Bible, July 24, 1969.

64. *Las Vegas Sun,* Aug. 30, 1952, Greenspun column; Len Carpenter to Patrick McCarran, June 16, 1952, McCarran Collection.

65. *Elko Free Press,* Sept. 5, 1952, *Fallon Eagle,* Sept. 6, 1952, *Reno Evening Gazette,* Sept. 6, 1952, scrapbook 48, McCarran Collection; Mary Ellen Glass, *Nevada's Turbulent '50s: Decade of Political and Economic Change.* Nevada Studies in History and Political Science, No. 15. (Reno: University of Nevada Press, 1981), pp. 99–100.

66. *Elko Free Press,* October 17, 1952, scrapbook 48, *Nevada State Journal,* Oct. 18, 1952, McCarran Collection.

67. Tom Mechling, "I Battled McCarran's Machine," *The Reporter,* VIII (June 9, 1953), 23–24.

68. Norm Biltz, "Memoirs of the Duke of Nevada," p. 144. Biltz asserts that McCarran was in tears before making his announcement; John Sanford, "Printer's Ink in My Blood," p. 343; John F. Cahlan, "Reminiscences of a Reno and Las Vegas Newspaperman, University Regent and Public Spirited Citizen" (Oral autobiography, University of Nevada-Reno Library, 1968), p. 257.

69. *Nevada State Journal,* Oct. 24, 1952, scrapbook 48, McCarran Collection.

70. *Nevada State Journal,* Oct. 25, 1952, scrapbook 48, McCarran Collection.

71. *Elko Free Press,* Oct. 25, 1952, scrapbook 48, McCarran Collection.

72. *Ibid.,* Oct. 27, 1952.

73. *Ibid.,* Oct. 30, 1952.

74. Norm Biltz, "Memoirs of the Duke of Nevada," pp. 141–42; *Reno Evening Gazette,* Oct. 29, 1952, scrapbook 48, McCarran Collection.

75. *Nevada State Journal,* Oct. 31, 1952, McCarran Collection.

76. *Nevada State Journal,* Nov. 1, 1952; *Reno Evening Gazette,* Oct. 29, 1952.

77. Interview with Ed Olsen, Nov. 26, 1974; Interview with Bryn Armstrong, Oct. 30, 1974; Pete Petersen, "Reminiscences of My Work in Nevada Labor, Politics, Post Office and Gaming Control," p. 64; Norm Biltz, "Memoirs of the Duke of Nevada," pp. 138–39.

78. *Reno Evening Gazette,* Nov. 8, 1952, scrapbook 49, McCarran Collection.

79. Interview with Ed Olsen, Nov. 26, 1974; Glass, *Nevada's Turbulent '50s,* pp. 101–2.

80. *Las Vegas Sun,* Oct. 28, 1952.

81. This refers to Mrs. Malone, who had the reputation of being aggressive.

82. Patrick McCarran to Mrs. McCarran, Sept. 23, 1952, McCarran Collection.

83. This was incorrect.

84. Patrick McCarran to Mrs. McCarran, Oct. 2, 1952, McCarran Collection.

85. Patrick McCarran to Mrs. McCarran, Oct. 20, 1952, McCarran Collection.

86. *Ibid.*

87. Patrick McCarran to Mrs. McCarran, Oct. 28, 1952. McCarran Collection.

88. Patrick McCarran to Mrs. McCarran, Nov. 4, 1952, McCarran Collection.

89. This material on Biltz's life is drawn from Freeman Lincoln, "Norman Biltz, Duke of Nevada," *Fortune,* L (Sept. 1954), 141–43 and Norman Biltz, "Memoirs of the Duke of Nevada," pp. 1–70.

90. Lincoln, "Norman Biltz," 141; Interview with Denver Dickerson, May 1, 1975; Interview with Ed Olsen, Nov. 26, 1974.

91. Norman Biltz, "Memoirs of the Duke of Nevada," pp. 33, 34; Lincoln, "Norman Biltz," 142, 146–48.

92. The phrase is from Eva Adams. Interview with Eva Adams, May 10, 1975.

93. Lincoln, "Norman Biltz," 141; Norman Biltz, "Memoirs of the Duke of Nevada," pp. 160, 238.

94. Nevada officially had seventeen state senators.

95. Norman Biltz, "Memoirs of the Duke of Nevada," pp. 211–12; Charles H. Russell, "Reminiscences of a Nevada Congressman, Governor, and Legislator," pp. 41, 221.

96. Pat McCarran to Norm Biltz, June 25, 1951, Biltz Papers, University of Nevada-Reno.

97. Pat McCarran to Norm Biltz, Jan. 7, 1954, Biltz Papers.

98. Eva Adams to Norm Biltz, Dec. 25, 1954, Biltz Papers.

99. See Patrick A. McCarran to Pete Petersen, May 25, 1951, McCarran Collection.

100. *Nevada State Journal,* "Nevada Politics," Feb. 11, 1951, scrapbook 38, McCarran Collection; Eric Moody, "Vail Pittman; His Life and Times in Nevada Politics, 1883–1964," (M.A. thesis, University of Nevada-Reno, 1971), pp. 160–61.

101. Interview with Charles Russell, November 26, 1974; Charles H. Russell, "Reminiscences of a Nevada Congressman, Governor and Legislator," p. 229.

102. Norm Biltz, "Memoirs of the Duke of Nevada," p. 153.

103. *Elko Independent,* April 26, 1951, scrapbook 38, McCarran Collection.

104. *Reno Evening Gazette,* March 24, 1951, scrapbook 38, McCarran Collection.

105. *Reno Evening Gazette,* May 21, 1951, *Las Vegas Sun,* May 22, 1951, scrapbook 39, McCarran Collection.

106. Patrick A. McCarran to Pete Petersen, May 25, 1951, McCarran Collection.

107. Charles H. Russell, "Reminiscences of a Nevada Congressman, Governor and Legislator," pp. 155–56.

108. *Ibid.,* p. 127; Biltz confirmed this in his oral history, "Memoirs of the Duke of Nevada," pp. 153–54.

109. Eric N. Moody, "Vail Pittman," p. 162.

110. Norman Biltz, "Memoirs of the Duke of Nevada," pp. 158–59.

111. *Ibid.,* p. 158.

112. Interview with Bryn Armstrong, Oct. 30, 1974; Interview with Charles Russell, Nov. 26, 1974.

113. Eric Moody, "Vail Pittman," pp. 162–63; Glass, *Nevada's Turbulent '50s,* pp. 103–4.

114. Norman Biltz, "Memoirs of the Duke of Nevada," p. 159.

115. *Las Vegas Review-Journal,* March 24, 1954, Chet Sobsey column, *Nevada State Journal,* Jan. 2, 1954, "Nevada Politics," scrapbook 52, McCarran Collection.

116. *Reno Evening Gazette,* Jan. 19, 1954, *Las Vegas Review-Journal,* Jan. 24, 1954, "Chet Sobsey column," Jan. 28, 1954, "Chet Sobsey column," scrapbook 52, McCarran Collection.

117. *Las Vegas Review-Journal,* Feb. 5, 1954, scrapbook 52, McCarran Collection; *Nevada State Journal,* Feb. 6, 1954.

118. *Reno Evening Gazette,* Feb. 12, 1954, scrapbook 52, McCarran Collection.

119. Pete Petersen to Patrick A. McCarran, March 23, 1954, Petersen Papers; Eva Adams to Sister Mary Mercy, May 11, 1954, McCarran Collection; Eric N. Moody, "Vail Pittman," p. 154; Charles Russell, "Reminiscences of a Nevada Congressman, Governor, and Legislator," pp. 233–34.

120. Patrick A. McCarran to Mrs. P. A. McCarran, May 24, 1954, McCarran Collection. James G. "Sailor" Ryan won the Democratic primary but lost the general election to Rex Bell, husband of former movie star Clara Bow. Ryan was from Las Vegas, President of the State Federation of Labor, and a former Speaker of the Assembly. McCarran ended up supporting him.

121. *Las Vegas Review-Journal,* June 3, 1954, scrapbook 52, McCarran Collection; Sister Margaret Patricia McCarran, "McCarran," XI, 5.

122. Interviews with Walter Baring, May 14, 1975; Grant Sawyer, Oct. 29, 1974; Howard Cannon, July 28, 1969; Charles Sobsey, July 24, 1969.

123. Interview with Charles Russell, Nov. 26, 1974; Charles Russell, "Reminiscences of a

Nevada Congressman, Governor, and Legislator," pp. 230–31; Patrick A. McCarran to Pete Petersen, July 29, 1954, Petersen Papers.

124. Interview with Sister Margaret Patricia McCarran, October 16, 1974; Interview with Eva Adams, May 10, 1975; Pete Petersen, "Reminiscences of My Work in Nevada Labor, Politics, Post Office and Gaming Control," pp. 76–77.

Chapter 10

1. *Las Vegas Review-Journal,* Dec. 20, 1946, scrapbook 20, *Nevada State Journal,* Aug. 31, 1947, scrapbook 23, McCarran Collection.

2. *Ibid., Ely Daily Times,* August 26, 1947; *Reno Evening Gazette,* Aug. 30, 1947, scrapbook 23, McCarran Collection.

3. *Reno Evening Gazette,* June 21, 1948, scrapbook 25; *Las Vegas Review-Journal,* Aug. 24, 1949, scrapbook 29, McCarran Collection.

4. *Reno Evening Gazette,* Nov. 1, 1951, *Nevada State Labor News,* Nov. 16, 1951, "Salmagundi," scrapbook 41, *Nevada Appeal,* Jan. 3, 1952, scrapbook 42, McCarran Collection.

5. Pat McCarran to Mrs. Avery Stitser, Feb. 6, 1952, *Reno Evening Gazette,* March 2, 1954, scrapbook 52, McCarran Collection; Interview with Sister Margaret Patricia McCarran, June 28, 1969, Interview with Eva Adams, May 10, 1975.

6. *Nevada State Labor News,* Aug. 10, 1951, "Salmagundi," scrapbook 41, McCarran Collection.

7. *Washington Post,* Aug. 7, 1953, McCarran Collection.

8. *Lovelock Review Miner,* Sept. 17, 1953, *Nevada State Journal,* Sept. 20, 1953, scrapbook 50, *Manchester Union Leader,* Oct. 7, 1953, McCarran Collection.

9. Edward A. Olsen, "My Careers as a Journalist in Oregon, Idaho, and Nevada; in Nevada Gaming Control; and at the University of Nevada" (Oral autobiography, University of Nevada-Reno Library 1969), pp. 157–58.

10. Senator Pat McCarran to Mary Mercy, Jan. 29, 1954, March 26, 1954, Pat McCarran to Winthrop W. Aldrich, March 25, 1954, Eva Adams to Rev. John F. Hurley, April 26, 1954, McCarran Collection.

11. Sister Mary Mercy McCarran to Sisters at the College of Holy Names, Nov. 4, 1954. Much of my information about the senator's last days comes from this letter; Eva Adams to Sister Margaret McCarran, Aug. 16, 1954, McCarran Collection.

12. Sister Mary Mercy McCarran to Sisters at the College of the Holy Names, Nov. 4, 1954, McCarran Collection.

13. *Ibid., Nevada State Journal,* Sept. 29, 1954; *Reno Evening Gazette,* Sept. 29, 1954; Interview with Eva Adams, May 10, 1975; Interview with Walter Baring, May 14, 1975.

14. *Nevada State Journal,* Sept. 29, 1954, *Reno Evening Gazette,* Sept. 29, 1954; *Las Vegas Sun,* Sept. 30, 1954, scrapbook 61, McCarran Collection; Interview with Bryn Armstrong, Oct. 30, 1974.

15. *Washington Post,* Sept. 30, 1954, McCarran Collection.

16. U.S. Congress, *Memorial Services Held in the Senate and House of Representatives of the United States, together with Remarks Presented in Eulogy of Patrick Anthony McCarran, Late a Senator from Nevada* (Washington, D.C.: G.P.O., 1955), pp. 3, 16, 21–22, 24, 51, 52.

17. The main sources for the funeral are Sister Mary Mercy McCarran to Sisters at the College of the Holy Names, Nov. 4, 1954, McCarran Collection; *Reno Evening Gazette,* Oct. 2, 1954; *Nevada State Journal,* Oct. 3, 1954; Silas Ross, "Recollections of Life at Glendale, Nevada, Work at the University of Nevada, and Western Funeral Practice," (Oral autobiography, University of Nevada-Reno Library, 1969), 593–595; Sister Margaret P. McCarran, "McCarran," XI, 6-7.

Bibliography

THE McCarran collection, housed at the Nevada Historical Society in Reno, was the single most valuable source for this study. Unfortunately, through the years the collection has undergone vicissitudes which have hindered its full utilization by scholars.

Shortly after Senator McCarran's death, his administrative assistant, Eva Adams, sent a letter to his closest political associates, stating that all correspondence of a "personal nature" was being returned to the associates so they "might dispose of it" as they thought best. Other political associates were invited back to Washington, D.C. to go through the files and remove material which they thought best to remove.* This having been accomplished, the files then reverted to the McCarran family.

In 1954, Sister Margaret P. McCarran placed manuscript and other material "on loan" to the Nevada State Museum in Carson City. In 1966, this material was "lent" and physically transferred to the Nevada State Archives. Other, smaller amounts of McCarran material independently found their way to the Nevada Historical Society. Sister Margaret, however, retained control of the great, and most valuable, bulk of her father's papers while she worked on a life of her father. Until 1978, this material was housed at the College of the Holy Names in Oakland, where she had served. The papers were organized and made accessible to scholars. This writer was among several who did research in the papers at the College. In 1978, the College told Sister Margaret that it needed space, and the papers were physically transferred to the Nevada State Archives, although never fully under the Archives' control. In September, 1981, the papers were donated to the Nevada Historical Society.

The collection is a large one, although spotty. It is frustrating to use because of its lack of professional and systematic organization. The integrity of the McCarran papers has also been compromised by the incorporation of extraneous, although valuable, material copied from the University of Nevada, the Truman, and the Roosevelt libraries. Differentiation by source has not always been noted.

Many personal letters of the Senator remain; fortunately the initial culling done by staff and friends does not appear to have been entirely systematic. Sister Margaret has added many valuable family letters to the collection. For many years and in many areas of McCarran's activities, the papers are extremely rich; for other years and areas, almost non-existent.

Of great help to researchers are the 60 newspaper scrapbooks which cover McCarran's senatorial years from 1933 to 1954. The papers, which were clipped for every mention of the Senator's name, include *all* Nevada newspapers, all Washington, D.C., newspapers, the *Baltimore Sun,* the *New York Times,* the *New York Herald Tribune,* the *New York Daily News,* and occasionally the *Chicago Tribune,* the *San Francisco Chronicle,* the *Los Angeles Examiner,*

---

*Eva Adams to "My dear friend," Nov. 15, 1954, McCarran Collection; John F. Cahlan, "Reminiscences of a Reno and Las Vegas, Nevada Newspaperman, University Regent and Public Spirited Citizen," p. 243.

and the *Los Angeles Times*. The staff was quite unbiased about its clippings—material both critical and uncritical of the Senator was included. Only the unmentionable *Las Vegas Sun* for 1952 and 1953 went beyond the pale and was not clipped.

Now that the collection is in Reno, the bulk of the manuscript and other unpublished material pertaining to Senator McCarran's political organization now resides in the state of Nevada. The Oral History Project at the University of Nevada, Reno, headed by Mary Ellen Glass, has also amassed considerable material on this subject. Particularly useful, among many oral histories, are those of Norm Biltz, Ed Olsen, Joseph McDonald, and Pete Petersen. Outside of the Nevada Historical Society, the largest repository of manuscript material pertaining to McCarran and his political organization is the Special Collections Department of the Library at the University of Nevada-Reno. The papers of Thomas Miller, Joe McDonald, and Vail Pittman contain important information; but the Pete Petersen papers, especially for the years 1939 to 1954, are indispensable. Petersen scissored out sections of his correspondence which he did not wish posterity to view, but what remains is an exceptionally vivid picture of raw politics. What was snipped must have been interesting indeed. Outside of Nevada are the important Key Pittman papers in the Library of Congress. These were only partially utilized, in their local, Nevada aspects, in Fred Israel's *Nevada's Key Pittman*.

Much has been published on Patrick McCarran. Especially important for this study are the two articles on her father written by Sister Margaret P. McCarran (*Nevada Historical Society Quarterly*, XI (Fall-Winter, 1968), 5–66, and XII (Spring, 1969), 5–75). Rich in detail, and undeviatingly loyal to her father, they give information unavailable anywhere else. Particularly illuminating is the first article, which concentrates on the Senator's background and career prior to 1938.

The following bibliography lists items used for this study. There has been no attempt to list the bibliographical material which pertains to activities of Senator McCarran outside the scope of this book, even though much of such material has been perused by the author.

Books

Allen, Robert S., and William V. Shannon. *The Truman Merry-Go-Round.* New York: Vanguard Press, 1950.

Alsop, Joseph, and Turner Catledge. *The 168 Days.* Garden City, N.Y.: Doubleday, Doran & Co., 1938.

Baker, Leonard. *Back to Back: The Duel between FDR and the Surpeme Court.* New York: Macmillan, 1967.

Block, Herbert. *The Herblock Book.* Boston: Beacon Press, 1952.

Brennan, John A. *Silver and the First New Deal.* Reno: University of Nevada Press, 1969.

Chan, Loren B. *Sagebrush Statesman: Tasker L. Oddie of Nevada.* Nevada Studies in History and Political Science, No. 12. Reno: University of Nevada Press, 1973.

Clark, Walter Van Tilburg, ed. *The Journals of Alfred Doten, 1849–1903.* 3 vols. Reno: University of Nevada Press, 1973.

Current Biography, 1947. New York: H. W. Wilson, 1948.

Darling, Arthur B., ed. *The Public Papers of Francis G. Newlands.* 2 vols. Washington, D.C.: W. F. Roberts, 1937.

Douglass, William A., and Jon Bilbao. *Amerikanauk: Basque in the New World* Reno: University of Nevada Press, 1975.

Elliott, Russell R. *History of Nevada.* Lincoln: University of Nebraska Press, 1973.

———. *Nevada's Twentieth-Century Mining Boom: Tonopah, Goldfield, Ely.* Reno: University of Nevada Press, 1966.

———. *Radical Labor in the Nevada Mining Booms, 1900–1920.* Carson City: State Printing Office, 1961.

Farley, James A. *Jim Farley's Story; The Roosevelt Years.* New York: McGraw-Hill, 1948.

Georgetta, Clel. *Golden Fleece in Nevada.* Reno: Ventura Publishing, 1972.

Glass, Mary Ellen. *Nevada's Turbulent '50s: Decade of Political and Economic Change.* Nevada Studies in History and Political Science, No. 15. Reno: University of Nevada Press, 1981.

Glasscock, C. B. *Gold in Them Hills: The Story of the West's Last Wild Mining Days.* Indianapolis: Bobbs-Merrill, 1932.

Gorman, Joseph Bruce. *Kefauver: A Political Biography.* New York: Oxford University Press, 1971.

Greenspun, Hank. *Where I Stand; The Record of a Reckless Man.* New York: David McKay, 1966.

Gunther, John. *Inside U.S.A.* New York: Harper & Brothers, 1947.

Hamby, Alonzo L. *Beyond the New Deal: Harry S. Truman and American Liberalism.* New York and London: Columbia University Press, 1973.

Hulse, James W. *The Nevada Adventure, A History.* Reno: University of Nevada Press, 1969. Revised edition.

———. *The University of Nevada, A Centennial History.* Reno: University of Nevada Press, 1974.

Israel, Fred L. *Nevada's Key Pittman.* Lincoln: University of Nebraska Press, 1963.

Koontz, John. *Political History of Nevada.* 5th edition. Carson City, 1965.

Levine, Edward M. *The Irish and Irish Politicians; A Study of Cultural and Social Alienation.* Notre Dame, Ind.: University of Notre Dame Press, 1966.

Lillard, Richard G. *Desert Challenge, An Interpretation of Nevada.* New York: Alfred K. Knopf, 1942.

Matusow, Harvey. *False Witness.* New York: Cameron & Kahn, 1955.

McCarran, Sister Margaret Patricia. *Fabianism in the Political Life of Britain, 1919–1931.* Chicago: The Heritage Foundation, 1954.

Moley, Raymond. *The First New Deal.* New York: Harcourt, Brace & World, 1966.

Montgomery, Ruth. *Once there was a Nun; Mary McCarran's Years as Sister Mary Mercy.* New York: G. P. Putnam's Sons, 1962.

Moody, Eric N. *Southern Gentleman of Nevada Politics: Vail M. Pittman.* Nevada Studies in History and Political Science, No. 13. Reno: University of Nevada Press, 1974.

Moore, William Howard. *The Kefauver Committee and the Politics of Crime, 1950–1952.* Columbia: University of Missouri Press, 1974.

Nevada State Federation of Labor. *Official Proceedings of the Second Annual Convention, 1944.*

Orton, Richard H. *Records of California Men in the War of the Rebellion, 1861–1867.* Sacramento: J. D. Young, 1890.

Ostrander, Gilman M. *Nevada, The Great Rotten Borough, 1859–1964.* New York: Alfred A. Knopf, 1966.

Patterson, James T. *Congressional Conservatism and the New Deal.* Lexington: University of Kentucky Press, 1967.

Pearson, Drew. *Diaries, 1949–1959,* ed. Tyler Abell. New York: Holt, Rinehart and Winston, 1974.

Pickford, Mary. *Sunshine and Shadow.* Garden City, N.Y.: Doubleday & Company, 1955.

Reid, Ed, and Ovid Demaris. *The Green Felt Jungle.* New York: Trident Press, 1963.

Roosevelt, Franklin Delano. *F.D.R.: His Personal Letters,* ed. Elliott Roosevelt. Vol. II. New York: Duell, Sloan and Pearce, 1950.

Scrugham, James G. *Nevada; A Narrative of the Conquest of a Frontier Land; Comprising the Story of Her People from the Dawn of History to the Present Time.* 3 vols. Chicago and New York: The American Historical Society, 1935.

Steinberg, Alfred. *The Man From Missouri; The Life and Times of Harry S. Truman.* New York: G. P. Putnam's Sons, 1962.
Swackhammer, William D. *Political History of Nevada, 1973.* Carson City, 1974.
Truman, Harry S. *Memoirs,* Vol. I. *Year of Decisions.* Garden City, N.Y.: Doubleday & Company, 1955.
———. Harry S. *Memoirs,* Vol. II. *Years of Trial and Hope.* Garden City, N.Y.: Doubleday & Company, 1956.
Truman, Margaret. *Harry S. Truman.* New York: William Morrow & Company, 1973.
Turner, Wallace. *Gambler's Money, The New Force in American Life.* Boston: Houghton Mifflin, 1965.
Wheeler, Burton K. with Paul F. Healy. *Yankee from the West.* Garden City, N.Y.: Doubleday & Company, 1962.
Zanjani, Sally Springmeyer. *The Unspiked Rail; Memoir of a Nevada Rebel* Reno: University of Nevada Press, 1981.

Periodicals, Articles

Barsalou, F. W. "The Concentration of Banking Power in Nevada: An Historical Analysis." *Business History Review,* XXIX (Dec., 1955), 350–362.
Donovan, Richard and Douglas Cater. "Of Gamblers, a Senator, and a Sun that Wouldn't Set." *The Reporter,* VIII (June 9, 1953), 25–30.
Edwards, Jerome. "Mary Pickford's Divorce." *Nevada Historical Society Quarterly,* XIX (Fall, 1976), 185–191.
———. "Patrick A. McCarran: His Years on the Nevada Supreme Court, 1913–1918." *Nevada Historical Society Quarterly,* XVIII (Winter 1975), 185–205.
———. "The *Sun* and the Senator," *Nevada Historical Society Quarterly,* XXIV (Spring 1981), 3–16.
Kennedy, Susan Estrabrook. "Nevada's Banking Holiday: 1932." *Nevada Historical Society Quarterly,* XVII (Fall, 1974), 125–130.
Lincoln, Freeman. "Norman Biltz, Duke of Nevada." *Fortune,* L (Sept., 1954), 140–154.
Martin, Anne H. "Nevada: Beautiful Desert of Buried Hopes." *Nation,* CXV (July 26, 1922), 89–92.
McCarran, Sister Margaret Patricia. "Patrick Anthony McCarran." *Nevada Historical Society Quarterly,* XI (Fall–Winter, 1968), 5–66.
McCarran, Sister Margaret Patricia. "Patrick Anthony McCarran, Part II." *Nevada Historical Society Quarterly,* XII (Spring, 1969), 5–75.
Mechling, Tom. "I Battled McCarran's Machine." *The Reporter,* VIII (June 9, 1953), 21–25.
Olson, James S. "Rehearsal for Disaster: Hoover, the R.F.C., and the Banking Crisis in Nevada, 1932–1933." *Western Historical Quarterly,* VI (April, 1975), 149–161.
Oshinsky, David M. "Labor's Cold War: The CIO and the Communists," in *The Specter: Original Essays on the Cold War and the Origins of McCarthyism.* Ed. Robert Griffith and Athan Theoharis. New York: New Viewpoints, 1974.
Smith, C. C., and Charles Kinsman, Jr. "Nevada," in *Presidential Nominating Politics in 1952.* Vol. V, *The West.* ed. Paul T. David, Malcolm Moos, Ralph M. Goldman. Baltimore: The Johns Hopkins Press, 1954.
Steinberg, Alfred. "McCarran, Lone Wolf of the Senate." *Harper's Magazine,* CCI (Nov. 1950), 89–95.
Time Magazine, LV (March 20, 1950), 18.
Wier, Jeanne Elizabeth, "The Mystery of Nevada," *Rocky Mountain Politics.* Ed. Thomas C. Donnelly. Albuquerque: University of New Mexico Press, 1940.

Unpublished Books and Manuscripts

Atkinson, Harry. "Tonopah and Reno Memories of a Nevada Attorney." Oral History, University of Nevada-Reno Library, 1970.

Barsalou, Francis Wilfred. "An Economic Analysis of Commercial Banking in Nevada." Ph.D. Dissertation, University of Southern California, 1953.

Bible, Alan. "Recollections of a Nevada Native Son: The Law, Politics, the Nevada Attorney General's Office, and the United Unites Senate." Oral History, University of Nevada-Reno Library, 1971.

Biltz, Norm. "Memoirs of the Duke of Nevada." Oral History, University of Nevada-Reno Library, 1967.

Binion, Benny. "Some Recollections of a Texas and Las Vegas Gaming Operator." Oral History, University of Nevada-Reno Library, 1976.

Bunker, Berkeley. "Life and Work of a Southern Nevada Church Leader, Legislator, U.S. Senator, and Congressman." Oral History, University of Nevada-Reno Library, 1971. Used with permission of author.

Cahill, Robbins. "Recollections of Work in State Politics, Government, Taxation, Gaming Control, Clark County Administration, and the Nevada Resort Association." Oral History, University of Nevada-Reno Library, 1976.

Cahlan, John F. "Reminiscences of a Reno and Las Vegas, Nevada Newspaperman, University Regent and Public Spirited Citizen." Oral History, University of Nevada-Reno Library, 1968.

Doyle, Sister Marie Olive. "The Political Career of James Scrugham, 1923–1945." M.A. Thesis, Catholic University of America, 1956.

Engelmann, Erin B. "Nevada, As Seen Through Her Newspapers, October 1, 1926–April 30, 1928." Paper for History 914, University of Nevada-Reno, Dec. 16, 1974. Personal Possession of Russell R. Elliott.

Guild, Clark J. "Memoirs of Careers with Nevada Bench and Bar, Lyon County Offices, and the Nevada State Museum." Oral History, University of Nevada-Reno Library, 1971.

Kaufman, Perry Bruce. "The Best City of Them All: A History of Las Vegas, 1930–1960." Ph.D. Dissertation, University of California, Santa Barbara, 1974.

Kofoed, Les. "Kofoed's Meanderings in Lovelock Business, Nevada Government, the U.S. Marshal's Office, and the Gaming Industry." Oral History, University of Nevada-Reno Library, 1971.

Lilley, William. "The Early Career of Francis G. Newlands, 1848–1897." Ph.D. Dissertation, Yale University, 1966.

McCarran, Patrick A. "Autobiography." Unpublished typeset ms., n.d. Personal Possession of Author.

McDonald, Joseph F. "The Life of a Newsboy in Nevada." Oral History, University of Nevada-Reno Library, 1970.

Miller, Thomas W. "Memoirs of Thomas Woodnutt Miller, a Public Spirited Citizen of Delaware and Nevada." Oral History, University of Nevada-Reno Library, 1965.

Moody, Eric N. "Vail Pittman, His Life and Times in Nevada Politics, 1883–1964," M.A. Thesis, University of Nevada-Reno, 1971.

Olsen, Edward A. "My Careers as Journalist in Oregon, Idaho, and Nevada; in Nevada Gaming Control; and at the University of Nevada." Oral History, University of Nevada-Reno Library, 1969.

Petersen, Peter. "Reminiscences of My Work in Nevada Labor, Politics, Post Office and Gaming Control." Oral History, University of Nevada-Reno Library, 1970.

Pittman, Von, Jr. "Senator Patrick A. McCarran and the Politics of Containment." Ph.D. Dissertation, University of Georgia, 1979.

Ross, Silas E. "Recollections of Life at Glendale, Nevada, Work at the University of Nevada, and Western Funeral Practice." Oral History, University of Nevada-Reno Library, 1969.

Russell, Charles H. "Reminiscences of a Nevada Congressman, Governor and Legislator." Oral History, University of Nevada-Reno Library, 1967. Used with permission of author.

Sanford, John. "Printer's Ink in My Blood." Oral History, University of Nevada-Reno Library, 1971.

Smith, Harold T. "New Deal Relief Programs in Nevada, 1933 to 1935." Ph.D. Dissertation, University of Nevada-Reno, 1972.

Thornton, Barbara. "George Wingfield in Nevada from 1896 to 1932." M.A. Thesis, University of Nevada-Reno, 1967.

Watson, Ronald Lee. "The Personality and Politics of Patrick Anthony McCarran." Paper for Political Science 497, University of Nevada-Reno, Aug., 1968. Personal possession of Jerome E. Edwards.

Whited, Fred E., Jr. "The Rhetoric of Senator Patrick Anthony McCarran." Ph.D. Dissertation, University of Oregon, 1973.

Manuscript Collections

Balzar, Fred. Papers. Nevada State Archives, Carson City.
Bartlett, George. Papers. Library, University of Nevada-Reno.
Biltz, Norman. Papers. Library, University of Nevada-Reno.
Carville, E. P. Papers. Nevada State Archives, Carson City.
Kirman, Richard. Papers. Nevada State Archives, Carson City.
McCarran, Patrick A. Papers. Nevada Historical Society, Reno.
McDonald, Joseph. Papers. Library, University of Nevada-Reno.
Miller, Thomas. Papers. Library, University of Nevada-Reno.
Petersen, Peter. Papers. Library, University of Nevada-Reno.
Pittman, Key. Papers. Library of Congress, Washington, D.C.
Pittman, Vail. Papers. Library, University of Nevada-Reno.
Pittman, Vail. Papers. Nevada State Archives, Carson City.
Russell, Charles. Papers. Library, University of Nevada-Reno.
Russell, Charles. Papers. Nevada State Archives, Carson City.
Storey County. Criminal Court Records. Virginia City, Nevada.
University of Nevada. Grades, 1897–1901. Registrar's Office, University of Nevada-Reno.

Interviews

Adams, Eva. May 10, 1975.
Armstrong, Bryn. October 30, 1974.
Baring, Walter. July 28, 1969, May 14, 1975.
Bible, Alan. July 24, 1969.
Bunker, Berkeley. October 31, 1974.
Cannon, Howard. July 28, 1969.
Collins, Ruth. June 11, 1969.
Craven, Tom. January 9, 1975.
Dickerson, Denver. May 1, 1975.
Laxalt, Robert. June, 1976.
McCarran, Sister Margaret Patricia. June 28, 1969, October 16, 1974.

McDonald, Joseph F. Jr. March 26, 1975.
Olsen, Ed. November 26, 1974.
Russell, Charles. November 26, 1974.
Sanford, John. March 13, 1975.
Sawyer, Grant. October 29, 1974.
Sobsey, Charles. July 24, 1969.
Sourwine, Jay. August 4, 1969, May 1, 1975.

Government Documents

Appendix to Journals of Senate and Assembly of the Eighth Session of the Legislature of the State of Nevada. Vol. III. Carson City: John J. Hill, 1877.
Appendix to Journal of Senate and Assembly, Nevada, 37th Session, 1935. Vol. 2. Carson City: State Printing Office, 1935.
Congressional Record. 1933–1954. *passim.*
Nevada Reports. Vols. 29, 36–42, 46 (1907, 1913–1919, 1922).
Statutes of Nevada. 1911.
U.S. Bureau of Census. *Census of Population: 1950.* vols. 1, 2. 1952.
U.S. Bureau of Census. *Fifteenth Census of the United States, 1930, Population.* Vol. 1. 1931.
U.S. Congress. *Memorial Services Held in the Senate and House of Representatives of the United States, together with Remarks Presented in Eulogy of Patrick Anthony McCarran, Late a Senator From Nevada.* 1955.
U.S. Congress, House. *Papers Relative to the Labor Troubles at Goldfield, Nevada, Message From the President of the U.S. Transmitting Report of Special Commission on Labor Troubles at Goldfield, Nevada, and Papers Relating Thereto.* 60th Cong., 1st Session, House Ex. Doc. 607, 1908.
U.S. Dept. of Commerce. *Statistical Abstract of the United States, 1934.*
U.S. Senate, Committee on the Judiciary. *Hearings before a Subcommittee . . . on the Nomination of William S. Boyle to be United States Attorney for the District of Nevada, 1939.* 76th Congress, 1st Session.
U.S. Senate, Committee on the Judiciary. *Nomination of Frank H. Norcross, Hearings before a Subcommittee of the Judiciary . . . and before William H. Neblett.* 73rd Congress, 2nd Session, 1934.
U.S. Senate, Committee on the Judiciary, Subcommittee to Investigate the Administration of the Internal Security Act and Other Internal Security Laws. *Communist Domination of Union Officials in Vital Defense Industry—International Union of Mine, Mill and Smelter Workers.* 82nd Congress, 2nd Session, 1952.
U.S. Senate, Special Committee to Investigate Organized Crime in Interstate Commerce. *Investigation of Organized Crime in Interstate Commerce, Hearings, Part 10, Nevada-California.* 1951.
U.S. Senate, Special Committee to Investigate Organized Crime in Interstate Commerce. *Third Interim Report.* 82nd Cong., 1st Session, S. Rept. No. 307, 1951.

Miscellaneous

Artemesia. 1900–1901. Archives, University of Nevada-Reno.
Las Vegas Age. Nov. 19, 1932.
Las Vegas Review-Journal. March 25, 1932.
Las Vegas Sun. March–November, 1952.

N. W. Ayers & Sons. *Directory, Newspapers and Periodicals, 1952.*
Nevada State Journal.
Reno Evening Gazette.
The Student Record. 1897–1901. Library, University of Nevada-Reno.
Territorial Enterprise (Virginia City). April 19, 26, May 29, 1889.
Tonopah Weekly Bonanza. Sept. 6, 1908.

INDEX

231